Copyright © 2023 by Benedict Maynard

All rights reserved. No part of this publication may be reproduced, stored or transmitted in any form or by any means, electronic, mechanical, photocopying, recording, scanning, or otherwise without written permission from the publisher. It is illegal to copy this book, post it to a website, or distribute it by any other means without permission.

Benedict Maynard asserts the moral right to be identified as the author of this work.

Benedict Maynard has no responsibility for the persistence or accuracy of URLs for external or third-party Internet websites referred to in this publication and does not guarantee that any content on such websites is, or will remain, accurate or appropriate.

Designations used by companies to distinguish their products are often claimed as trademarks. All brand names and product names used in this book and on its cover are trade names, service marks, trademarks and registered trademarks of their respective owners. The publishers and the book are not associated with any product or vendor mentioned in this book. None of the companies referenced within the book have endorsed the book. Cboe images and trademarks provided as a courtesy by Cboe Exchange, Inc. (Cboe).

Disclaimer notice: Please note the information contained within this document is for educational and entertainment purposes only. All effort has been executed to present accurate, up to date, reliable, complete information. No warranties of any kind are declared or implied. The book does not consider an individual's specific circumstances and is not intended to be a source of financial or legal advice. Making adjustments to a financial strategy or plan should only be undertaken after consulting with a professional, and they must be consulted before attempting any techniques outlined in this book. The publisher and the author make no guarantee of financial results obtained by using this book and readers acknowledge that the author is not engaged in the rendering of financial or professional advice. By reading this document, the reader agrees that under no circumstances is the author responsible for any losses – whether direct or indirect – that may be incurred from using the information contained within this document, including but not limited to errors, omissions, and / or inaccuracies.

First edition 2023

CONTENTS

Foreword	1
Chapter 1: What Are Equity Options and Why Trade Them?	3
Chapter 2: Option Pricing	12
A Collection of Risks—The Greeks	19
Chapter 3: Delta	21
Chapter 4: Vega	27
Chapter 5: Theta	30
Chapter 6: Gamma	34
How Equity Options Trade	37
Chapter 7: The Options Exchange and Clearing House	38
Chapter 8: Selecting a Broker Platform	43
Single Option Strategies	48
Chapter 9: Long Call	49
Chapter 10: Long Put	67
Chapter 11: Short Call	83

Chapter 12: Short Put	93
Multiple Option Strategies	**103**
Chapter 13: Long Call Spread	104
Chapter 14: Long Put Spread	116
Chapter 15: Collar	126
Chapter 16: Risk Reversal	140
Chapter 17: Long Call Condor and Butterfly	158
Ratio Option Strategies	**165**
Chapter 18: Long Ratio Call Spread	166
Chapter 19: Long Ratio Put Spread	174
Chapter 20: Long Ratio Call Spread Risk Reversal	182
Portfolio Considerations	**190**
Chapter 21: Managing Risk	191
Glossary	209

FOREWORD

Great investors understand how to use options.

Options are immensely versatile financial assets. Among their many uses, they can generate far greater returns than simply investing in the stock market and can reduce the risk of stock market investing also. The purpose of this book is to explain to the average stock investor what equity options are, how they work, what risks they carry, and the way to select an option brokerage platform to begin their journey as an option user. In the book, I remove the mystique of trading options and use no complicated mathematics. Employing real-market examples, the book explains conceiving and constructing option strategies to reduce risk and to enhance returns relative to simply using the stock market.

However, options are dangerous if mishandled. The book illustrates how to handle them correctly, using only strategies that cannot expose the user to greater risk of loss relative to stock market investing. It also explains how risks are managed within the context of an option portfolio once you begin your happy life as an option user. Happy trading and happy returns!

CHAPTER 1: WHAT ARE EQUITY OPTIONS AND WHY TRADE THEM?

To begin, what is an equity?

The *equity market* (or *stock market* or *share market*) is a term used to describe any stock exchange or number of stock exchanges where shares are officially listed and traded. A share is a unit of equity ownership of a listed company, whose holder is entitled to a "share" of any residual profits that the company makes, if the board decide to distribute them, in the form of dividends. Share prices are therefore very sensitive to the economic fortunes of the companies that issue them.

Stock exchanges (such as the New York Stock Exchange) have exacting listing requirements that a company must meet. Once listed, their shares become tradable on the exchange. Exchanges facilitate the fair trading of shares, which allows for the determination of a market equilibrium price for them at any point during the trading day, where buy orders match sell orders to create transactions at trade prices. This also allows for the calculation of stock indices (or *equity indices*), whose values derive from trade prices of listed shares selected by specific criteria. The London Stock Exchange, for example, owns the FTSE Group that, in principle, calculates the value of the FTSE 100 Index of largest listed companies in the UK, based on the price of its shares multiplied by the number of shares the company has issued. I refer to a share as equity or stock interchangeably throughout this book.

I frequently also refer to exchange-traded funds (ETFs). ETFs trade on stock exchanges just like regular equites but can contain many types of investments, such as stocks, commodities, bonds, or a mixture of different investments. They therefore allow investors exposure to a variety of different investment markets but with a fraction of the cost of investing in traditional funds. Many ETFs track equity indices, such as the "SPDR S&P 500 ETF Trust" (ticker SPY), which tracks the S&P 500 Index—the main US equity index.

So what is an equity option?

An option is a type of **derivative**, meaning that its price is derived from the price of another **underlying asset**—in this case, the price of an equity. Exchanges also list equity options, although they are invariably separate to the exchange where the underlying assets trade. The CBOE Options Exchange is the largest options exchange in the US, and it facilitates trading of options on the S&P 500 Index and Nasdaq Index, and options on the individual stocks that make up both indices as well as on a huge array of different ETFs.

Contracts or **lots** are units of options, and **option premium** is the money spent (or received) on buying (or selling) options. There are two different types of basic (or **plain vanilla**) options: (1) a **call option** and (2) a **put option**.

Buying a **call option** contract gives you the right but not the obligation to buy a specific quantity of the underlying asset at a specific price by a specific point in time in the future.

Buying a **put option** contract gives you the right but not the obligation to sell a specific quantity of the underlying asset at a specific price by a specific point in time in the future.

Listed options have specific standardized characteristics that beget greater volume of trading and hence better liquidity in the market. Large volumes of option contracts are also traded "Over-the-Counter" (OTC). These are primarily between investors and investment banks, often are not plain vanilla in nature, but have non-standardized characteristics and payoffs and trade away from an options exchange. OTC options are not within the scope of this book.

Listed equity options all have the following characteristics:

- They are either a put or a call.
- They all have an underlying asset, which is an equity, ETF, or equity index.
- They have a **strike price** (also referred to as an **exercise price**), which is the price you can (1) buy the underlying asset for in the case of call options or (2) sell the underlying asset at in the case of put options.
- They all have an expiry date.
- They are all traded on an options exchange.
- The premium value paid (or received) when an option is traded = number of contracts × option price × multiplier.

The **multiplier** is a fixed standardized quantity of underlying shares that an option contact is based upon as determined by the options exchange that listed them. Different exchanges sometimes have different multipliers. For example, all US equity options exchanges have multipliers of one hundred, so each option contract is on one hundred shares quoted in US dollars; however, UK-listed equity options have one thousand multipliers, so each option contract is on one thousand shares quoted in pence.

Ok, so why trade them?

This is best illustrated with an example. Imagine: it is October 2022, and you are extremely bullish on JPMorgan Chase & Co. (JPM) shares, which trade on the New York Stock Exchange at $102. You have been following the stock very closely and anticipate a sizable move higher over the next month.

You buy two JPM call option contracts that expire in one month from today and have a strike price of $110, at a cost of $2.34 per contract. The total option premium spend is $468 (number of contracts × option price × multiplier = 2 × $2.34 × 100). When the call option expires one month from now, the amount of money you make or lose (your profit or loss, or **P&L**) depends entirely on what the price of JPM shares is at that point in time. Assuming that they are somewhere between $50 and $160, your P&L is somewhere on the blue line in Figure 1.1.

Figure 1.1.

There are a couple of initial points to take from this graph:

1. If JPM shares are <u>anywhere</u> **below** the strike price of $110 when the call options expire, then the entire $468 premium is lost (i.e., the option contracts expire worthless). The call option is **out-the-money**.
2. If JPM shares are <u>anywhere</u> **above** the strike of $110 when the call options expire, then they do not expire worthless but have a value that is directly related to how high above the strike. The call option is **in-the-money**. In fact, anywhere above the strike the call options are making the same dollar-for-dollar appreciation as directly owning two hundred JPM shares in this example.

The end of the second point above is important to understand: Anywhere above the call option strike at option expiry, you make the same dollar-for-dollar amount of money as if you owned an equivalent quantity of shares—i.e., your exposure above the call option strike is identical.

The **notional exposure** of an option trade is the value of the stock position that underlies it.

Notional exposure = number of contracts × multiplier × share price of underlying

In this example, the notional exposure of the call options when they were bought was $20,400 (2 contracts × 100 multiplier × $102 underlying share price). Since the notional exposure of a stock trade is simply the share price multiplied by the number of shares, two hundred shares of JPM bought at $102 also had a notional exposure of $20,400 (200 shares × $102 share price).

Going back to our original example, instead of buying two contracts of our JPM one-month expiry 110 strike call options for $2.34 when the stock was trading at $102, you might have bought two hundred JPM shares to get the same notional exposure. Figure 1.2 displays the P&L for the stock purchase alongside the call option P&L graphed from before.

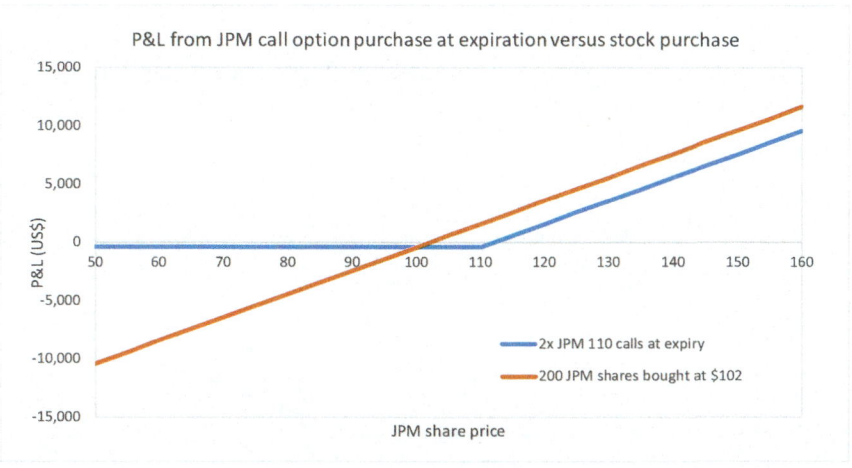

Figure 1.2.

The key differences that this graph highlights are as follows:

1. The orange line showing the P&L of owning JPM stock is a straight diagonal line—i.e., if JPM stock goes up 20 percent, you make 20 percent on your money; if it goes down 20 percent, you lose 20 percent of your money. It therefore has a **linear payoff.**
2. The blue line showing the P&L from owning the JPM call options, as we have already seen, is not linear—i.e., you stand to make much

more money from a 20 percent move higher in JPM shares than you stand to lose if JPM shares fall 20 percent. It therefore has a positive **asymmetric payoff**.

The ability to make asymmetric returns from options is one key reason why investors trade them, because it means that your potential to make more is bigger than your potential to lose.

Another key reason why investors trade options is apparent when we think back to our example again. Owning two hundred JPM shares and owning two JPM calls have the same notional exposure. So above the call option strike at expiry, they make the same dollar-for-dollar profit when JPM shares increase. However, the stock position cost $20,400 to get this return, which is a large sum of money compared to the $468 paid for two call option contracts. So, despite having the same notional exposures, buying the call options involve a fraction of the cost in this example. That is because options have **leverage**.

Options give both positive asymmetry and leverage to their buyers, and this gives the potential for large trading profits. Consider the returns available from the trade example again.

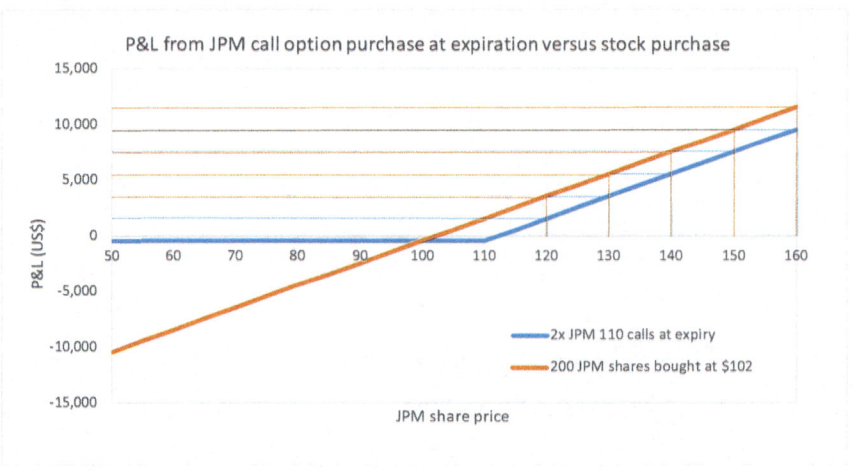

Figure 1.3.

Figure 1.3 is the previous graph overlaid with lines showing what profit is made on both the option and the stock positions, given a JPM stock price of

$120, $160, and every $10 interval in between. Figure 1.4 shows tables giving the monetary values and percentage profit for each JPM stock price interval.

US$ returns for both trades at different JPM share prices

JPM share price at option expiry	120	130	140	150	160
2x JPM one month expiry 110 strike call options	$1,532	$3,532	$5,532	$7,532	$9,532
200x JPM shares	$3,600	$5,600	$7,600	$9,600	$11,600

% return on money invested

JPM share price at option expiry	120	130	140	150	160
2x JPM one month expiry 110 strike call options	327%	755%	1182%	1609%	2037%
200x JPM shares	18%	27%	37%	47%	57%

Figure 1.4.

Therefore, if, for example, JPM shares reached $130 by the expiry of the option after one month, then the profit on the option position would be $3,532. This is simply how much the JPM share price moved higher in excess of the call option strike, multiplied by the number of contracts and the multiplier, then subtracting the initial cost of the options.

(($130 share price – 110 strike price) × 2 contracts × 100 multiplier) – $468 premium paid = $3,532

Since the initial spend is $468 and one month later it is worth $3,532, the return is 755 percent. This compares favourably with the 27 percent return possible from just buying the same notional exposure of JPM shares and illustrates the benefits of leverage, which is inherent when buying an option.

So what happens if JPM shares do not reach the 110 call strike by expiry?

It is all or nothing with trading options. If the bullish view is incorrect and JPM shares do not trade above $110 by the expiry date of the call option, then they expire worthless—i.e., the entire $468 spent on option premium is lost, and so you lose 100 percent of the money.

Still, losing $468 is a far better outcome than instead spending $20,400 on two hundred JPM shares and seeing them fall drastically in price. If the stock had fallen to $85, for example, you would have been nursing a $3,400 loss rather than a loss of just the $468 option premium.

This highlights another key reason why people buy options: any potential **loss is limited to the premium paid.** Buying a call option bestows the right but not the obligation (i.e., the option) to buy before a specific point in the future (expiry) at a specific price (the call strike). If JPM shares fall to $85 by option expiry date, you are under no obligation to buy them at the 110 call strike but can just write off the relatively small loss you have made from buying the call option premium.

Retail option usage

The benefits of positive asymmetry, leverage, and limited loss are encapsulated in one instrument when you buy an option. This makes options powerful investment and trading tools. However, only hedge funds, investment banks, and other sophisticated investment managers have traditionally used them. Even some large traditional investment firms do not focus on option usage because their expertise lies elsewhere and their end-clients have a mistrust of derivatives, fostered by a lack of proper understanding of the huge potential options have when used correctly.

Until recently, retail investor participation in equity option markets has also been low. This changed dramatically over the last few years, however, as brokers slashed trading fees to compete for retail client business, which has exploded in volume and at times has been the dominant market force driving stock markets. Global volume of option contracts traded reached a new record in 2022, with over forty-nine billion reported, according to data from the Futures Industry Association (Figure 1.5). Trading of single stock options surged during 2020 and continued to be buoyed by accelerating volumes in 2022, particularly in Asia. Competition has also driven the development of increasingly user-friendly and intuitive broker platforms with which retail clients can access the equity option market. Increasing integration of technology across broker platforms will sustain these trends into the future and help democratize option markets to allow retail investors the opportunity to participate in the wealth it can help generate.

Figure 1.5.

CHAPTER 2: OPTION PRICING

The previous chapter highlighted the huge benefits available to the owner of an option, which can be summarized as **leveraged positive asymmetry with limited loss**. It also outlined a number of criteria that any listed equity option must have, some of which are as follows:

- they are either a call option or a put option
- an underlying listed equity, equity index, or ETF
- a strike price
- an expiry date

When an option reaches expiry, if it has a value, it is simply determined by how much it is in-the-money. The JPM 110 strike call option from the previous chapter has no value if JPM shares are below $110 at the point of expiry and a value equal to the JPM share price minus $110 if in-the-money at expiry.

As for how the option price is determined at any point in time prior to expiry, there is a large amount of work (and mathematics) devoted to the subject. For the purpose of this book though, it is just important to know that economists Fischer Black and Myron Scholes published a mathematical model called the Black-Scholes Model (BSM) in 1973, which is still used today to price equity options. The four criteria listed above are inputs to the model as well as the following:

- the value of dividends that the underlying equity, equity index, or ETF will pay between now and the option expiry date
- the **risk-free** interest rate, which is the yield on a government bond (and hence borrowing that has little risk of default) that matures at the same time as the option expiry date

These last two criteria are the basis of pricing equity futures, which are another type of financial derivative that is not within the scope of this book. It is important to note, however, that owners of options are not entitled to dividends in the same way that owners of the underlying stock are. The option price is essentially adjusted to compensate for this, which is why they are included in the BSM computation.

There is one remaining input into the BSM that is not mentioned above, which is **implied volatility**. This is a key concept required for understanding options, because when using the BSM to calculate the price of them, all the other criteria listed above are known with certainty (or near certainty in the case of dividends and the risk-free interest rate). This makes implied volatility the key determinant for the price of an option: (1) increase implied volatility, and all option prices increase; or (2) decrease implied volatility, and all option prices decrease. Essentially, implied volatility is an estimation of the future level of volatility the underlying asset will experience between now and expiry of the option as determined by the option market.

What is volatility?

Without delving into mathematics, volatility is an annualized measure of how far the price of the underlying asset moves from its average price level each day, during a given time period. The two measures of volatility that option users routinely look at are the following:

1. **Realized volatility** (also called **historic volatility**), which is calculated from the history of usually end-of-day daily closing prices of

the underlying stock or stock index. Realized volatility is therefore <u>backward looking</u>.

2. **Implied volatility**, which is <u>forward looking</u>. Since implied volatility is the key variable input into the BSM to calculate an option price, any option price contains the option market's estimate of the future volatility that an underlying asset will have.

Realized volatility

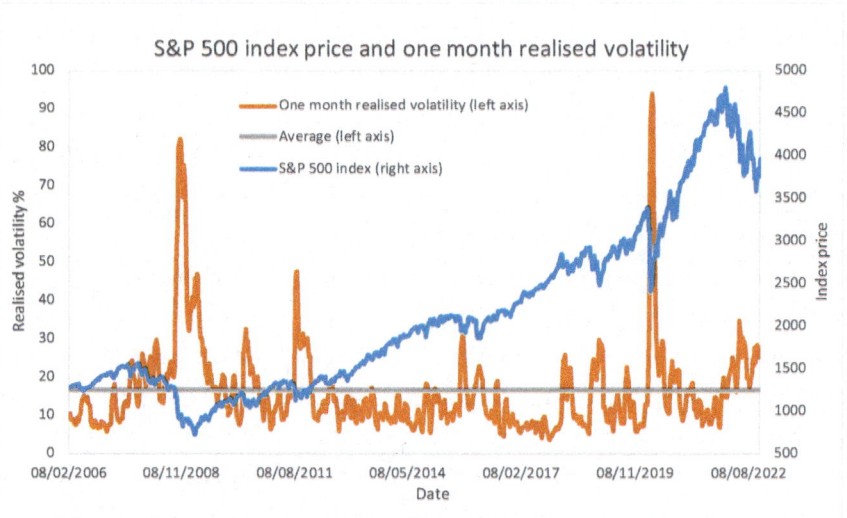

Figure 2.1

Figure 2.1 shows the price return history of the S&P 500 Index in blue, overlaid with its one-month realized volatility in orange. Each point on the orange line is therefore the value of volatility calculated over the preceding one-month period (thirty calendar days). The horizontal grey line shows the average level of the one-month realized volatility during the entire period.

One of the first things to appreciate is that equity realized volatility has a negative correlation with equity markets: when the index rises, volatility stays low; when the index falls, volatility increases. The largest spikes in volatility during this period occurred during the onset of the global pandemic in 2020 and the Global Financial Crisis in 2008.

It is usual to see volatility expressed as an annualized number. So, looking at either a one-month realized volatility (as in the graph above) or a three-month realized volatility calculated over the preceding ninety calendar days, direct comparisons can be made across different measures. They are also expressed in percentage terms, although this does not mean that volatility cannot exceed 100 percent. The highest S&P 500 Index one-month realized volatility in the above graph was 95.6 percent, so many of the index constituent stocks would have recorded realized volatilities in excess of 100 percent at that time.

Single stocks, such as JPM in our example in the previous chapter, generally have higher volatilities than indices like the S&P 500 Index. This is because equity indices comprise a number of stocks, which usually span different sectors and industries, thereby making them well diversified. Since different stocks within an index have different magnitudes and even direction of movement, indices are generally less volatile than the individual stocks within them.

The **rule of 16** is a useful yardstick when considering realized volatilities. Without delving into the maths behind it, a stock or index that moves on average 1 percent every day in any direction during the period in question will have an annualized realized volatility of roughly 16 percent. Coincidentally, the average one-month realized volatility of the S&P 500 Index during the period in the previous graph is just over 16 percent, suggesting that on average during a thirty-day period the index moved a little over 1 percent a day during this time. The rule of 16 works in multiples, such that a realized volatility of 32 percent implies an average daily movement of 2 percent, a realized volatility of 8 percent implies an average daily stock move of half a percent, a realized volatility of 112 percent implies an average daily stock move of 7 percent, etc.

Also apparent from the graph is that volatility tends to **mean revert** over the very long term, meaning that volatility has a tendency to move toward its average level over time. Therefore, volatility does not tend to stay extremely elevated for extended periods, but the largest spikes tend to be short lived when viewed over a long-time history. The fact that the orange line representing S&P 500 Index one-month realized volatility has spent only 2 percent of its time in the top half of its total range illustrates this property. However, over short-time horizons, it is usual to see evidence of **volatility clustering**, which is to say that from one day to the next, larger moves in volatility often beget other large moves before reverting toward its mean over the long term.

Volatility also displays differing **volatility regimes** due largely to changes in the macroeconomic backdrop. The medium and high volatility regime that began in mid-2007 was the build-up to the great financial crisis, which then kept equity market volatility elevated through to 2009. The years that followed the eurozone crisis in the mid-2010s were a long period of very benign market equity volatility that formed an elongated low volatility regime, aided by an exceptionally long US business cycle and highly accommodative central bank policy. The global pandemic punctuated this lull in equity market volatility in 2020, and in 2022, it was consistently elevated once again as central banks raised interest rates to combat inflation.

Implied volatility

The realized volatility of an equity or equity index is the starting point for determining how volatile it is likely to be in the near future and therefore the level of **implied volatility** appropriate for calculating the price of an option using the BSM.

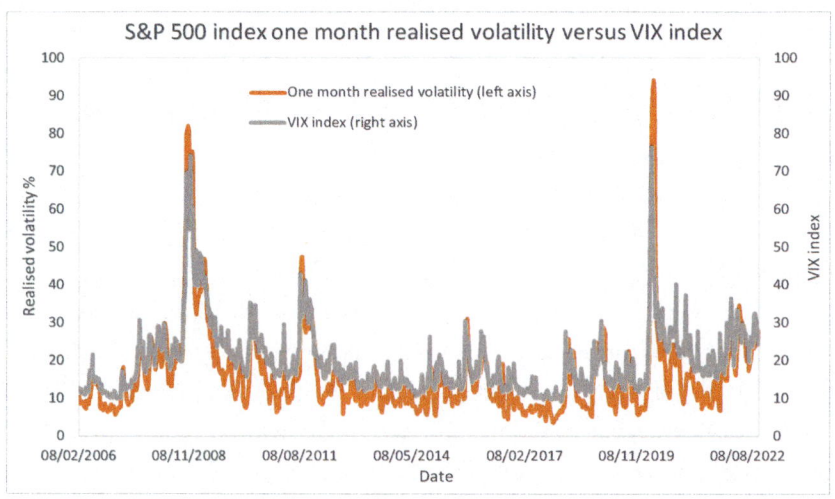

Figure 2.2.

Figure 2.2 shows the same S&P 500 Index one-month realized volatility as Figure 2.1, but overlaid with the **VIX Index**. The VIX Index is calculated from the implied volatility of options on the S&P 500 Index with 30 days to expiration and therefore gives a sense of how volatile the option market expects the S&P 500 Index to be over the next thirty days. Two concepts discussed later in the book are (1) put option skew and (2) the volatility risk premium, and these largely account for the structurally higher level of the VIX Index the majority of the time. Nevertheless, the two are extremely similar and demonstrate that particularly for short-dated options (i.e., those with a month or so until expiration), the current and very recent level of market volatility gives a good indication as to how costly options are priced by the market.

Market participants' buying options causes levels of implied volatility to rise. If there is an upcoming economic data release, for example, there might be an increasing demand for options that causes implied volatility to increase noticeably. However, for a liquid underlying such as the S&P 500 Index, a large difference between implied volatility of shorter-dated options and realized volatility is unlikely to persist for any great length of time. It is resolved either by the market's becoming more volatile to match levels of implied volatility or by implied volatility falling to become more in line with realized volatility, since market participants are able to sell expensive options if implied volatility is priced too richly, which lowers the level of implied volatility.

Longer-dated options that have expiries well in excess of thirty days often do trade with implied volatilities that can be more detached from realized volatility. When markets are quite benign and realized volatility is quite low, longer-dated options often are priced with much higher implied volatility than shorter-dated options on the same underlying stock. This is because further out in the future, there is less certainty of the correct level of realized volatility that will persist throughout the life of the option, so a premium is additionally priced.

It is more common for implied volatility to deviate from realized volatility for individual stock options than it is for options on equity indices. Individual stocks have regular events that may generate short-term volatility to their share prices over a few days (such as earnings announcements every quarter) and also carry unsystematic risk—another concept that will be covered later in the book.

Implied volatility is therefore the market's best estimation of what the realized volatility of an equity is going to be over the life of the option. If the level of implied volatility begins to look too low relative to realized volatility, market participants will buy options, thereby raising implied volatility. If it begins to look too high, market participants will sell the options, thereby lowering implied volatility.

As discussed earlier in the chapter, implied volatility is the only variable not known with a high degree of certainty when calculating an option price. Therefore, the price of any option you see in the market is interchangeable with an implied volatility number—it is just the same thing run through the BSM. Option traders will talk exclusively of implied volatility instead of monetary values for options when talking about prices, which makes it far easier to compare different options at different strikes, expiry dates, and times in the past.

A COLLECTION OF RISKS—THE GREEKS

Once an option expires, its value is either zero or, if it expires in-the-money, fixed at a price determined by how far in-the-money it is relative to its strike price. Prior to expiry, however, a listed option contract has a price that is visible on an options exchange throughout the entire trading day. The previous chapter outlined how market participants determine the price of an option prior to expiry, while this section explains the different risk factors that affect option prices.

The price of a listed option contract can change in value due to a variety of different factors prior to expiry, and each of these is attributable to a specific risk with a different name. These collectively are referred to as **The Greeks**, because many are given a letter of the Greek alphabet.

Each of the Greeks mathematically quantifies the sensitivity that an option price has to a specific risk factor, which acts to either increase or decrease the value of the option. The Greeks all affect an option price simultaneously, so understanding the main ones is important when assessing how an option price will behave in a portfolio.

The following chapters cover **delta**, **vega,** and **theta**, which are all **first-order Greeks**, so called because they quantify changes to the option price due to a change in another variable. **Gamma** is also covered, which is a **second-order Greek**, so called because it quantifies the change to a first-order Greek (delta) due to the change in another variable. This list is not exhaustive by any means but is sufficient for a retail option trader to understand price movements within a retail option portfolio.

CHAPTER 3: DELTA

Delta is the first Greek to understand if hoping to profit from movements in the underlying equity. An option's delta is a measure of the risk to the option price resulting from a movement in the price of the underlying asset.

Figure 3.1 shows data for December 17, 2021 expiry calls and puts (left and right in blue and pink, respectively) for Apple Inc. shares (AAPL). The details were taken from a broker platform on September 28, 2021, so the options had eighty-one days to expiry.

Apple Inc. December 17th 2021 expiry option details.

	CALL					PUT		
theta	delta	impl vol	last price ($)	strike	last price ($)	impl vol	delta	theta
-0.042	0.74	32.5%	15.43	130	3.50	32.1%	-0.25	-0.043
-0.044	0.67	30.2%	11.80	135	4.79	30.2%	-0.33	-0.046
-0.046	0.57	28.7%	8.59	140	6.57	28.6%	-0.43	-0.048
-0.044	0.46	27.4%	5.95	145	9.10	27.4%	-0.54	-0.046
-0.041	0.35	26.8%	4.00	150	12.00	26.8%	-0.65	-0.043
-0.035	0.26	26.2%	2.55	155	15.55	25.8%	-0.75	-0.036

Apple Inc share price: $141.91

Figure 3.1.

The central column in white shows strike prices, and the price of AAPL shares is $141.91 as noted at the bottom of the table. Looking at the 155 strike options on the bottom row and moving to the left gives information about the listed AAPL December 17, 2021 expiry 155 strike call option.

We can see that at that point in time this option had a 0.26 delta and a price of $2.55. This means that if AAPL shares were to <u>increase</u> by $1 to $142.91 per share, you could expect this call option to <u>increase</u> in value by 26c ($1 x 0.26) from $2.55 to $2.81. Conversely, if AAPL shares fell by $1 we should (roughly) expect the option price to fall from $2.55 to $2.29, in other words, as follows:

Change in option price = change in underlying price × option delta

However, this is true for only small incremental changes in stock prices. For larger moves in the underlying equity, an option's gamma also must be considered, which is covered in chapter 6.

A useful way of thinking about delta is that it quantifies how much of the underlying equity exposure there is in the option. As covered in chapter 1, a stock, ETF, or equity index has a linear payoff and therefore has a delta of one—i.e., if it were to go up or down 10 percent, you gain or lose 10 percent. The AAPL December expiry 155 call had a delta of 0.26, so it roughly a quarter of the exposure of AAPL shares. Do not forget, however, that US option have multipliers of 100, so one December expiry 155 call has the exposure of 26 AAPL shares. If AAPL shares go up 1 percent, you are making (roughly) a 1 percent return on 26 AAPL shares through the increase in the value of the call option.

Moving up the table in Figure 3.1 (and down the strikes) from 155 all the way up to 130, the deltas increase along with the price of the options. This is because the call option strike has moved closer to the stock price, and so the option gains more stock exposure and hence becomes more expensive to buy. Indeed, the 140, 135, and 130 strike calls are below the AAPL share price and therefore are in-the-money.

So, for example, the 145 strike call is closer to the $141.91 stock price than the previous 155 strike call and so has a higher delta of 0.46 (i.e., has the exposure of 46 AAPL shares). Consequently, this costs more to buy, at $5.95 ($595 per contract), and the call option price will change by almost half of the magnitude of any small movement of the AAPL share price due to its 0.46 delta. The 130 strike call option has a strike that is in-the-money and therefore below the $141.91 AAPL share price. It has an even higher delta of 0.74, which means this option price will change by almost three-quarters of magnitude of any small movements in the price movement of AAPL shares. One contract will roughly make the same return today as owning 74 AAPL shares, but you pay considerably more for it at $15.43 (i.e., $1,543 when multiplied by 100 multiplier).

When an option is in-the-money, it is said to have **intrinsic value**. This is just a measure of how much in-the-money an option is. The 130 strike call option, for example, has an intrinsic value of $11.91 with the AAPL share price at $141.91. If an option is not in-the-money, it has an intrinsic value of zero (i.e., intrinsic value is never negative, but always either zero or positive).

Intrinsic value of in-the-money call option = stock price – call option strike

When we compare call options with the same underlying asset and the same expiry date, in-the-money or **at-the-money** options (options that have strike price closest to the stock price) have higher deltas and therefore cost more than **out-the-money** call options (i.e., those that have call strikes higher than the stock prices). The further out-the-money you go, the cheaper the cost and the lower the delta.

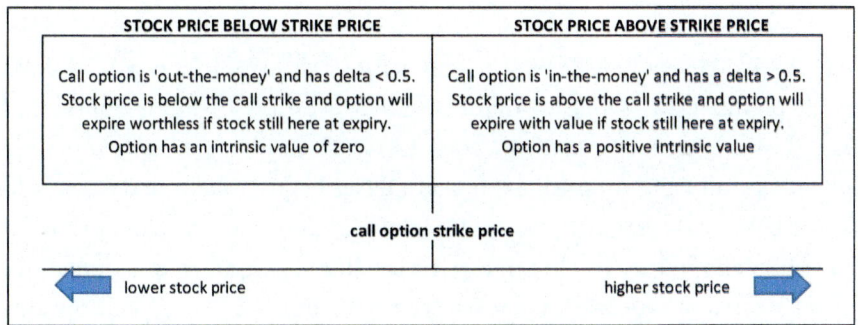

Figure 3.2.

An option delta also has another useful interpretation. Delta can be viewed as an estimated probability of the option ending up in-the-money at expiry and therefore not expire worthless. For instance, the 155 strike AAPL call option in the last example can be thought of as having a 26 percent probability of ending up in-the-money. An at-the-money call option will have a delta of around 0.5, as it has a roughly 50/50 chance of ending up in-the-money and therefore expiring with some value. An in-the-money call option already has the stock price above the strike price, so it has a higher probability of expiring in-the-money and therefore has a delta somewhere above 0.5.

Once a call option reaches expiration, the option has a value if the underlying is above the call strike, or it expires worthless. There is no longer any fractional probability of it expiring in or out-the-money, and so the delta becomes either one (i.e., the same exposure as the notional equivalent of the underlying stock) if it expires in-the-money or zero if it expires out-the-money. All call options therefore have a delta somewhere <u>between</u> zero and one before expiry and a delta <u>of</u> zero or one at expiry.

Option deltas are not static but are moving constantly as the underlying equity price moves. Delta is also affected by several other variables throughout the life of the option, which are quantified by second-order Greeks. Gamma is a second-order Greek that affects delta and is covered in a following chapter. **Charm** is another, which quantifies the change in delta due to the passage of time, and is evident with in-the-money call options whose delta increases as expiry approaches, as it becomes more and more probable that the option will expire in-the-money. For example, the AAPL December 17 expiry 130 strike call option had a 0.74 delta on September 28, which is high because it is an in-the-money option. If AAPL shares were to remain at around $142 throughout the rest of the life of the option right up until expiry on December 17, then the delta would steadily increase from 0.74 to one, as the probability of the call option expiring in-the-money (and therefore acting like a long stock position above the 130 strike) increases. Conversely, all the out-the-money call options with strikes of 145 or higher currently have deltas below 0.5. Their deltas would fall steadily to zero if AAPL shares stayed at the same price up until expiry on December 17.

Put option deltas

Call options, like the underlying equity, have positive deltas and therefore profit when the underlying equity increases in price. Put options, on the other hand, have negative deltas and therefore, like a **short stock** position, increase in value when the underlying equity falls in price. A short stock position entails borrowing a stock for a fee and then selling it in the hope of buying it back at a later date at a lower price for a profit.

Since buying a put option contract gives you the right but not the obligation to sell a specific quantity of the underlying asset at a specific price before a specific point in time in the future, whether you own the underlying asset or not, all put options have negative deltas.

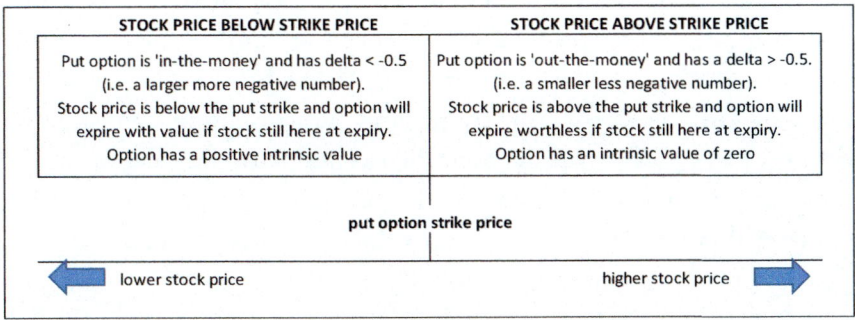

Figure 3.3.

Opposite to call options, put options with strikes numerically <u>above</u> the current stock price are in-the-money and so have larger (negative) deltas and hence are more expensive relative to out-the-money put options with the same expiry. Referring back to the AAPL December 17 expiry options from earlier in the chapter (Figure 3.1), the 155 strike put has a delta of -0.75 and therefore has the same delta exposure as being **short** 75 AAPL shares. It has a cost of $15.55 (i.e., $1,555 per contract) and so is more expensive to buy than the 130 strike put option, which has a delta of -0.25 (and therefore delta equivalent to being **short** 25 AAPL shares) and costs $3.5 (i.e., $350 per contract). If AAPL shares were to increase in price by $1 to $142.91, then the 130 strike put option would fall in price by roughly $0.25 to a value of $3.25. If AAPL shares decreased by $1, then the 130 strike put would increase in value by roughly $0.25 to $3.75.

As with call options, in-the-money put options have intrinsic value, so the 155 strike put has $13.09 of intrinsic value with AAPL shares trading at $141.91, whilst the 130 strike put has zero intrinsic value because it is out-the-money.

Intrinsic value of in-the-money put option = put option strike − stock price

Also, as is the case with call options, a put option delta can be interpreted as a rough probability that the put option will be in-the-money at expiry. Its negative sign is ignored in this instance, so a put option with a -0.30 delta has roughly a 30 percent chance of expiring in-the-money in the same way that a 0.30 delta call option has.

All put options have a delta somewhere between minus one and zero prior to expiry and a delta of minus one or zero at expiry. A put option that expires in-the-money has a delta of minus one and is the delta equivalent of a short stock position below the put strike. Prior to expiry, the negative delta of an in-the-money put option will become increasingly negative if the underlying stock does not move, as the probability increases that the put option will expire in-the-money, and the delta approaches minus one.

CHAPTER 4: VEGA

Vega is a measure of the risk to the option price resulting from a movement in its implied volatility. **Kappa** is sometimes used instead of vega in academic literature (kappa is a *bona fide* Greek letter, unlike vega).

In chapter 2, where the concept of implied volatility was introduced, I explained that demand from market participants buying options increased the level of implied volatility and that selling pressure decreased levels of implied volatility. Vega quantifies how such movements in implied volatility translate to changes in the prices of options themselves.

Any bought options benefit from a gain in implied volatility and suffer when implied volatility falls. Vega is therefore always positive for both put and call options prior to expiry. At expiration, options no longer have any vega exposure. Implied volatility is always expressed in percentage terms, and vega is the value that is added to (or subtracted from) an option price as a result of a 1 percentage point rise (or fall) in implied volatility of that option. Vega therefore quantifies the likely profit or loss on an option position due to a change in the market level of implied volatility for that option.

For example, if an option has a theoretical value of $2, an implied volatility of 25 percent, and a vega of 0.1, its value would become $2.5 if demand for options on that underlying equity caused implied volatility to rise by five implied volatility points to 30 percent. Conversely, the option price would reduce to $1.5 if selling of options caused it to fall five implied volatility points to 20 percent.

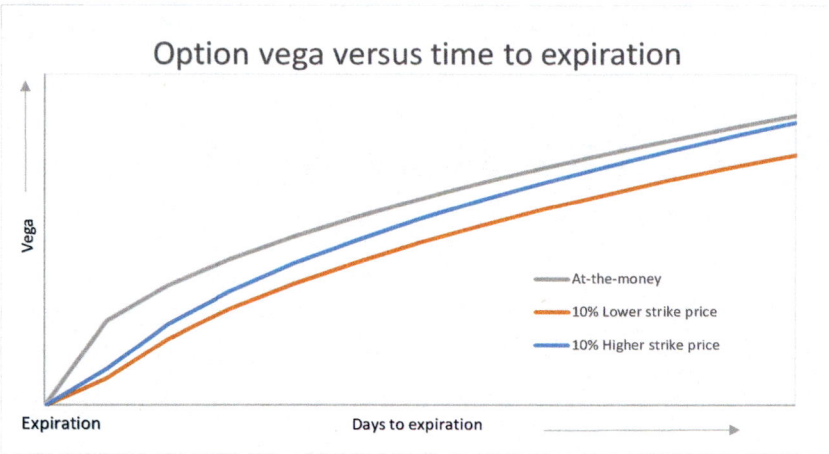

Figure 4.1.

Not all options have similar vegas, and Figure 4.1 illustrates this with respect to option strike and time to expiry. Of note firstly is that longer-dated options have higher vegas than shorter-dated options. Furthermore, vega falls at an increasingly fast rate for an at-the-money options as expiry approaches. Lastly, at-the-money options have the highest vega relative to other options with the same expiry, and those with higher strikes will have higher vega than those with lower strikes if the strikes are equidistant from the underlying stock price (this is a slight oversimplification).

Purposefully taking large vega exposures is not ordinarily a motivation for most retail option users, and this book explicitly focuses on strategies that profit instead from an option's delta, whilst offering either better returns and/or less risk than stock investing. However, an option's vega is important to understand, as it can often have a meaningful impact on potential profits prior to expiration.

When market volatility has pushed up implied volatility levels, it can be frustrating to buy a call option with a large vega exposure to play a rebound in a particular market, for example. You may find that you have paid too much for your call option, since higher implied volatility raises the cost of all options, and that as the market rebounds, implied volatility naturally falls, creating a far smaller gain in your call option price than you would otherwise expect, as profits from delta gains are offset by vega losses.

It is important to have a sense of the volatility regime that markets are currently in because this assists in determining what vega exposure to accept and hence which option strategy to use. For example, if markets are in a high volatility regime, then one can have greater confidence that markets will be less volatile over the next year or so, because implied volatility is mean reverting over long periods, and highly volatile markets historically do not persist indefinitely. It would be unwise to buy longer-dated options during these circumstances, because owning large vega exposure may generate losses prior to expiry that outweigh potential profits from an option's delta, if markets normalize and implied volatility falls. Strategies that employ shorter-dated options and have net short vega exposures may be better suited in this environment, for example. The strategies laid out in later chapters have different vega exposures, and reference will be made regarding the suitability of each in different volatility regimes.

CHAPTER 5: THETA

An option's theta is a measure of the risk to the option price resulting from the passage of time. Specifically, an option price falls in value by its theta in one day.

Apple Inc. December 17th 2021 expiry option details.

	CALL					PUT			
theta	delta	impl vol	last price ($)	strike	last price ($)	impl vol	delta	theta
-0.042	0.74	32.5%	15.43	130	3.50	32.1%	-0.25	-0.043
-0.044	0.67	30.2%	11.80	135	4.79	30.2%	-0.33	-0.046
-0.046	0.57	28.7%	8.59	140	6.57	28.6%	-0.43	-0.048
-0.044	0.46	27.4%	5.95	145	9.10	27.4%	-0.54	-0.046
-0.041	0.35	26.8%	4.00	150	12.00	26.8%	-0.65	-0.043
-0.035	0.26	26.2%	2.55	155	15.55	25.8%	-0.75	-0.036

Apple Inc share price: $141.91

Figure 3.1.

Repeating Figure 3.1 and the example of the AAPL December 17, 2021, expiry stock options from chapter 3, the first thing to note is that all options have a negative theta—in this example, of around $0.04 a day. Any bought option will have a negative theta, since premium is paid for either a put or a call option and that ultimately it will expire either at zero or at their intrinsic value at some point in the future. Theta is at work, eroding the premium paid for an option from the first day it is purchased, which is why it is often referred to as **time decay**.

The AAPL December 17, 2021, expiry 150 strike call option costs $4 ($400 in total premium due to the 100 multiplier) on September 28, 2021. One day later, on September 29, that option price will have fallen by its theta of -$0.04 (rounded up to the nearest cent), from $4 to $3.96 ($396 in total premium), assuming that all other variables, including the AAPL share price and the option's implied volatility, remain unchanged.

Theta is therefore a constant daily drain on the value of an option. Effectively, when purchasing a put or call option you are implicitly trying to benefit from gains to the option price, resulting primarily from its delta and/or vega, in excess of the drain of theta decay on its value.

Figure 5.1 takes the AAPL December 17, 2021, expiry 145 strike call option from Figure 3.1, costing $5.95, and shows a recalculated price for it, using the BSM, assuming changes in the price of AAPL shares. The lightest line shows these prices as they would have appeared on September 28, 2021, with 81 days remaining until expiry on December 17, 2021. Each subsequent line shows the same option revalued twenty days later (assuming no change in any other variable except the share price) up until expiry of the option. Figure 5.1 therefore graphically shows how the price of a call option decays over time. The shape of the darkest line, denoting the values for the option at expiry, has the same shape as the JPM call option example in Figure 1.1.

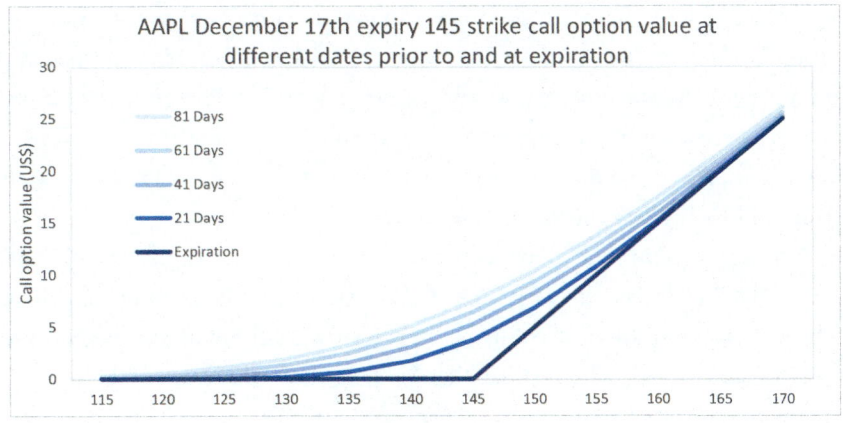

Figure 5.1

Prior to expiry, all options have **time value**. Time value is simply the amount of an option price that is in excess of its intrinsic value. Since the AAPL Inc. share price was $141.91 in Figure 3.1, the 145 strike call has no intrinsic value because it is not in-the-money and the entire $5.95 cost is made up of time value. The 130 strike call is in-the-money, however, and has an intrinsic value of $11.91 ($141.91 − 130) and therefore its remaining cost of $3.52 ($15.43 − $11.91) is its time value.

Option price prior to expiry = time value + intrinsic value

Because an option price at expiry is purely its intrinsic value (i.e., it is either worthless if it is out-the-money or if in-the-money, it is worth how much it is in-the-money by), this means that theta decays only an option's time value to leave just intrinsic value at expiry. Time value is therefore a measure of how much of an option's price is eliminated by theta at expiry if the underlying equity does not move.

In Figure 5.1, at extremes of the option being deeply in-the-money, with the share price at $170, for example, or deeply out-the-money, with the share price at $115, there is very little time value added to the option's intrinsic value. Consequently, theta is low for deeply in or out-the-money options. There is a great deal more time value and hence higher theta for at-the-money options.

Close inspection also shows that the rate at which time decay occurs, and therefore the size of an option's theta, increases as expiry approaches. Since the lines are all spaced twenty days apart, this is evidenced by the increasing size of the spacing between the lines and is particularly apparent when the option is at-the-money—i.e., when the share price is at the 145 option strike in Figure 5.1. At-the-money options have greater time values and hence more decay is necessary for the price to reach its intrinsic value at expiry. Theta actually increases exponentially for at-the-money options as they approach expiry and is highest the day before expiry.

Changes in implied volatility also affect an option's theta. Higher implied volatility increases the prices of all options, and, assuming that there is little change in the underlying share price, this simply increases the time value of an option, which means there is more to decay away before the option reaches its intrinsic value at expiry. Options with higher implied volatility therefore also have higher theta. This relationship is linear for at-the-money options, so if implied volatility were to double, then theta decay of that option would also double.

CHAPTER 6: GAMMA

An option's gamma is a measure of the risk to the option's delta resulting from a movement in the underlying asset. It is therefore a second-order Greek, because it quantifies changes not to the option price but specifically to the change in an option's delta resulting from a one-unit change in the value of the underlying stock (i.e., a $1 change in a dollar-denominated stock).

Delta at times does a poor job of accurately quantifying changes to an option price due to a move in the underlying stock, if the move is moderately large. Furthermore, if the option is at-the-money, its effectiveness decreases as expiry approaches. Figure 6.1 helps illustrate why this is the case, using the earlier example of the AAPL December 17 expiry 145 strike call option.

AAPL December 17th expiry 145 strike call option value at different dates before expiration

- 81 Days
- 21 Days
- 81 Days and recalculating option price just using its 0.5 delta
- 21 Days and recalculating option price just using its 0.5 delta

Figure 6.1

It shows only the values of the call option for different prices of AAPL shares with just 81 days and 21 days before expiration. Both lines are **convex** in shape, which is a feature of any long option payoff prior to expiry, before reaching the asymmetric payoff at expiry. **Convexity** is a highly beneficial property of an option because, in the case of a call option like the one in Figure 6.1, as the market rises the call option increases in value at a faster rate, and as the market falls the call option loses money at a slower rate. In the case of a put option, when the market falls, it increases in value at a faster rate, and as the market rises, it loses value at a slower rate.

Figure 6.1 shows also that whilst the prices for this option with twenty-one days remaining to expiry, represented by the darker blue line, due to the effect of theta decay are lower than the light blue line, which denotes prices for the option with eighty-one days before expiry, it also has a more convex shape. This highlights the fact that shorter-dated options have greater convexity. In order to illustrate gamma and convexity, the dotted lines represent the effect of repricing the 145 strike call option when it is at-the-money, using just the option's delta. Since an at-the-money option has a delta of 0.5, this would involve adding (or subtracting) $0.5 for every $1 up (or down) in the price of AAPL shares. This shows the problem with using delta alone to try to recalculate the value of an option, following large moves in the underlying stock. The delta calculation is linear in nature, whereas option prices have convexity. Gamma therefore adjusts the option delta to give the option price convexity. The reason that call options increase in value at a faster rate than the underlying stock when it rises is that gamma adds more delta to the call option. The reason why they lose money at a slower rate as the market falls is that gamma reduces the call option's delta. Since shorter-dated options have greater convexity, they therefore have greater gamma. Figure 6.1 also shows that the greatest point of convexity is also when the stock is at the strike price. Therefore, at-the-money options also have greater gamma than out-the-money options have.

Another feature of gamma is that if you buy an option, gamma is always positive, which is to say that convexity is always working in your favour. How this works with a call option is outlined above, but in the case of a put option, when the market rises, gamma reduces the negative delta, and when the market falls, gamma increases the negative delta. For example, an at-the-money call and put option have a delta of 0.5 and -0.5, respectively. Assume they have the same expiry date and both have a gamma of five (since puts and calls with the same strike price and expiry have the same gamma). If the underlying stock moves up one unit (whatever its currency of denomination), then the call delta increases to 0.55 and the put delta increases to -0.45. If the stock instead moves down one unit, then the call delta decreases to 0.45 and the put delta decreases to -0.55, since the positive gamma is subtracted when the stock move is negative.

The downside of owning gamma is that gamma and theta are closely related. Theta and gamma are almost always of opposite signs but are of similar magnitude. Owning an option with a large amount of convexity therefore will also suffer from significant theta decay.

HOW EQUITY OPTIONS TRADE

CHAPTER 7: THE OPTIONS EXCHANGE AND CLEARING HOUSE

Equity options that retail investors are able to trade are listed instruments quoted on an options exchange, such as the CBOE Options Exchange in the US, Eurex in Europe, or NSE in India.

As set out in chapter 1, listed equity options all have the following characteristics:

1. They are either a put or a call.
2. They all have an underlying asset, which is an equity, ETF, or equity index.
3. They have a strike price, which is the price you can buy the underlying asset for in the case of call options or sell the underlying asset at in the case of put options.
4. They all have an expiry date.
5. They are all traded on an options exchange.
6. The premium value paid (or received) when an option is traded = number of contracts × option price × multiplier.

Listed option contracts are highly standardized by the exchange to facilitate trading. The options exchange determines which underlying equity they will list options on, which option expiry dates to use, which strike prices will be available to trade, and which multiplier it will use as standard.

The quantity of expiry dates that the exchange will list for a particular underlying equity will be a reflection of the volume of option trades that are undertaken. For example, the SPDR S&P 500 ETF Trust (SPY) is an ETF that tracks the S&P 500 Index and attracts retail and institutional investors. It regularly has the largest demand for option trades by investors and consequently a huge array of expiry dates to choose from—from over two years into the future to each day of the week. This allows investors to make very specific bets on price movements on the SPY ETF. Conversely, stocks that attract less demand for option usage may have monthly expiry dates listed by exchanges or even just quarterly.

For each expiry date for each underlying asset, the exchange lists a variety of out-the-money, at-the-money, and in-the-money call and put option strikes that investors are able to trade. Again, the quantity of strikes that are listed for each expiry date is to a large extent dependent upon the volume of option trading that each underlying asset attracts. On the SPY ETF alone, there may be over thirty expiry dates and one hundred different available strikes to trade for each expiry date, making thousands of put and calls available to trade on the ETF at any one time.

The exchange works with a clearing house, which may be an agency of the exchange or a separate corporation. It provides a number of essential roles once a trade occurs on the exchange, aimed at reducing risks and maintaining the integrity of the market. As well as becoming legal counterparty to each option trade undertaken, it also establishes the parameters around **margin** requirements.

Margin is collateral, in the form of cash for retail investors, that is demanded by the clearing house when entering into any trade that has a contingent liability. Contingent liabilities essentially carry the risk of requiring additional funds at some point in the future if there are adverse market movements. Since buying an option does not leave the owner open to a contingent liability, because there is no additional loss that the holder can suffer in excess of the premium paid, margin is not required by the clearing house.

However, options are also sold short in the same way that stocks can be sold short. When a stock is sold short, it is with the intention of buying it back in the future (to **buy to close** the **short position**) hopefully at a lower price. When an option is sold short, it is with the intention of collecting the option premium. Sold options are either bought to close or left to expire. When an investor sells a call option short, it leaves them potentially open to an unlimited loss, whilst selling a put option short potentially leaves them open to a substantial loss if the underlying share price falls to zero. Because selling an option may create a contingent liability, the clearing house can demand a margin payment to collateralize it. Selling options can carry significant risk, and strategies that involve selling options in this book have strict requirements to mitigate these risks.

The clearing house also performs trade settlement and recording of all trades undertaken on the options exchange. On the expiry day of an option, using a published methodology, the exchange where the underlying asset trades determines its **settlement price**, which is the price that will apply for all put and call option contracts expiring that day. Figure 7.1 shows the process undertaken.

Exchange determines settlement price of ABC stock on expiry day

◄──── lower ABC option strikes ──── | ABC SETTLEMENT PRICE | ──── higher ABC option strikes ────►

put strike below settlement price	call strike below settlement price	put strike above settlement price	call strike above settlement price
put expires worthless	CH automatically exercises call	CH automatically exercises put	call expires worthless

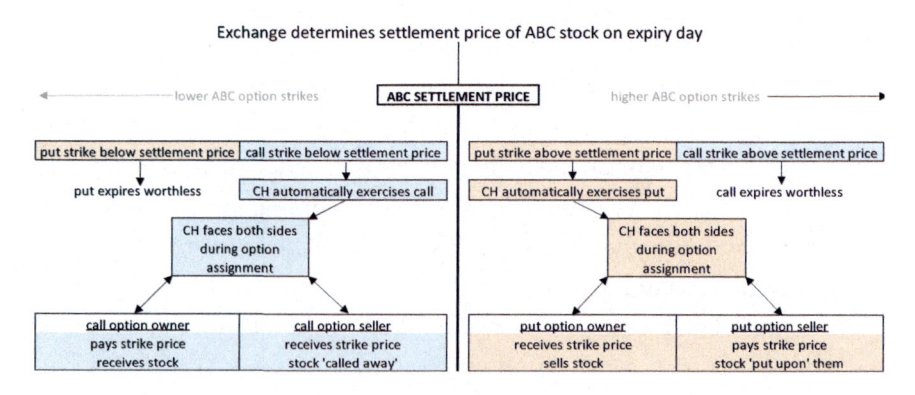

CH faces both sides during option assignment

CH faces both sides during option assignment

| call option owner pays strike price receives stock | call option seller receives strike price stock 'called away' | put option owner receives strike price sells stock | put option seller pays strike price stock 'put upon' them |

Figure 7.1

Out-the-money options expire worthless at the conclusion of the expiry day, but in-the-money options are automatically exercised by the clearing house. The process of **option assignment** follows the option exercise and refers to the transfer of ownership of stock and cash in order to fulfil the contractual obligation that was entered into when the option was originally bought or sold. Owners of in-the-money put options sell stock at the strike price to the clearing house and receive money, and owners of in-the-money call options buy stock at the strike price and pay money to the clearing house. Every put and call option that has been bought has an investor(s) who has made a corresponding sale of that option. The clearing house acts as intermediary to "put" the stock onto the corresponding seller of the in-the-money put options and take payment equal to the put strike, and to "call away" the stock from the call option seller and make payment equal to the call strike.

The process is simpler with listed index options because they are **cash-settled**, so there are no transfers of stock, just the cash value of the option based on the settlement price of the underlying equity index. However, retail investors do not generally use index options, since the exposure sizes are much larger.

American versus European style options

The majority of listed options are American style options. This name has nothing to do with their country of origin; rather, it is the term given to options that are exercisable at any day prior to, as well as on, expiry day. This is entirely at the prerogative of the option buyer, who has the right to exercise their American style option at any time. However, it makes little economic sense to do so except under a few specific circumstances, since once an option is exercised, any remaining time value for the option, which always has some monetary value prior to expiry, is lost. Therefore, only when the desire to own the shares underlying a call option is greater than the value lost when exercising early, is it worth consideration. This might be due to a dividend ex-date approaching. Owning a call option alone does not entitle the buyer to any dividends, so if the dividend is more valuable than the remaining option time value, in order to own the stock and therefore receive the dividend on payment date, a call option owner may exercise early. Also, it may be desirable to exercise a call option early if a takeover of the company is, or is likely to be, in progress. It usually makes little sense to exercise a put option early, however, although it does sometimes happen in the last few days prior to expiry. This may occur when the remaining time value becomes increasingly negligible, particularly deeply in-the-money puts, and if put holders are keen to receive the put strike payment to reinvest, or when interest rates and the put strike are large enough to earn a return in excess of the remaining time value.

European style options, conversely, are not exercisable at any time until the point of expiry of the option. European style options list on some European exchanges though, so it is always important to check which type you are trading.

CHAPTER 8: SELECTING A BROKER PLATFORM

Your broker platform is the window through which you interact with global option markets. It relays information directly from the options exchanges, showing what products they have listed for trading and where buy and sell orders from every other investor have aggregated to form a market with a single bid and an offer price. The platform will also relay the exchange's information to you regarding the standardized specifics for contracts you can trade, such as the multiplier, whether it is stock-settled or cash-settled, whether American or European style, etc. Most important, the platform also allows you to select a contract of your choice and submit an order in it (for a fee) that is relayed instantly to the options exchange for execution according to your wishes. It then acts as a live ledger for your portfolio, showing the profit or loss relative to current prices disseminated by the exchanges for option and stock positions you have traded.

That is the basics, and there is a growing number of platforms to choose from that can provide this for you. Once you have a shortlist of contenders that have passed the initial due diligence, your selection comes down to the additional functionality they offer, the price you pay to use it, and your personal preferences. The good news is that platforms and the technology that power them have become increasingly sophisticated over recent years, whilst competition has driven down the trading costs to individual investors as option volumes have grown significantly. This chapter aims to provide some guidance in selecting the right one for you.

Due diligence

The services offered and products available to trade on online broking platforms vary greatly. Not all platforms facilitate the trading of equity options, and even some that do will allow you to trade only a restricted range of contracts. It is therefore primarily necessary to determine the platforms that offer the largest range of option contracts to trade. This may require using more than one platform to cover not only the largest exchanges but also contracts on other global options exchanges for complete market coverage if you wish. Since different platforms also have differing strengths and weaknesses, using a couple of platforms that complement each other can be a good strategy.

Although there is no agency in the world that will safeguard you against market risk—i.e., the risk of falling markets negatively affecting the prices of investments you have made—investor protections safeguarding you in the event of your chosen broker going bust do exist. For example, the Securities Investor Protection Corporation (SIPC) is a US organisation that protects investors if a broker firm declares bankruptcy, runs into financial trouble, or if customer's assets go missing. The broker must be a SPIC member, but then even non-US citizens and non-residents have up to $500,000 of protection.

A national or supranational regulatory body within the jurisdiction of a major financial centre must also regulate your chosen broker. This ensures that their financial stability and conduct are of the highest standard and that an ombudsman is in place to address any potential grievances. These details will feature prominently on their website.

They should also have rigorous online security and account protection to safeguard you and your personal information. Two-factor authentication login should be a minimum protection when accessing your account, and all communications should be secure and encrypted.

Functionality

Once you have whittled down a shortlist of potential broker platforms, it is time to investigate what they can offer you in terms of functionality. Many make this easier by offering a demo account, which lets you play around on the platform and make simulated trades so that you are able to experience almost exactly what the platform would be like to use. Others allow you to go through the sign-up process and then investigate their platform prior to funding your account. Either way, the ability to use the platform yourself will inform your choice much more than reading the broker's promotional material. There is usually some online tutorial to help you navigate the platform as well.

Among the top selection priorities should be some capability to assess how expensive or cheap the implied volatility priced into an option is. A Bloomberg terminal used by an investment professional gives them the ability to graph a long history of specific implied volatilities for any asset that has listed options, relating to different expiries and to different strikes, both in terms of percentage of stock price and option delta. They display current implied volatilities relative to a multi-year average in order to assess whether they look expensive or not relative to their history, as well as how they compare with current realized volatility. This requires an immense amount of data, which is expensive to buy, so it is unlikely that your broker platform will have such a high degree of analytical capability. However, since implied volatility is a primary determinant of an option price, it is essential that the broker platform you select have as much analytical capability as possible. Spend time researching this, as it will improve your trading outcomes.

Other important functionality includes the capability to build graphs easily, preferably with the ability to do so versus another asset so you are able to view relative performances. Most will allow you to overlay graphs with a variety of technical indicators if you wish. An extremely useful function that some platforms offer is the ability to undertake some risk analysis on a portfolio of options. The more technologically advanced platforms will allow you to build customizable screens where it is possible to see the exposures that a portfolio or a single option position has. The ability to view aggregated values for each of your Greek risk exposures is extremely important. The best platforms will take this a step further and provide "what-if analysis" to show the effect of market or implied volatility shifts and the passage of time on your portfolio as well. Being able to make informed trading decisions and manage your risks properly will enhance your trading performance.

Fees

After you have tried out the platform offerings from as many suitable brokers as possible, your final decision for which platform(s) to use will also come down to the fees they charge. Trading costs eat directly into your profits, and so you need to be very clear about exactly what they are. Unavoidably, some relatively small fees will be levied by the exchange or clearing house and passed through to you via the broker platform when you trade, but those that will be charged directly to you by the broker operating the platform require scrutiny.

Any regulated broker must clearly state all fees and contingent cost so there will be no hidden surprises once you begin trading. There are two types of fees that a broker platform will charge—account fees and trading commissions. You should not have to pay for using a broker platform, but some may charge account fees to use a more technologically advanced version, which is unnecessary for novices. Others may charge account maintenance fees, possibly related to the size of account and frequency of trading, for live price feeds of options and stocks while offering slightly delayed pricing free, or fees for additional news services and stock trade recommendations. Trading commissions are costs for executing trade orders, quoted per contract for options or at a fixed fee or percentage of trade size for stock trades.

Your aim is to select potential broker platforms that charge no account management fees, or as small an amount as possible, particularly if you are just starting out. Trading commissions are unavoidable, but their amounts do vary from broker to broker. Spend some time comparing the costs of different platforms and weighing them up against what they offer, recognizing that at the start your trading will be relatively small and that costs need to be minimized whilst you gain trading experience.

Submitting orders

Once you have selected the most suitable platform and funded your account, you will be in a position to start formulating trade ideas and eventually submitting orders for execution by your broker via their platform. There are varieties of different possible trade orders, and you should read or watch relevant educational material if provided by your broker on this subject if you are not familiar with them. The basic ones, however, are (1) a **market order**, which is an instruction to trade immediately at the prevailing market price and (2) a **limit order**, which is to trade only if the price reaches a predefined limit of your choice.

As mentioned in the previous chapter, it is possible to sell an option that you do not currently own, which is referred to as **selling short**, to create a short position that you hope to buy back at some point in the future at a lower price, or to let expire worthless. Selling short an option, whether a put or a call, is also referred to as **writing** an option. This necessitates the distinction when submitting a trade order to either **buy to open** or **sell to open** when trading a new position, or to either **buy to close** or **sell to close** when trading an existing position. The opposite of a short option, or short stock position, is one that you have bought, which is a **long option**, or **long stock position.**

SINGLE OPTION STRATEGIES

CHAPTER 9: LONG CALL

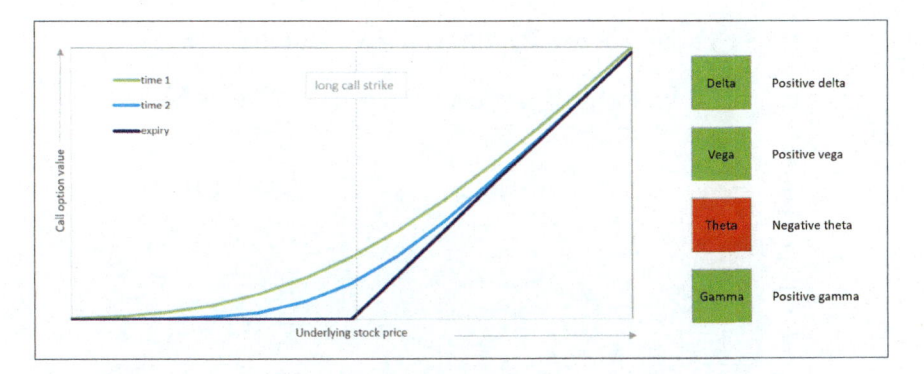

Figure 9.1.

Buying a call option is the simplest option strategy for gaining positive exposure to an underlying asset. It encapsulates all the previously highlighted benefits of using options—i.e., positive convexity or asymmetry, leverage, and limited loss. A long call is bought by submitting a single buy to open instruction on a broker platform.

The dark blue line in Figure 9.1 shows the payoff profile of a long call option at expiry. The other two lines show the value of the call option at the two different points in time prior to expiration. The light green line shows how the call option value initially changes in relation to moves in the underlying stock, denoted by "time 1". The light blue line shows how its value has changed due to theta decay by two thirds of the way through its life, denoted by "time 2". Subsequent chapters have similar schematics for each option strategy, following the same rules.

Once it has been decided which asset to gain exposure to via a call option, which call option is the correct one to buy when the SPY ETF, for example, has around thirty different expiry dates and one hundred strikes listed for each expiry? In order to answer this question, it is first necessary to appreciate the way the following affects the call option price: (1) the call option's time to expiry and (2) the option's being in, at, or out-the-money (its **moneyness**). Figure 9.2 attempts to explain these relationships in general terms.

Effect of strike and expiry on call option premium cost

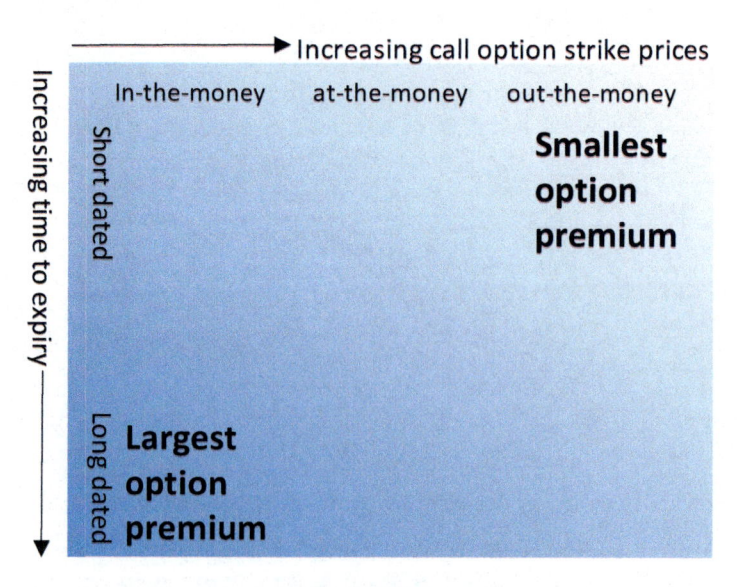

Figure 9.2.

As Figure 9.2 suggests, far out-the-money, shorter-dated call options have lowest call option premiums. Intuitively this makes sense, when further out-the-money options have a smaller delta and therefore smaller probability of expiring in-the-money, while those already in-the-money have higher deltas, greater stock exposure and are therefore more valuable. Intuitively also, longer-dated options with more time to expiry have a greater time value and thus cost more to purchase than shorter-dated options with less time value.

Consequently, short-dated, out-the-money options have the lowest likelihood of making the owner any money and so are the cheapest to buy. However, because they are so cheap, the potential returns can be enormous, so are more akin to lottery tickets.

Overlaying the determinant factors of moneyness and time to expiry on a call option price is also its amount of implied volatility. All call option prices increase (decrease) as implied volatility rises (falls), and the amount by which it does is quantified by the option's vega, as covered in chapter 4.

With these relationships in mind, it is also necessary to be clear about each of the following points in order to select the appropriate call option strike and expiry and ultimately submit a trade:

1. What is the purpose of the trade? Is it speculation or investment?
2. Conservatively, how much upside is there to the price of the underlying equity and over what time frame?
3. How much conviction is there in this view, and what are the risks to it?
4. Is the implied volatility attractively priced?
5. What is the correct trade size?

Figure 9.3 uses these points to construct a flow chart to aid the decision process when formulating a long call option trade and highlights that speculating and investing are separate approaches. Speculation involves capitalizing on anticipated market moves over a short time frame, whereas investing involves using longer-dated call options to gain exposure to assets in a limited risk capacity because they have attractive long-term return potential. However, both require an assessment of whether option prices have implied volatility that is high, medium, or low.

HAPPY RETURNS

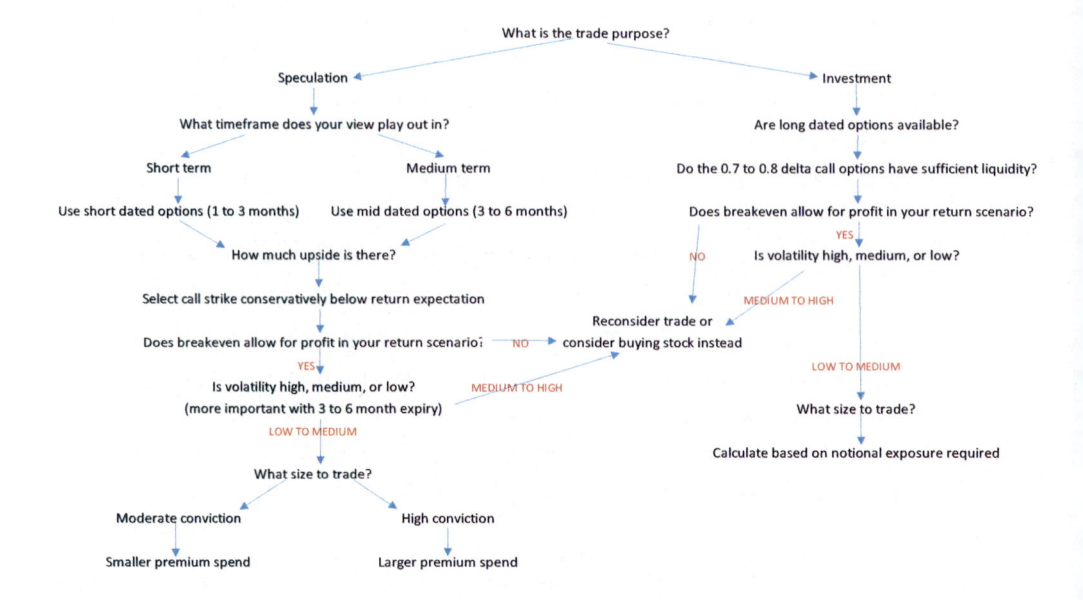

```
                          What is the trade purpose?
                         /                          \
              Speculation                            Investment
                   |                                      |
    What timeframe does your view play out in?    Are long dated options available?
         /                    \                           |
   Short term            Medium term          Do the 0.7 to 0.8 delta call options have sufficient liquidity?
       |                      |                           |
Use short dated options   Use mid dated options   Does breakeven allow for profit in your return scenario?
  (1 to 3 months)         (3 to 6 months)                 |
       |                      |                    NO ---/  \--- YES
       How much upside is there?                    |           |
              |                            Is volatility high, medium, or low?
  Select call strike conservatively below return expectation
              |                                   MEDIUM TO HIGH
   Does breakeven allow for profit in your return scenario?
                    NO ---/  \--- YES       Reconsider trade or
                              |             consider buying stock instead
         Is volatility high, medium, or low?        |
         (more important with 3 to 6 month expiry)  LOW TO MEDIUM
                    MEDIUM TO HIGH                  |
                              |              What size to trade?
                         LOW TO MEDIUM              |
                              |              Calculate based on notional exposure required
                     What size to trade?
                        /         \
             Moderate conviction    High conviction
                  |                       |
          Smaller premium spend    Larger premium spend
```

Figure 9.3.

Is the implied volatility high, medium, or low?

To answer this question precisely requires detailed analysis of implied and realized volatility data. This is because implied volatility is not static; on the same underlying equity, implied volatility will be different for each specific option strike and expiry. If you were trading options for a large investment company, this data is readily available on a Bloomberg terminal. So, if you were buying a SPY three-month 5 percent out-the-money call option, you would be able to look at a continuous history over the last ten years of data for that specific implied volatility and calculate its average and the number of standard deviations the current market price is from it. However, Bloomberg licences are expensive, and implied volatility data to that degree of granularity is difficult to obtain without paying large subscription fees.

This first point of reference, therefore, will be the chosen broker platform. Any worth their salt will have some degree of functionality in this respect, although undoubtedly less sophisticated than a Bloomberg terminal. However, this underlines the importance of selecting one that allows as much implied volatility analysis as possible for a chosen underlying equity. Implied volatility is a primary determinant factor in an option price, so a means of assessing it relative to its history is extremely important. This should be possible by either graphing its history or having a function whereby the platform calculates current implied volatility as a percentile of its recent history. This gives an initial read on whether an option's implied volatility is high, medium, or low.

Another way of assessing whether an option is richly priced is by comparison with the realized volatility of the underlying asset. This becomes somewhat complicated by the fact that for any chosen expiration date, out-the-money equity put options naturally have a higher implied volatility than at-the-money options, and out-the-money call options naturally have lower implied volatility. This is referred to as **implied volatility skew** and is a topic that I discuss later in this book. Nevertheless, comparison of at-the-money implied volatility of the same expiration date with realized volatility is a common method of determining whether option pricing looks attractive. One-month realized volatility is suitable for this comparison, or three-month realized volatility for any implied volatilities of options with over three months to expiration. Again, the chosen broker platform should have sufficient functionality to view realized volatilities for equities. However, it is also possible to download historical price data for the underlying asset in order to calculate realized volatility. Several internet sites can help, such as "How to Calculate Historical Volatility in Excel," https://www.macroption.com/historical-volatility-excel/. Implied volatility that appears to be at a large premium to realized volatility is at the greatest risk of falling and thereby generating a vega loss for an option prior to expiry, so you should avoid it.

In any event, it remains that during periods of heightened market volatility, options become more expensive to buy. This is especially so for longer-dated options because they have the highest vega exposures and therefore are disproportionately more expensive and generate the highest vega losses if volatility normalizes. Therefore, I recommend not to buy anything other than short-dated options during periods of heightened market volatility and even then, to utilize more advanced strategies than simply buying options so that vega exposures are reduced.

Finally, it is also possible to get a general sense of how expensively priced shorter-dated equity index options are by looking at a graph of the **VIX Index** or the **VSTOXX Index**. These indices derive their prices from the implied volatility of options with thirty days remaining to expiry on the S&P 500 Index and the Eurostoxx Index, respectively. Assessing how far current levels are from a one-year average, denoted by the dotted lines in Figure 9.4, gives a general sense of how expensive short-dated index options are on these indices relative to recent history.

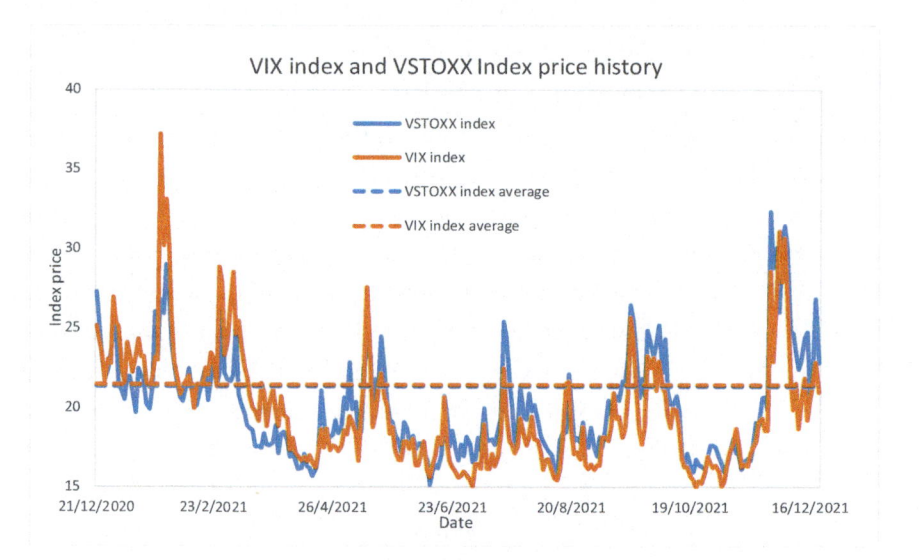

Figure 9.4.

Speculating with call options

Speculating on anticipated shorter-term moves to a stock or a stock index, whether prompted by your own analysis or signals from elsewhere, generally requires the use of graphs to study the price behaviour of the asset. Studying how it has moved in the past will inform you to some extent about the magnitude and the time frame of an anticipated move that you are wishing to profit from. Forming an opinion on how much "upside" there is to the stock price and on how much time it will take to get there can inform the selection of strike and expiry.

Being clear on the time frame is crucial when speculating with options because they have a limited life. On the one hand, you may wish to buy the most suitable shortest-dated option, since shorter-dated options are cheaper than longer-dated options. On the other hand, your entire option premium will expire worthless if the anticipated move does not materialize before expiry. It makes sense to err on the side of caution and buy a slightly longer-dated call option than you think you need because it is always possible to sell your call option at any point prior to expiry once your view has played out. Since theta accelerates in the last month of the option's life, it is often not desirable to hold an option during this period either.

The **breakeven** for a long call option refers to how much the underlying equity has to move by expiry so that you have not lost any money on the trade. Since the entire premium is lost unless the underlying stock exceeds the call strike at expiry, the breakeven is the call strike plus the option premium.

Call option breakeven = call option strike + cost of the call option

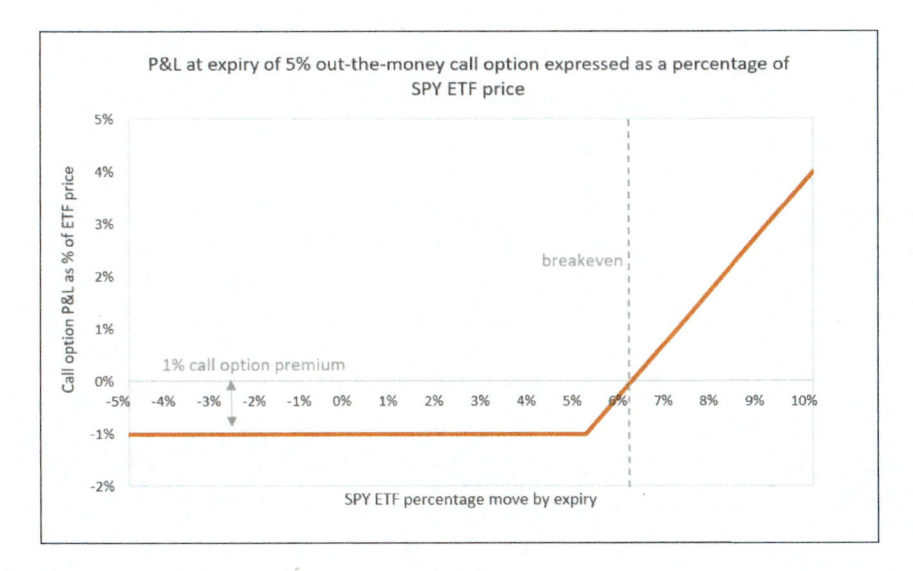

Figure 9.5

For example, a 5 percent out-the-money call option costing 1 percent of the underlying SPY ETF price would require a 6 percent move higher in the ETF by expiry to breakeven. Should the ETF climb 10 percent, the option would make 4 percent profit, which is four times the premium spent. Were the index to climb 5 percent or less by expiry, the entire 1 percent premium would be lost. It is therefore crucial that your call option breakeven is sufficiently below your return expectation in order to ensure an acceptable profit.

Example

It is early February 2022, and you want to speculate on Chevron Corp. (CVX), given the bullish fundamentals in the oil price and comparatively low valuation. Its share price has lagged its peers recently, notably Exxon Mobil Corp., and looks set to reach $165 by mid-May, from its current price close to $138, if continues its current trend.

Figure 9.6.

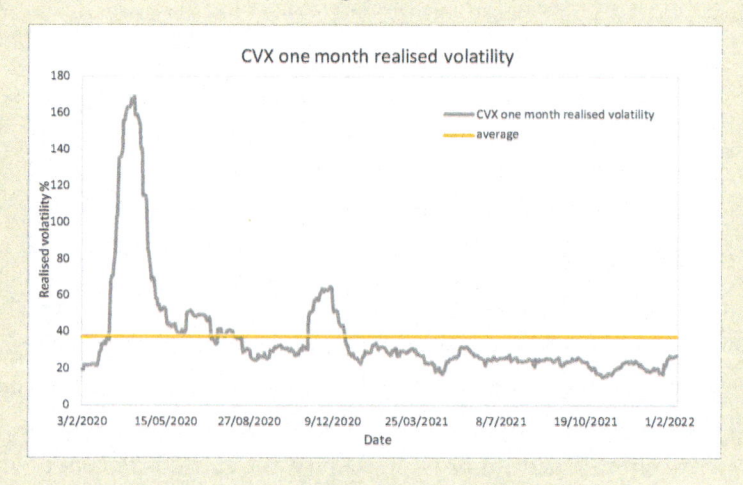

Figure 9.7.

You look at the available listed expiries for CVX call options on your broker platform and see that those on May 20 and June 17 cover your mid-May time frame. You calculate breakevens and profit potential for each strike, based upon your expectation that the stock will reach $165 by that point, and compile the tables in Figure 9.8.

May 20 expiry call option details

				(call strike + call cost)	($165 - breakeven)	(expiry profit/call cost)
strike	call mid price	implied volatility	delta	breakeven	expiry profit	% profit
140	6.72	28.5%	0.46	146.72	18.28	272%
145	4.68	27.7%	0.37	149.68	15.32	327%
150	3.15	27.1%	0.28	153.15	11.85	376%
155	1.98	26.3%	0.20	156.98	8.02	405%
160	1.23	25.9%	0.14	161.23	3.77	307%

June 17 expiry call option details

strike	call mid price	implied volatility	delta	breakeven	expiry profit	% profit
140	7.71	28.7%	0.47	147.71	17.29	224%
145	5.63	27.9%	0.38	150.63	14.37	255%
150	4.03	27.4%	0.31	154.03	10.97	272%
155	2.74	26.7%	0.23	157.74	7.26	265%
160	1.87	26.4%	0.17	161.87	3.13	167%

Figure 9.8.

The lower table tells you that despite the June expiry calls' having more time and therefore more chance for the stock to appreciate to the level you expect, the profit potential is too low. Ideally, you want the ability to generate four times your premium spend if your return expectation for the stock is correct, so you decide against the June expiry options. It is with some regret because the May options expire on the 20th, and although you expect the stock to reach $165 by mid-May, this leaves you with around only a week-and-a-half safety margin.

Focusing on the May expiry table, you see that there is only one call option that generates in excess of your desired 400 percent return under your expectation for the stock move, which is the 155 strike call. The delta is 0.2 for this call option, which is just about acceptably high enough. Any lower and the trade would be overly speculative, you feel.

You utilize the implied volatility functionality of your broker platform and see that the 28.5 percent implied volatility price for the May 140 strike at-the-money call appears to be around its two-year average. This looks in line with the current level of one-month realized volatility also (Figure 9.7). The average realized volatility is closer to 40 percent over the last couple of years, which, although skewed by the extreme volatility of the global pandemic, gives you some satisfaction that it is moderately acceptable to pay the current level of implied volatility.

Although you have a reasonable conviction on the trade rationale, your conviction is moderated by the smaller safety margin of having to use May expiry options and the only somewhat acceptable level of implied volatility being paid. You categorize your conviction as moderate and use an accordingly smaller premium spend limit of $1,000. You submit an order via your broker platform to buy to open five contracts of the CVX May 20, 2022, expiry 155 strike call options for $1.98, costing $990 (5 contracts × $1.98 call option price × 100 multiplier).

Investing with call options

As mentioned previously, investing with options involves using longer-dated call options to gain exposure to assets with attractive long-term return potential in a limited risk capacity. It is an alternative to buying stock, while risking only a fraction of the price. The rest remains in cash or in very safe and liquid interest-bearing assets. If there is a market crash or a severe profit warning from the company, only the option premium purchased is at risk. This is a considerably less risky activity than buying stock **on margin** through a broker platform, where a similarly small percentage of the stock price is required at initiation, but the remaining funds are borrowed from the broker. Not only the interest due on these borrowed funds is often much higher than market rates, but large drops in the stock may precipitate a **margin call**, needing either additional deposited funds or a sale of the stock—potentially locking in losses.

A large proportion of the cost of long-dated deeply in-the-money options is intrinsic value. The remaining cost is time value, which decays away to zero by expiry. The rationale for using long-dated in-the-money call options is that the theta decay is lower for longer-dated options, the delta is higher for in-the-money options, and also that the time value that is lost through time decay is less for in-the-money options compared with out-the-money or at-the-money call options.

However, it is important that long-dated options are bought at a compellingly low implied volatility because they have the high vega exposures. This means that a vega loss can be generated prior to expiry if expensively priced implied volatility falls closer to its long-term average, or into a low volatility regime. It is therefore a prerequisite to invest only during periods of relative market calm.

Trading in very-long-dated option positions with expiration dates of a few years requires a great deal of specialism. Prices are highly dependent upon their implied volatility, requiring investment professionals to undertake detailed analysis of the **implied volatility surface** of a stock or a stock index—a three-dimensional map that graphs implied volatility against percentage option strike and time to expiry. This they compare with historical surfaces, as well as patterns of realized volatility, in order to determine the correct level of implied volatility at which to trade. The level of expertise and the granularity of data required to trade these effectively are therefore beyond the majority of retail investors.

Furthermore, an option-pricing model such as the BSM calculates an option price based not upon the current price of a stock but around the future price of the stock, which requires assumptions on both future levels of interest rates and the amount of dividends that the stock will pay. The further into the future, and hence the longer the date of expiry for an option, the less certainty there is regarding the correct values for both of these assumptions. The diminishing liquidity and widening bid/ask spreads of longer-dated options reflect this reality.

It is therefore necessary to limit the use of call option investments in a portfolio. If not already in a low volatility regime, volatility can transition to one over time and even catch out investment professionals who focus on the subject; if volatility is already in such regime, it can persist for years. Being selective with opportunities and limiting them to contracts with sufficient liquidity and within an expiration date of a maximum of two years is sensible.

In-the-money call strikes with deltas between 0.7 and 0.8 are best suited to call option investing, since they act very much like the underlying stock in a rising market. However, this adds a further layer of complexity to your trying to assess whether implied volatility is attractive to buy or not due to the implied volatility skew. As mentioned earlier, implied volatility skew is a feature of equity option markets, and it means that an at-the-money (0.5 delta) call option always trades with a lower implied volatility than an in-the-money (such as 0.7 delta) call option does. An 0.8 delta call option generally has a higher implied volatility than an 0.7 delta call option does, and so on. Option skew will change over time due to supply and demand for options, and unfortunately, without a high degree of data granularity, it is not possible to tell whether the amount of skew is low or high. Skew frequently tends to increase during periods of general market volatility, which reinforces the mantra not to invest using long-dated call options during heightened volatility. Ideally, your chosen broker platform will have some functionality for analyzing the implied volatility of your selected option to ensure that it is not above average levels, and realized volatility of your underlying equity should also be calculated to ensure that it is not above average also.

Illiquidity is also a challenge when investing in call options. Shorter-dated options have greater trade volumes and therefore greater liquidity than the ones longer-dated ones have, and the relative lack of liquidity manifests as wider spreads between bid and offer prices of longer-date options. Usefully, many broker platforms show a theoretical price for an option along with its associated implied volatility, which gives a steer as to where to buy within a wide bid/offer spread. A limit order ensures that trades are undertaken at only acceptable prices. This may require a great deal of patience and discipline over a number of trading sessions, as well as diligence, since market variables, including the underlying stock price in particular, are obviously in constant flux. It is therefore necessary to continue monitoring and reviewing limit orders right up until execution to ensure that your limit order to buy corresponds to a compelling implied volatility. This is particularly important when entering a new investment compared to **rolling** an existing position, which involves a somewhat smaller net exposure to trade. To roll a position involves submitting one instruction on a broker platform, to sell to close an existing position and to buy to open a new call option, using a limit order for the net price of the two transactions.

Open interest quantifies how many existing open trades there are for specific strikes and expiration dates, which is helpful in distinguishing whether contracts have sufficient liquidity to be tradable. It is sensible to avoid contracts that have wide bid/offer spreads and low open interest. It is painful to overpay for an option due to paying the wrong price within the spread and find that the contract is too illiquid to sell at a reasonable price also.

Example

It is mid-January 2022, and you want to own British Petroleum (BP) American Depositary Receipts (ADRs). ADRs are simply how foreign shares—in this case, a UK stock—are able to trade on a US stock exchange. You are attracted by the high free cashflow yield, cheap valuation, and belief in a structurally bullish story for the price of oil over the next few years. You conservatively anticipate around a 15 percent price return per year but, given high valuation for the overall market in the US and potential onset of an interest-rate-tightening cycle, ideally want to invest via a long-dated call option to reduce your risk.

You assess the available expiries of in-the-money call options and conclude that there is sufficient open interest and that bid/offer spreads are sufficiently tight to trade. You decide to look for a two-year in-the-money call option with a delta between 0.7 and 0.8 and find one with the following characteristics:

Underlying	BP	Call option mid price	$7.51
Underlying price	$31.19	Intrinsic value	$6.19
Call option strike	25	Time value	$1.32
Expiry	January 19 2024	Delta	0.75
Days to expiry	737	Vega	0.123
Implied volatility	33.7%	Theta	-0.004

Figure 9.9.

You calculate the breakeven to be $32.51 (25 call option strike + $7.51 call option price) at expiry in two years, which is 4.2 percent higher than the current price. This is just 2.1 percent per year, so well below your return expectation of 15 percent, and you are happy to tolerate the average relative drag of 2.1 percent per year in exchange for limiting your entire risk to the investment at 24 percent of the current share price ($7.51 call option price / $31.19 underlying price).

You use the available functionality that your broker platform has for analyzing the implied volatility. The 25 strike call has an implied volatility of 33.7 percent, with unfortunately no ability to assess whether the implied volatility skew is excessive, but the implied volatility for an at-the-money call option for the January 2024 expiration date is 30.3 percent. This looks to be near the bottom of its recent history, given what you can see, but you decide to calculate realized volatility also. You find that the current level of three-month realized volatility is 30.5 percent, but that the average for the last three years is around five percentage points higher (Figure 9.10). You are satisfied that while not excessively cheap, the implied volatility is not prohibitively expensive. Since you have very few other long-dated options in your portfolio and have strong conviction in the long-term outlook for the stock, you decide to continue with the trade.

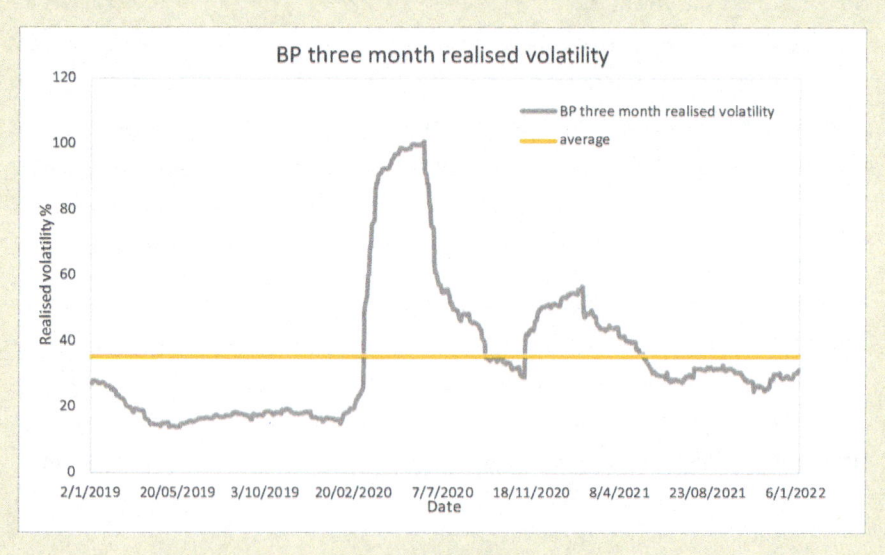

Figure 9.10.

You would ordinarily allocate around $25,000 to buying BP ADRs at the current price of $31.19, so instead place an instruction through your broker platform to buy to open eight contracts of BP January 19, 2024, expiry 25 strike calls, using a limit order at $7.51. This has a notional exposure of $24,592 (8 contracts × $31.19 ADR price × 100 multiplier) but a premium spend of $6,008, so you invest the remaining $18,944 in a liquid money market fund to earn some additional interest.

Taking this example further, Figure 9.11 shows the relative merits of investing $24,592 in eight hundred ADRs of BP at $31.19, shown by the dotted black line, or buying eight call options and keeping the remaining $18,944 in cash. The thin orange area shows the portfolio of calls option and cash on the day of purchase, and the blue and grey areas show the modelled call option value after one year's time decay (all else being equal) and the cash, respectively.

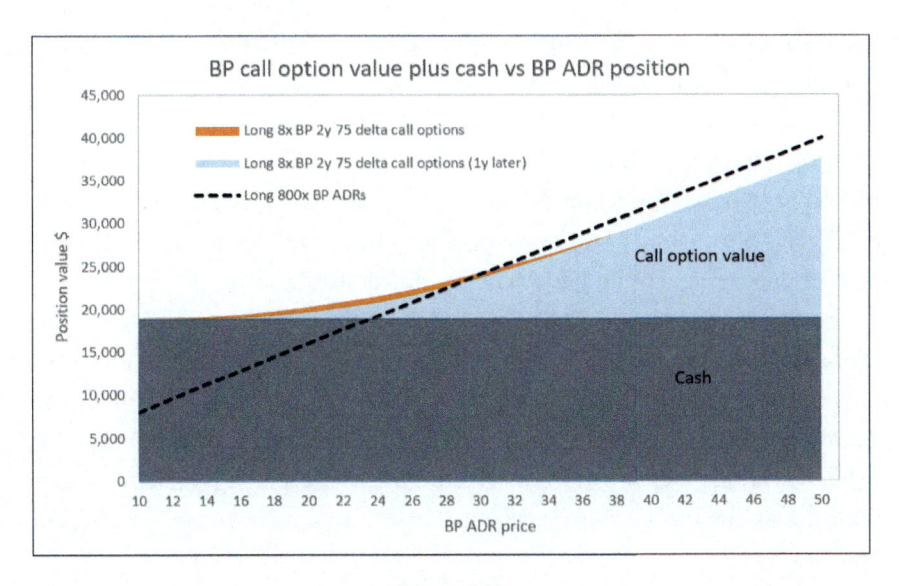

Figure 9.11.

As you can see, the majority of the investment remains in cash when investing with call options. The graph assumes that there is no return on this, although it is best invested in a low-risk, interest-bearing asset to provide additional return. If the underlying stock falls heavily, then the maximum loss that can occur for the call option investor is the premium paid for the call option, whereas the stock investor is at risk of much heavier losses. A further benefit is that under such circumstances, the call option investor is able to deploy the cash to buy stock at very low levels if desired, in the event of a large fall in share prices.

In this example, the notional exposures are the same (the multiplier is one hundred, so one call option is equivalent to one hundred ADRs), so at higher BP ADR prices, owning eight call options will not fully match the profit potential of owning eight hundred ADRs. This is because the calls will always have a delta of less than one, and there is always time value in the price of an option, which decays due to theta. Selecting a more in-the-money strike or a somewhat shorter-dated expiry will increase the delta and reduce the time value should you wish, thereby reducing the underperformance relative to owning the equivalent ADRs. Simply owning more call options can also be justified if the return potential is particularly high.

This example looks at the potential return today and in one year for a BP 25 strike call option with slightly over two years to expiration. However, what should you do with the investment in one year? If there has been an unusually large profit, it may be desirable to sell the option, but otherwise it may be beneficial to roll it into another 0.75 delta call option with another two years to expiry if the original rationale for the trade still holds.

Figure 9.12 shows the rate of time decay for the call option in the example that would apply if BP ADRs were to remain at $31.19 and all other variables were to remain fixed except the passage of time. Also included is the daily theta decay rate if the stock were 20 percent higher and lower.

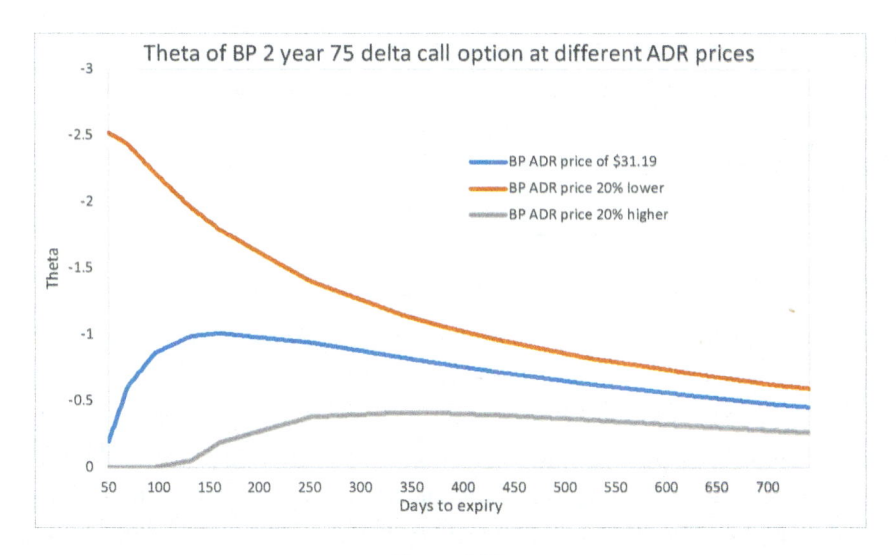

Theta of BP 2 year 75 delta call option at different ADR prices

Figure 9.12.

As Figure 9.12 shows, the longer-dated you keep the investment the less theta decay you suffer. However, if the underlying asset has risen meaningfully in price after one year (as you hope it will), not only will the call option delta have risen meaningfully so the call option will be behaving very much like the underlying stock, but the theta decay will also be less onerous—as shown by the grey line. If you are still happy with the investment case for owning BP, it is legitimate to keep the call option if at that point you were more comfortable with the risk of effectively owning a long stock position, as if there were another solid year of appreciation in BP equity the profits would be greater. The decision to roll into a new call option would then come down to a matter of whether prudently it is wise to lock in the gains you have made.

However, if after one year you are not fortunate enough to have benefited from a meaningful appreciation of the underlying asset (and hence your call option value), then firstly it is necessary to re-evaluate the original investment case. If you still believe in it, then it may be wise to roll the position. The orange line shows the increased level of theta decay that the existing call option would suffer if BP equity fell 20 percent closer to the strike price, which begins to get punitive into the final year of the option's life. Assuming you are again able to buy another deeply in-the-money call option with two years to expiry at an implied volatility level that is appealing, use a limit order to roll the position (i.e., simultaneously selling to close the existing call option and buying to open the new call option position). This allows sufficient time to complete the trade before theta decay begins to climb further.

Long call option assignment

If a long call option is in-the-money at expiration, it will be automatically exercised. This will involve buying stock at the strike price under the assignment process. However, more frequently, buyers of call options will wish not to own the stock that they have bought call options on but simply to speculate on its appreciation. In such cases, the call options should be sold prior to expiration to ensure that the holder of the option does not go through the assignment process. An in-the-money option can be sold at intrinsic value or better prior to expiration. For a call option that is at-the-money, which may or may not have small intrinsic value, time value is at its greatest before expiry. Therefore, these too also have a positive value, which can be realized at any point up to and including the day of expiration.

There is therefore no need to go down the route of the assignment process unless the underlying stock is desired and there is no additional risk from a call option above the premium paid. Cash will be required on a broker account to pay for the stock if a long call option is assigned, but it is not necessary to hold this cash against the position for this eventuality, as will be discussed later is the case for a short put option position.

CHAPTER 10: LONG PUT

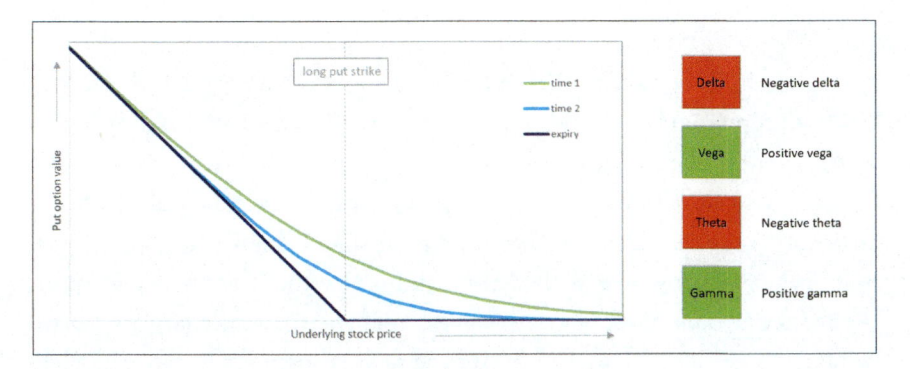

Figure 10.1.

Buying a put option is the simplest option strategy for gaining negative exposure to an underlying asset. As with buying a call option, buying a put option encapsulates all the benefits of using options—i.e., positive convexity or asymmetry, leverage, and limited loss. However, a put option has a negative delta, so the positive convexity of a put option price occurs from a fall in value of the underlying asset. As such, long equity put options provide a hedge against a stock portfolio dropping in value.

Effect of strike and expiry on put option premium cost

[Figure: A chart with "Decreasing put option strike prices" arrow at top (pointing left) and "Increasing time to put option expiry" arrow on left (pointing down). Columns labeled: out-the-money, at-the-money, in-the-money. Rows labeled: Short dated, Long dated. "Smallest option premium" is in the top-left (short-dated, out-the-money) and "Largest option premium" is in the bottom-right (long-dated, in-the-money).]

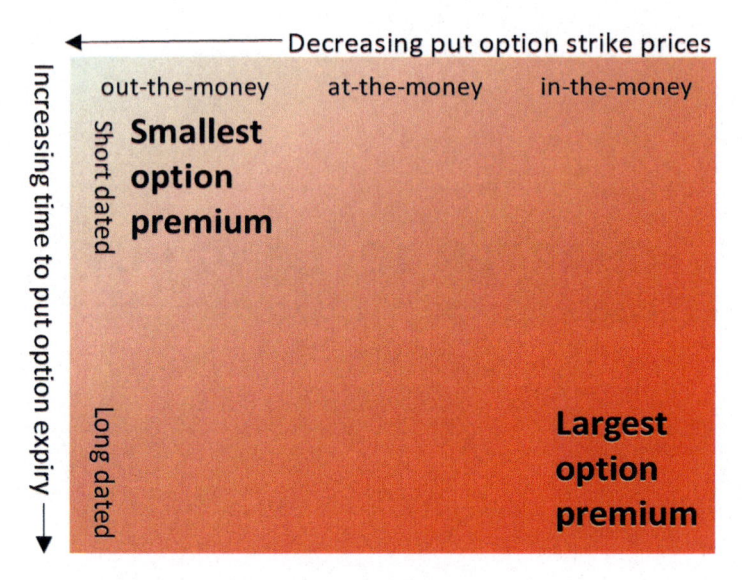

Figure 10.2.

Figure 10.2 shows the relationships in general terms between the cost of put option premium and moneyness versus time to expiry. A put option is in-the-money when the stock price is below the strike price (which is the opposite of a call option). Out-the-money put options have increasingly lower strike prices, with lower put option premiums and smaller negative deltas. Since delta is synonymous with the probability that the option will end up in-the-money at expiration, put options with higher strikes have larger negative deltas, are more likely to make a profit, and so are consequently more valuable. As with call options, longer-dated put options have a greater time value and thus cost more to purchase than shorter-dated options with less time value. Short-dated, out-the-money, low-strike put options have the lowest likelihood of making the owner a profit and so are the cheapest to buy. Since they are so cheap, the potential returns can be enormous and so are akin to lottery tickets.

Overlaying the determinant factors of moneyness and time to expiry on a put option price is also its amount of implied volatility. All put option prices increase (decrease) as implied volatility rises (falls), and the amount by which it does is quantified by the option's vega, as covered in chapter 4.

Long put options usually doubly benefit from falling equity prices. Not only does their negative delta exposure increase, but they also (like long call options) have a positive vega exposure. Since realized volatility and consequently implied volatility generally rise when markets fall, owners of put options usually get the additional kicker of vega appreciation as well as a delta profit. Hence, it is possible to make large returns from small long put options premiums if a market sell-off is timed correctly.

Because equity markets generally rise over the long term, so have a positive expected return, put options are not generally investment vehicles in the same way that call options can be. More commonly, put options are used to hedge existing positions or to speculate on the likelihood of a stock, or stock market falling in value. Figure 10.3 splits out these two trade purposes and provides steps for each to help formulate a long put option strategy.

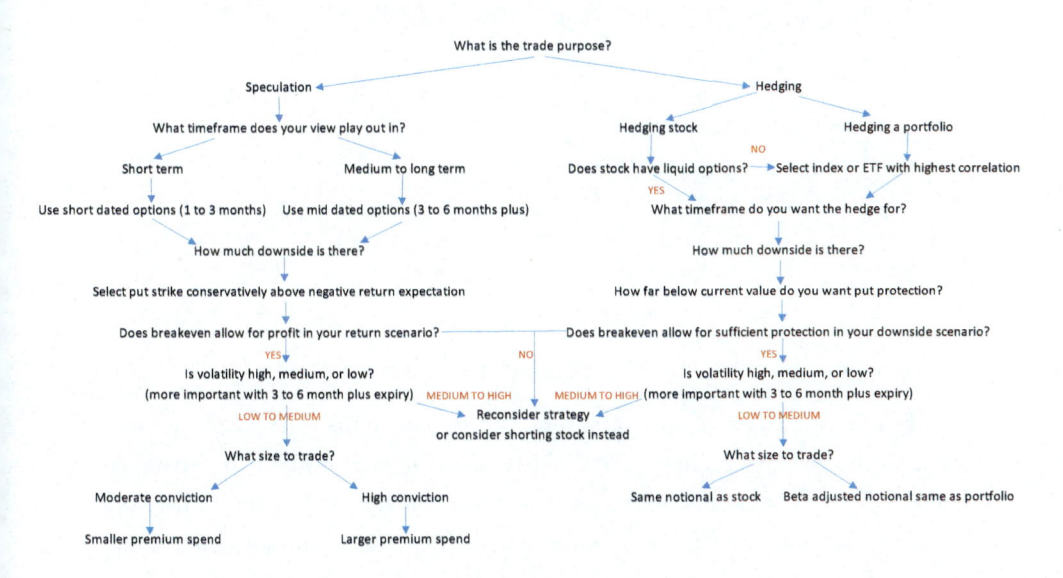

Figure 10.3.

Hedging with long put options

Hedging refers to the process of using an asset to offset the effects of price fluctuations on another asset or portfolio of assets owned. Put options are a common choice for hedging equities because a comparatively small option premium is paid, which is the maximum that can be lost, while the leverage offers a much larger hedged exposure.

Although spending a small percentage of your stock price on protecting it against large falls in value sounds attractive in theory, there are some drawbacks. Firstly, lower strike options have higher levels of implied volatility, and therefore put price, to pay due to implied volatility skew. Figure 10.4 is a snapshot of the price of put options on the SPY ETF and their implied volatilities from mid-January 2022. Although put options that are further out-the-money cost less, as you would expect because they have a smaller delta, their implied volatility is higher due to implied volatility skew. This inflates the cost of put options that have a smaller probability of making a profit.

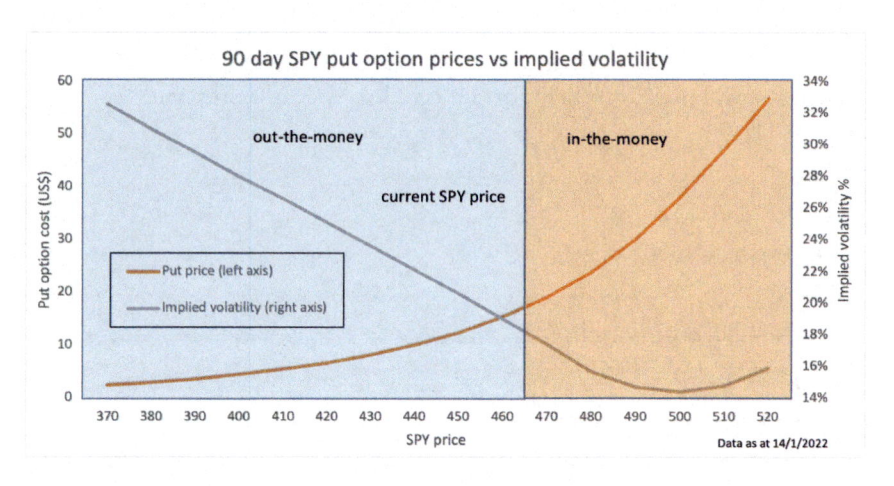

Figure 10.4.

Furthermore, over the very long term, stock markets tend to rise. Therefore, buying relatively inflated prices for put options to routinely hedge portfolios against extreme sell-offs has historically been a drag on returns and eschewed by portfolio managers, who instead have used them tactically in investment portfolios when they believe that markets are at a greater risk of falling. Notwithstanding this, their continued use testifies to the fact that large returns, whether hedging or speculating, are possible from owning put options during falling markets.

Strategies that are more complex are derived by the investment management industry to try to reduce the cost of hedging large investment portfolios with the goal of engineering the panacea of an effective, low-cost solution that works over the long term. Although this is ultimately unobtainable—if it were, portfolios would never suffer large losses and risk management departments would not need to exist—market conditions over the last few years have highlighted the benefits of a simple long put position.

Figure 10.5 shows the CBOE S&P 500 Tail Risk Index in blue (PPUT3M) versus the S&P 500 Total Return Index (SPXTR)—i.e., the index return including dividends paid—in orange. PPUT3M is an index maintained by CBOE (https://www.cboe.com/us/indices/dashboard/PPUT3M/), which comprises a hypothetical investment in the S&P 500 Index to generate its total return and a long three-month put option bought every quarter (i.e., March, June, September, and December) with a strike 10 percent out-the-money and held to expiry. The dotted grey line shows the outperformance of the PPUT3M Index. It demonstrates that a simple long put strategy has been successful in reducing risk and generating higher returns during this period.

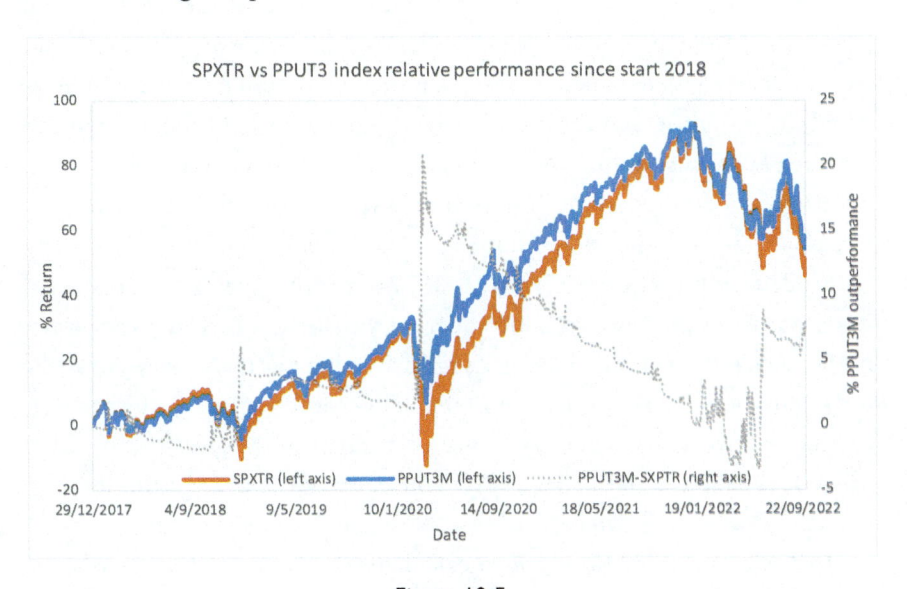

Figure 10.5.

Hedging a stock position

Assuming that a stock has liquid options, the process of formulating a hedging strategy begins with determining how long the hedge is required and at what level of put protection is needed. As with formulating a long call option trade, to answer these questions it is necessary to have a view regarding how much of a fall in the price of the underlying equity is anticipated and over what time frame. Again, studying graphs of past episodes of weakness in the stock price helps reach conclusions on this.

Once a time frame for the hedge is determined, a range of expiration dates that cover it with time to spare requires consideration—specifically, a comparison of the implied volatilities for each of the option expiries using the same put strike. Focus should be on any of the expiries that have a meaningfully lower implied volatility than the rest, and if similar, then ideally on one that is at least a month in excess of the period in question. This builds in some additional safety if the share price weakness takes longer to materialize as well as allows to potentially sell the option prior to expiry at a higher implied volatility if it has served its purpose.

Choosing a put strike among the listed options available is a matter of judgement, knowing that the lower strike you choose the more inexpensive the put option will be, but also the less protection it will provide. The magnitude of any profits already made on a portfolio will also likely play a role in deciding how much to pay for an option and hence which put strike to use. If sitting on a particularly large gain from a stock, it may feel more palatable to pay a relatively high premium for a put option that is nearly at-the-money with a delta approaching -0.5, which will protect the stock position around its current level. Alternatively, surrendering the first few percent in the event of the stock selling off and buying a slightly further out-the-money put strike for slightly less premium may be preferable in some instances. Either way, a delta somewhere between -0.45 and -0.25 balances the level of protection offered and some benefits of positive convexity of the put option, if a -0.5 delta put option feels too expensive.

In any event, it is important to calculate the breakeven for the selected put strike, as this is the true level of protection that the stock will have, since it factors in the cost of buying the put. Furthermore, the breakeven must be meaningfully high relative to the anticipated stock sell-off. There is little point in hedging an anticipated 10 percent fall in a stock, using a long put hedge that has a similar breakeven.

Put breakeven at expiry = put option strike – put option premium paid

Once you have settled upon which put option to buy, the implied volatility requires checking to ensure it is not prohibitively expensive. The functionality of your selected broker platform should be utilized for analysing implied volatility to confirm it is at or below its average. However, implied volatility skew ensures that further out-the-money puts naturally have a higher implied volatility than at-the-money options, which makes assessing how cheap or expensive they are far more difficult without very detailed data. Unless your broker platform has this, assessing the at-the-money implied volatility for the selected expiration date would suffice. Ensuring that realized volatility is not excessive compared with its history is also important. If implied or realized volatility looks high, then consider instead using a put spread, as detailed in a later chapter.

Finally, the appropriate number of put option contracts to buy is then calculated by dividing the number of shares owned by the option multiplier.

Example

It is mid-January 2022, and you have made a reasonable profit over the last couple of years from owning one hundred shares of Apple Inc. (AAPL). Despite remaining bullish on the stock, you are concerned that the stock market is highly valued and might fall from current levels over the next few months. You could sell the shares, but you also think that they could appreciate much further too, and you do not want to miss out if they do. You decide to consider buying a put option to hedge your long stock position.

You generate a price history chart on your broker platform of AAPL and decide that you would like to protect the gains you have made up to a price of $160. It was trading there around a month ago, and you think that if the share price broke below that price, it could lead to further losses to the stock.

You decide to look at an April 21 expiry 160 strike put option because it has three months to expiry, which you feel is long enough to get a better understanding of where the stock market may be heading throughout the rest of the year. You utilize the available implied volatility analysis on your broker platform and see that the at-the-money options have an implied volatility of 28 percent for your chosen April expiry, which looks in line with the recent average for implied and one-month realized volatility over the last couple of years.

Your broker platform shows that with AAPL shares trading at $173.07, the April expiry 160 strike put options have a mid-price of $4.80 and a delta of -0.27. This gives a breakeven of $155.20 for the put hedge, which you are happy with, since you are primarily concerned with a sharp sell-off should the stock trade below $160. You place an order to buy to open one contract of the AAPL April 21 expiry 160 strike put options at a limit price of $4.80, costing $480 in premium (1 contract × $4.80 put price × 100 multiplier).

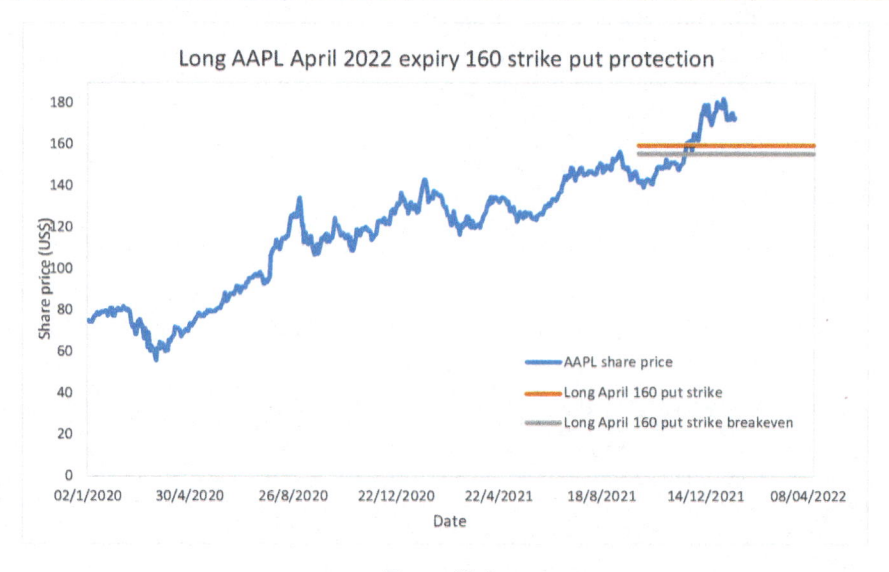

Figure 10.6.

Figure 10.6 shows a price history for AAPL shares, annotated to show the put protection offered by the strategy in the example. The grey line shows the breakeven for the trade, which is the level below which the put option strategy will make a profit at expiry. Since the notional exposures are the same—one contract with a 100 multiplier has one hundred underlying shares—the put option profit will exactly offset any losses made on the stock below the grey line.

Synthetic call option

Figure 10.7 builds on this example and shows the P&L of the combined position of one hundred AAPL shares and one long $160 strike put option contract with three months to expiry (orange line) and at expiry (blue line), along with the original position of just the one hundred AAPL shares without a put option (black dotted line).

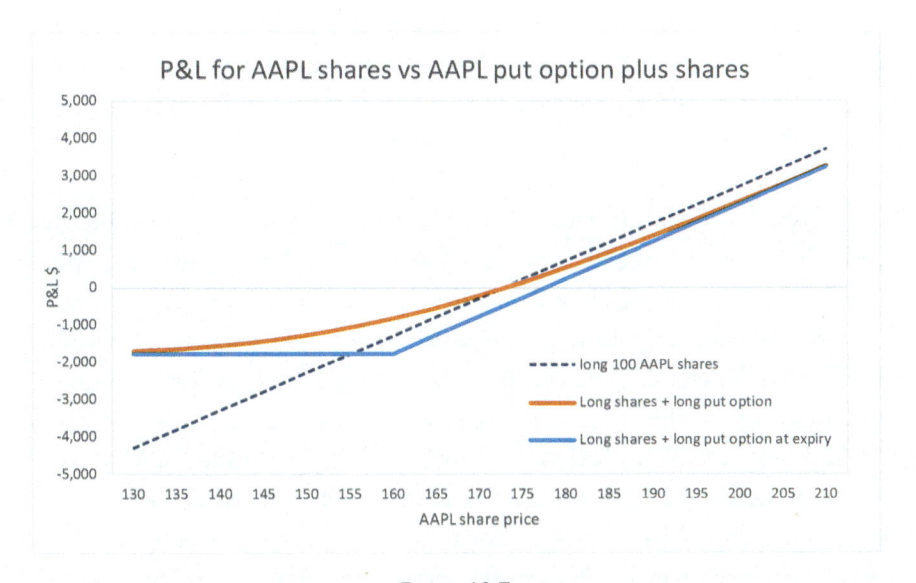

Figure 10.7.

The put option truncates the potential loss at the $160 strike at expiry and then compensates dollar for dollar any losses that the stock makes below this, whereas the long stock position would continue to lose you money if AAPL shares fell further. The point that the dotted black line intersects the blue line is the breakeven for the option trade, represented by the horizontal grey line in Figure 10.6. At higher prices, the potential profit of the combined position is less than the long stock position by the $480 put premium paid, which is lost if the AAPL share price is above the $160 put strike at expiry.

The combined long stock and long put position in Figure 10.7 has exactly the same payoff as a long call option, such as in Figure 9.1. Similarly, a profit is made if the stock rises in value, but the loss is limited by the put strike. This is the same profile as owning a call option, where a profit is made if the underlying equity rises, but loss is limited to the call premium paid. Hence, a **synthetic call option** can be created from a long stock position with a long put option.

Using a portfolio hedge

Frequently, however, investors will wish to apply some put protection to an entire portfolio if they become concerned about the outlook for the market. This is sometimes compared with insurance because the mechanics are similar to an insurance contract, in that a premium is paid to protect a portfolio with a contract that has a predetermined length of time before it expires.

This is less straightforward than hedging an individual stock with its listed put options because portfolios contain a variety of different equities. It may be appropriate to buy some put options on individual stocks if a portfolio is particularly concentrated in them; however, if a portfolio is well diversified, then it is easier and cheaper to buy put options on an index or an ETF that tracks an index.

Although unable to hedge a portfolio perfectly, the index or ETF used as the underlying must be selected on the strength of its **correlation** to the portfolio to ensure that the two have a close historical relationship. It is also necessary to calculate the **beta** of the portfolio relative to the chosen underlying index or ETF, which is a measure of how historically volatile it has been relative to it. Your chosen broker platform should have some capability for calculating the portfolio beta relative to an index.

Most large recognized equity indices around the world—defined by country, style, or even sector—will likely have an ETF that tracks it. Many of these ETFs, particularly those traded in the US, have listed options also. An internet search will yield the most actively traded ETFs per underlying category, and then the tradability of options listed on the ETF (if any) can be checked by looking at the open interest and acceptability of bid/offer spreads via your broker platform. Clearly, ETF used must be in the same currency as the highest concentration of stocks in the portfolio.

The same considerations for selecting expiration date and strike for a put protection hedge for a stock apply when selecting them for a portfolio. However, the required quantity of contracts to buy is calculated relative to the size of the portfolio being hedged and the beta the portfolio has to the underlying equity ETF or index.

Number of put option contracts to buy = (Portfolio value × portfolio beta) / (index price × option multiplier)

Example

It is January 2022, and you own a large portfolio of American tech stocks currently valued at $350,000 that has generated very strong returns over the last few years, but you have become concerned that the market might experience a sizable pull back over the next month or so that might be as much as 20 percent. Instead of selling the portfolio and missing out on further gains if you are wrong, you want to investigate buying some put option protection to hedge your portfolio in case of near-term turbulence.

The portfolio consists of twenty stocks priced in dollars. You suspect that the portfolio is quite correlated to the Nasdaq Index, and graphing its performance on your broker platform alongside that of your portfolio suggests that it is. Your broker platform is also able to calculate that your portfolio has a beta of 1.1 relative to the Nasdaq Index, suggesting it has a volatility that is 10 percent higher. You decide to look at put options on the Invesco QQQ Trust Series 1 (QQQ), since it is an ETF on the Nasdaq Index with highly liquid listed options.

You study the available near-dated put option expiration dates on your broker platform for QQQ and see that the at-the-money put options trade with similar implied volatilities, which is also extremely close to the two-year average of one-month realized volatility on the ETF. Whilst your broker platform does not have sufficient functionality for much further analysis, because you are intending to use just short-dated options, you are happy to proceed. You decide to investigate the April expiry put options because it meets your immediate concerns and provides a little additional safety in case your market fears take longer to play out.

You decide upon an at-the-money strike because you have some sizable profits that you wish to protect. With the QQQ ETF trading at a price of $380.11, the April 14, 2022, expiry 380 strike put options have a mid-price of $18.24. This equates to spending 4.8 percent of the ETF on protecting it ($18.24 put cost / $380.11 ETF price) and a breakeven of 361.76 (380 put strike - $18.24 put cost). Surrendering around 5 percent of the portfolio to protect it around current levels for a three-month period feels reasonable, given the large gains you have made on the assets to date.

Finally, you calculate the quantity of your chosen put options to buy. The QQQ ETF is currently trading at $380.11, and so each put option is on $38,110 of underlying shares, since US options all have a 100 multiplier. The number of contracts to buy, rounded to the nearest whole number, therefore is ten = ($350,000 portfolio value x 1.1 portfolio beta) / ($380.11 ETF price x 100 multiplier). You place an instruction on your broker platform to buy to open ten contracts of the QQQ April 14, 2022, expiry 380 strike put options at a price of $18.24, giving a premium spend of $18,240 (10 contracts × $18.24 put price × 100 multiplier).

Speculating with put options

Positive speculative returns can be made from a stock falling in value as easily as from it rising in value. The necessary short exposure traditionally comes from shorting the stock, with the hope of buying it back at a later date at a lower price for a profit. The ability to short stocks is an important feature of an efficient market, since it allows overvalued stocks to fall in price and trade closer to their fundamental fair value.

However, selling stocks short can be risky not simply because stock markets tend to rise over the long term, but because at any point during the trading day information may be disseminated to the market that undermines the fundamentally bearish view on a stock and causes it to move higher. Unlike owning a stock where all you can lose is your investment if its price falls to zero, a share can theoretically have infinite upside, therefore exposing the shorter of a stock to an almost unlimited loss. Furthermore, stocks that have large short positions from several investors are prone to a **short squeeze**, where its price begins to rise and investors scramble to buy back their short stock positions, perpetuating the price spike and causing large losses. Other investors sometimes target stocks where large known short positions exist, in the hope of engineering a short squeeze in order to make a quick profit at the expense of those that have shorted it.

Buying a put option instead of shorting stock greatly limits these risks because although a put option has leveraged short exposure to the underlying equity, all the owner can lose is their premium, which is always a fraction of the current stock price. This makes buying put options the only "safe" means of gaining short exposure because risks are contained and your maximum loss is quantified. A **stop loss** order on a short equity position in theory also has a quantified maximum loss, but it is at the risk of locking in a guaranteed loss if a certain price barrier is touched, even very briefly.

Speculating with put options is approached in the same way as with call options. The intention is to gain exposure—short exposure in this case—to an equity that is not owned, so the same questions help when formulating the trade. Correctly anticipating a fall in the price of an equity or an equity index is difficult, however. John Maynard Keynes is claimed to have said in the 1930s, "The market can remain irrational longer than you can remain solvent." Equities generally rise in value, and overvalued equities can remain overvalued for an inordinate length of time.

This again argues for selecting an option expiration date that is somewhat longer than believed to be required for a speculative view to play out. Since longer-dated options have greater vega exposures, and a falling equity price will generally boost implied volatilities, this also supports this course of action. Nevertheless, if there is a specific event in the near future that will likely have a significant negative effect but has not been fully priced into an equity or index, then a shorter-dated put option can be used, provided it covers sufficient time for the repricing to occur.

Speculating rather than hedging with put options allows for the use of slightly lower strike, further out-the-money puts with a somewhat lower delta. Since the goal is not to protect an existing position, which requires a large negative option delta exposure from the outset of the trade, smaller delta puts are used, which can deliver greater percentage profits. However, the option strike must be selected in the context of the anticipated move in the stock, such that a meaningful return can be generated from the stock falling far enough in excess of the put option breakeven. This requires a very precise view on where a stock will fall to. Studying graphs of previous periods of weakness in a stock will help determine the likely magnitude and the time frame of any move.

As mentioned in previous sections, implied volatility of any potential long option trade must be analyzed using the tools at hand to ensure that it is not expensively priced.

Example

It is the start of February 2022. You believe that the tobacco sector in the United States is likely to experience weakness this year and have singled out Altria Group (MO) as overvalued at $50.88 a share. You expect some moderate selling pressure over the first quarter but think that the next earnings announcement on April 29, 2022, will provide a catalyst for further ongoing weakness. You study the graph and conclude that there is a high probability that the shares will fall back at least to the October 2020 lows of $36 but a moderate probability that they will find some support at the 2021 low of $42 instead if the earnings announcement is not quite as bad as you believe.

You decide to look at using a put option because the sector has already underperformed the broader stock market over the last few years and are concerned that it may rise if you are wrong, as investors buy areas of the market that have lagged. You compile a chart of realized volatility, using a three-month measure as you anticipate using a put option expiry in excess of three months, and see that it is around 21 percent and at the lower end of its range, as well as comfortably below the two-year average of 27.5 percent (Figure 10.9). This encourages you to look at put option pricing, since implied volatility is likely to be similarly undemanding. If true, implied volatility will have room to rise if you are correct in your view on the MO share price, which will potentially give an additional vega profit prior to expiration.

Figure 10.8.

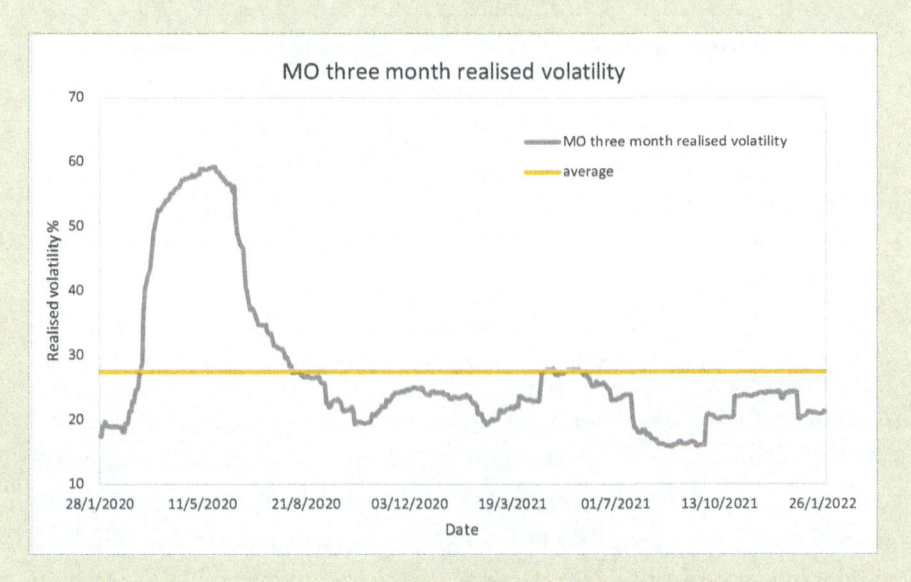

Figure 10.9.

You decide to look at all the listed expiries for MO that you can trade via your broker platform. Beyond the current month, there are March,

June, and September listed expiries this year. You want one that captures the earnings announcement, so ignore the March expiry. June and September look similarly priced, with at-the-money implied volatility at 23 percent, so either would work. You decide to focus on June expiry options, since they expire on June 17, 2022, and so amply cover the period of the earnings announcement; however, because they are shorter-dated, they have a lower premium cost than September expiry options. Had September expiry options been priced with a much lower implied volatility than June, you would have focused on those instead.

You look at the available out-the-money June put strikes and costs to calculate the breakeven for each. You then calculate profit at expiry for each of the available put options under your two return scenarios, noting that there is no profit to be made under scenario A for some of the options if the stock falls to only $42 (Figure 10.10).

MO June 17 2022 expiry put option details					scenario A: $42		scenario B: $36	
June put strike	put mid price	implied volatility	delta	breakeven (put strike - put cost)	expiry profit (breakeven - $42)	% profit (expiry profit/put cost)-1	expiry profit (breakeven - $36)	% profit (expiry profit/put cost)-1
50	3.10	22.9%	-0.44	46.90	4.90	58%	10.9	252%
47.5	1.90	23.0%	-0.32	45.60	3.60	89%	9.60	405%
45	1.25	24.0%	-0.22	43.75	1.75	40%	7.75	520%
42.5	0.85	26.3%	-0.15	41.65	not profitable		5.65	565%
40	0.62	30.0%	-0.11	39.38			3.38	445%
37.5	0.46	33.8%	-0.08	37.04			1.04	126%

MO stock price: $50.88

Figure 10.10.

Erring on the side of caution, you chose the June 47.5 strike put at a cost of $1.90. It makes over twice the return of the 45 strike put in scenario A if the share price falls to the more conservative level of $42, whilst still returning over 400 percent in scenario B. You ordinarily spend $2,000 on a high conviction trade and $1,000 on a moderate conviction trade. You have high conviction in this idea so decide to buy ten contracts. You place an order on your broker platform to buy to open ten MO June 17, 2022, expiry 47.5 strike put options at $1.90, costing $1,900 in premium (10 contracts × $1.90 put price × 100 multiplier).

CHAPTER 11: SHORT CALL

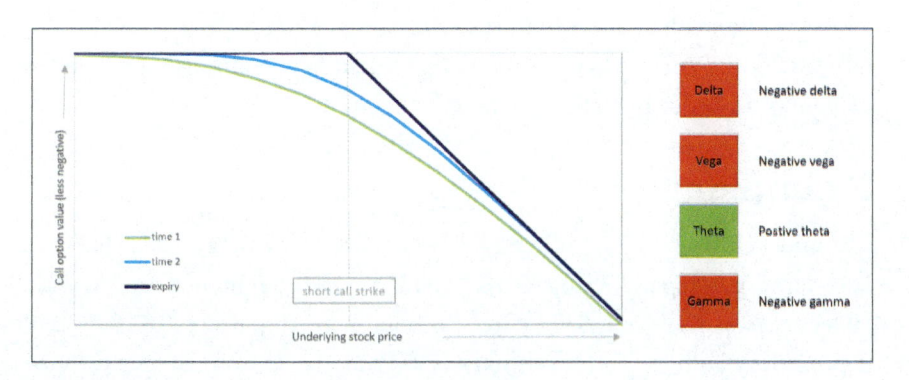

Figure 11.1.

As Figure 11.1 shows, a short call is the inverse of a long call. A short call position is established by submitting an order on a broker platform to sell to open a call option. Whereas a long call option gives the owner theoretically infinite upside potential for the price of the premium paid, a short call option makes the seller liable for a theoretically infinite loss in exchange for the premium received. That might sound like rather poor trade-off and at odds with the idea of participating in the stock market with reduced risk and/or higher returns, and yet under certain conditions it does both.

To appreciate this, it is necessary to distinguish between **covered call** selling and **naked call** selling. A covered call (also known as an **overwrite** or **buy-write**) refers to a call option sold by an investor who also owns a sufficient quantity of the underlying stock to meet their obligation should the option be exercised and the stock called away. An investor who does not own a sufficient quantity of the underlying stock sells a naked call.

Covered call selling

If the call is covered, the seller owns the stock already so exercise is not a problem, other than they miss making additional profits above the strike price if the stock has gone up greatly in value. The motivation to engage in covered call selling is to receive the premium from selling the call option, whilst using a call strike where the overwriter is happy to sell the underlying stock. In effect, this is receiving payment of the option premium for using a limit order for selling a stock.

Example

It is mid-February 2022, and you have been holding five hundred shares in U.S. mining company Alcoa Corp (AA) that you bought at a significantly lower price over a year ago. The stock has just spiked in price to $78.20 and approaching your target for selling at $85. You decide to consider overwriting your stock by selling a call option and look at available listed strikes on your broker platform. You see that the March 18 expiry 85 strike call has an attractively high implied volatility and so will generate a meaningful amount of premium from selling it. You submit an order to sell to open five contracts of AA March 18, 2022, expiry 85 strike call options at a limit of $2.70, for $1,350 in premium (5 contracts × $2.70 put price × 100 multiplier).

Figure 11.2.

Option details

March call strike	expiry	call mid price	implied volatility	delta	theta
85	March 18 2022	2.70	60.2%	0.34	-0.084

Trade details

contracts	premium	$ delta	$ theta	days to expiry
-5	$1,350	-$13,294	$42	28
	(2.7 x 5 x 100)	(-5 x 78.2 x 100 x 0.34)	(-5 x 100 x -0.084)	

AA price: $78.20

Figure 11.3.

When selling short any option, it is desirable that it has a high implied volatility, since this will correspond to a high premium value. Shorting any asset creates a liability on a portfolio, which gets smaller if the position is making a profit. With a short option position, this profit comes from theta as the option decays on a daily basis, incrementally reducing the value of the option premium that has been sold short until, hopefully, the option expires worthless.

Overwriting stocks in this way requires the use of short-dated options because they have higher theta, which means that income earned is at a higher rate per day. The overwrite must generate sufficiently meaningful premium to make the trade worthwhile—in the example, $1,350 of premium is 3.5 percent of the $39,100 value of the stock position (500 shares × $78.20 share price). This is over just a 28-day period and annualized the return is 45 percent, so meaningful enough. Each day the premium value is reduced by the theta earned, which is $42 per day at the outset of the trade, in this example. If the stock price remains below the $85 call strike, the liability is reduced by theta every day until at expiration, the option will have a value of zero and the entire $1,350 premium amount has been earned. If the stock rises above the $85 call strike, then the short premium liability may grow in size, generating a loss on the option trade, but this is more than offset by a gain in the long AA stock position that is also held. At expiry, if the stock is above the $85 call strike, then the short call option is automatically exercised, and under the assignment process, the stock is "called away"' and $85 per share is paid via the clearing house.

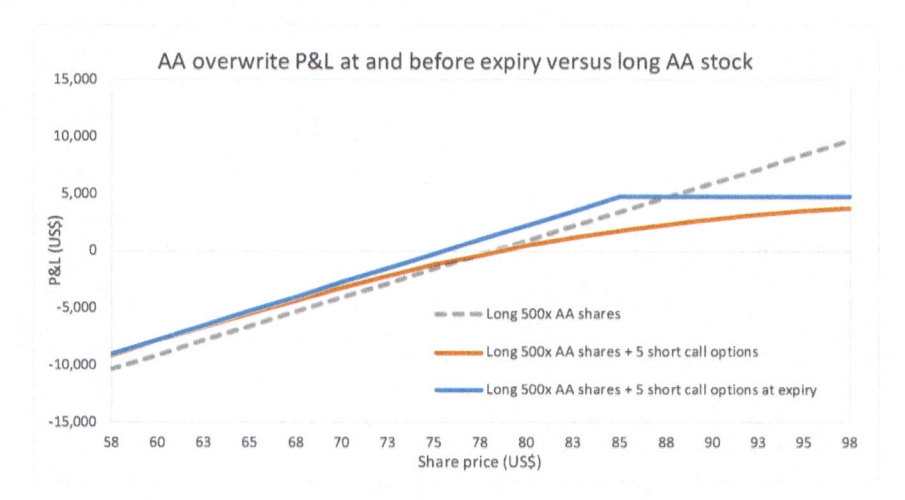

Figure 11.4.

Figure 11.4 summarizes the P&L from owning five hundred AA shares at $78.20 (dotted line) or deciding to overwrite five hundred shares with the short $85 strike call options that expire in twenty-eight days. The overwrite, consisting of the long stock position and short call options, truncates the potential P&L upside by the short call strike at $85. At expiry, the maximum P&L for the overwrite is the 85 strike plus the $2.70 premium received for selling the call option.

Overwrite breakeven = short call strike + call premium received

As long as the stock does not exceed $87.70 (85 short call strike + $2.70 call premium) at expiration, then the overwrite will have made more money. If the stock exceeds $87.70 by the expiration date, a profit is still made, just less than would have been the case had AA not been overwritten. If the shares fall after the call option is sold, then money is lost from holding the shares, but this loss is somewhat cushioned by the premium earned from selling the call option.

Figure 11.3 shows that the short call options have a negative $ delta exposure of -$13,294 at initiation (-5 call options × 78.20$ share price × 100 multiplier × 0.34 call delta). Since a stock has a delta of one, the stock delta is $39,100 ($78.20 share price × 500 shares). Consequently, the net delta of the overwrite is $25,806 ($39,100 + -$13,294). Prior to the option's expiry, as the shares rise in value, the short call loses money whilst its delta exposure gets more negative, and as the shares fall in value, the short call makes money whilst its delta exposure gets less negative. In this way, the short call cushions the price volatility of the overwritten stock in either direction. The volatility of an position is synonymous with its risk, so an overwritten stock therefore has less risk than the stock on its own, and if the stock is below the breakeven at expiration of the call option, a greater return also.

An important additional consideration when overwriting is the **dividend ex-dates** for the underlying stock. The ex-date of a stock is the day on which new buyers are no longer entitled to the next dividend payment. Since the majority of listed option are American style and therefore able to be exercised by the holder at any point, if a dividend ex-date falls a short time before the date of option expiry and the dividend due is of a reasonable size, short call positions are at risk of being exercised early. This is because it may be financially beneficial for the holder of a long call position to exercise the option early to obtain the stock and hence entitlement to the next dividend. It is therefore not advisable to overwrite a stock, using a short call option that expires soon after an ex dividend date, if certainty of entitlement to its dividend is wanted.

In terms of performance of the systematic use of overwriting as a strategy, the CBOE provide data that offer a note of caution regarding blindly using it. They calculate a variety of hypothetical overwriting indices that show the performance of systematically selling call options against a long equity position. The CBOE S&P 500 2% OTM BuyWrite IndexSM (BXY) is one of those, which shows the P&L from holding the S&P 500 Index and overwriting by successively selling consecutive one-month S&P 500 Index call options with a strike that is 2 percent out-the-money. Although overwriting generates income and reduces volatility of an overall position, selling call options does limit your maximum upside potential in strongly rising markets, such as prior to and following the global pandemic, as shown in Figure 11.5, where the S&P 500 Total Return Index is shown in orange. Many fund managers will therefore generally use overwriting opportunistically on individual stocks when market conditions are right and the stock has reached extreme valuations.

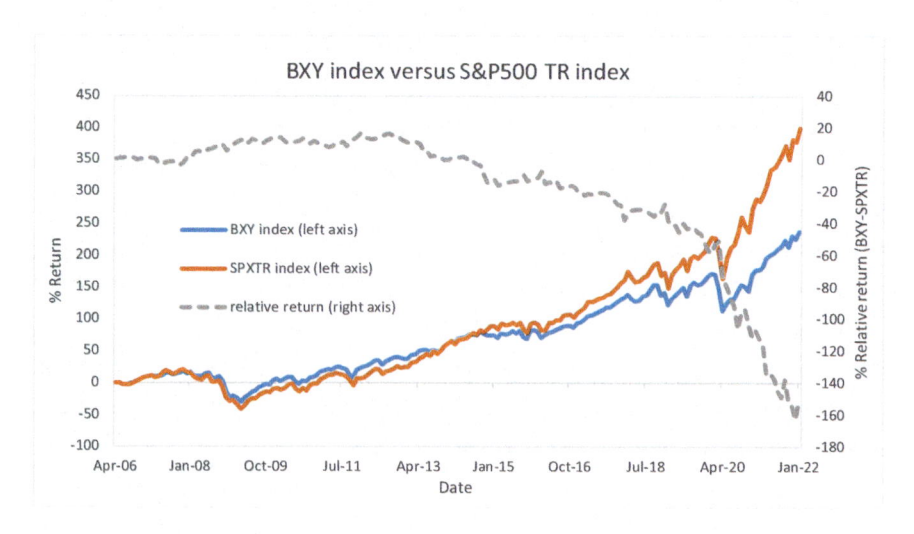

Figure 11.5.

Naked call selling

Naked call option selling carries a high degree of risk because there is no stock to cover the liability, and theoretically, the stock price underlying the short call option can rise infinitely high. Correspondingly, the clearing house may require meaningful margin to collateralize the risk, while the broker being used could also demand an additional margin payment.

The focus of this book is on using options to generate superior returns and reduce risk on equity portfolios relative to using the stock market alone. For investors that participate in the stock market via only long stock positions, naked call selling is not relevant, and any short call option positions must be covered by the requisite quantity of underlying stock. However, for investors that already participate in shorting stocks, which also has a potentially infinite loss, shorting a call option arguably poses somewhat less risk. Although not able to participate in as much profit if the stock falls heavily because the maximum profit achievable is the call premium received, unlike a stock short trade, there is receipt of an option premium. Furthermore, if selling a call option with a strike that is 10 percent above the current share price, for example, not only is premium received, but a loss at expiry is only generated above the breakeven over 10 percent higher. This is a less risky proposition than shorting the equivalent underlying stock at the current market price.

A common reason for having a short stock position is as part of a **pairs trade**. A pairs trade describes buying a stock and at the same time selling another stock against it, usually so that the net notional exposure or beta-weighted notional exposure is zero. This is sometimes referred to as **statistical arbitrage** if there is a reasonable statistically significant correlation between the two stocks but one has begun trading out of line with the other.

A pairs trade that is constructed with call options is called a **call switch**, where a short call is used in place of the short stock and a long call with the same expiry date in place of the long stock position. A call switch is used instead of a pairs trade if the pricing of the options makes it advantageous, or if some conditionality is desired—i.e., because you want to have the trade only if the market is going up, but do not want the exposure if the market is going down. Whatever the reason, the resulting call switch can inherently have less risk relative to the associated pairs trade.

Example

It is mid-February 2022, and you believe that for the remainder of the year there is likely to be better returns from owning pan-European large cap stocks rather than US large cap stocks, which you consider relatively overvalued. You are tempted to enter a pairs trade, selling the SPDR S&P 500 ETF Trust (SPY) and buying the Vanguard FTSE Europe ETF (VGK) in equal notional sizes. However, you are concerned that in the event of a large market sell-off that caused both ETFs to fall heavily, VGK would additionally suffer versus SPY, as European currencies could depreciate versus the US dollar. This would potentially create a loss for the pairs trade under that scenario, you believe.

You decide to consider a call switch instead, selling SPY call options and buying VGK call options. On your broker platform, you look at the VGK options first because you know that they will have less liquidity than SPY options, and ensuring that there is sufficient liquidity to trade them will be one factor in assessing whether the trade is viable. You see that there is a January 20, 2023, option expiry listed, giving about eleven months until expiration, which looks liquid and with plenty of open interest. There is also a corresponding expiry for the same date for options listed on the SPY ETF, so the call switch trade looks like it may have potential.

You look at all the out-the-money January 2023 expiry call options listed for VGK and match each option delta with the closest corresponding delta on SPY call options for the same expiry, compiling the table in Figure 11.6.

VGK call option details			price: 64.71		SPY call option details			price: 434.23		Price ratio
				strike / ETF					strike / ETF	VGK:SPY
call strike	delta	ask price	implied volatility	% strike	call strike	delta	bid price	implied volatility	% strike	6.71
75	0.15	0.79	16.2%	115.9%	505	0.18	6.06	16.5%	116.3%	7.67
70	0.33	2.05	17.2%	108.2%	475	0.33	14.77	18.3%	109.4%	7.20
68	0.41	2.89	18.3%	105.1%	465	0.40	20.94	19.2%	107.1%	7.25
67	0.45	3.33	18.6%	103.5%	450	0.45	26.50	20.5%	103.6%	7.96
66	0.48	3.85	19.1%	102.0%	445	0.48	28.93	21.0%	102.5%	7.51

Figure 11.6.

Encouragingly, the implied volatility for the SPY call options is higher, suggesting that call options with an equivalent delta for SPY may sell for a higher price than those you are looking to purchase on the VGK ETF. You calculate the number of VGK call options that you can buy from selling SPY call options for each combination and find that it is almost possible to buy eight times the quantity of 67 strike VGK calls for every 450 strike SPY calls sold. This is much better than the ratio for the pairs trade, which would involve buying just 6.7x VGK ETF for every SPY sold.

Figure 11.7.

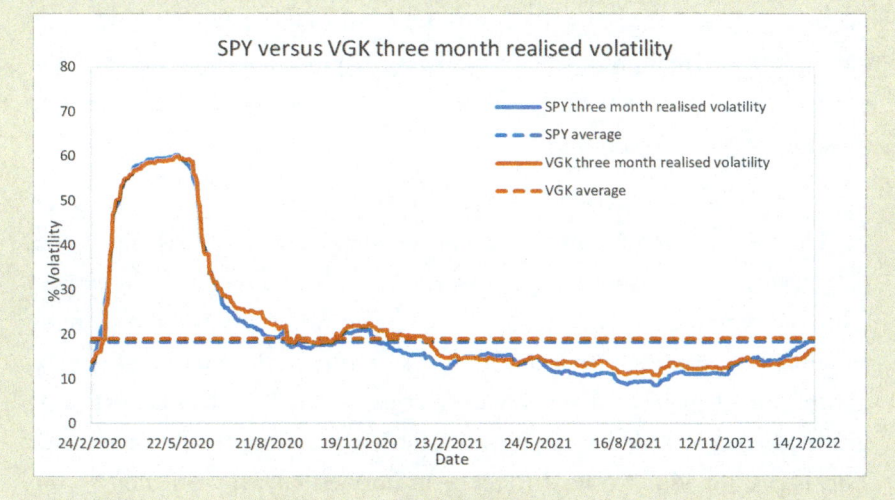

Figure 11.8.

Unfortunately, you are unable to see data history for one-year implied volatility on your broker platform for these options. Ideally, you would be able to see both and judge whether the spread between them looks compelling—i.e., that SPY options look rich and VGK options look cheap relative to their histories. Nevertheless, you graph three-month realized volatility of both ETFs and find them to be very similar. SPY realized volatility is currently marginally higher and touching its average, which probably explains why SPY options are trading at a higher implied volatility and why you are able to trade the call switch at attractive levels. You are satisfied that the trade is a good way to express your view on the two ETFs.

You size the trade upon the exposure you are comfortable with, arising from the short call option side, since this is the riskiest side of the call switch. One short SPY 450 strike call would leave you with a short position of one hundred shares at $450 at expiry, which is $45,000 notional. You are comfortable with this trade exposure on the short leg of the trade. This generates $2,650 (1 contract × $26.5 call price × 100 multiplier) in option premium, which almost allows you to buy eight VGK January 20, 2023, expiry 67 strike call options at $3.33 each, spending $2,664 (8 contracts × $3.33 call price × 100 multiplier). This would give you a long position of eight hundred shares at $67 at expiry, which is a $53,600 (8 contracts × 67 call strike × 100 multiplier) notional positive exposure. You may not hold the call switch to expiry, however, but you may possibly close them out beforehand depending on how the trade develops.

The above example illustrates how a call switch can be inherently less risky than the corresponding pairs trade. If both ETFs fall from current levels by expiry, then both call options expire worthless and there are no remaining exposures. However, if both rise in tandem, then the short exposure side of the trade has a smaller notional size than the long exposure side of the trade and therefore gives a positive asymmetry to the returns. This is possible due to the difference in implied volatility of the two options, which enables the mismatch in notional sizes when trading a call switch at or close to zero cost.

CHAPTER 12: SHORT PUT

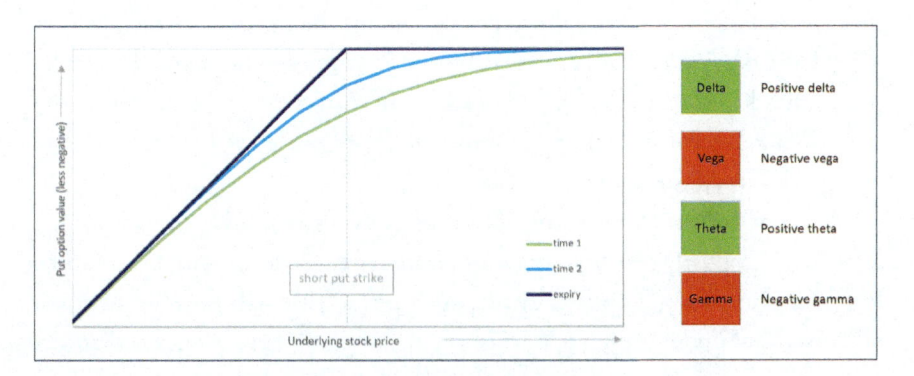

Figure 12.1.

As evident in Figure 12.1, a short put is the inverse of a long put. Whereas the put buyer has the right to sell stock at the strike price, so experiences a maximum gain if the stock falls to zero, the put seller is obliged to pay the strike price for stock, so experiences a maximum loss if the stock falls to zero. The inherent risk of a short put position may require the clearing house to levy a meaningful margin, to which the broker could also add an additional margin requirement (as with a short call option position).

Under certain conditions, however, a short put strategy can be viewed as an extremely defensive position to take and can be used as a means of reducing risk relative to investing directly in the underlying stock. Short put option positions (like short call option positions) can be categorized as either covered or naked, depending on how they are employed, and a short put strategy is often referred to as an **underwrite**, **put-write** or **sell-write**.

Selling covered puts

Short put options are covered not with stock but cash. Since a short put option potentially leaves the put seller obliged to buy the underlying stock at the strike price in exchange for the premium received, if sufficient cash is set aside in the portfolio to pay for the stock, then it is referred to as a **covered put.** Hence, underwriting stock is akin to being paid the option premium for leaving a limit order to buy stock at the strike price.

A covered put is therefore generally less risky than owning the relevant quantity of underlying stock, because not only does the covered put option seller receive premium for selling the option, but the majority of the position is held as cash, which has zero volatility, in anticipation of paying the strike price. In addition, the put strike used is often some percentage below the current market price, and therefore if the short put ends in-the-money at expiry, the stock is bought at a discount.

A major influence on a put option price is its implied volatility, which along with implied volatility skew can reach extremes during market sell-offs. Elevated prices for put options during such times, although possibly justified, offer excellent underwriting opportunities if cash levels have been raised anticipatorily and stocks have become fundamentally cheap. Underwriting is a good way of utilizing that cash to potentially buy cheap stock whilst earning a return.

Example

It is late February 2022, and you have been holding cash in your portfolio for some months. You want to begin earning a return on that cash as well as to begin gaining exposure to stocks that have fallen heavily in price this year. Sunnova Energy (NOVA) is currently trading at $14.96, having fallen heavily since its 2021 high. You are happy to own the stock at $12.50 and decide to investigate an underwrite, knowing that the stock is volatile and therefore that you are likely to achieve a meaningful premium for doing so.

Figure 12.2.

Option details

March put strike	expiry	put mid price	implied volatility	delta	theta
12.5	18 March 2022	0.55	101.2%	-0.21	-0.021

Trade details

contracts	premium	$ delta	$ theta	days to expiry
-10	$550	$3,142	$21	22
	(0.55 x 10 x 100)	(-10 x 14.96 x 100 x -0.21)	(-10 x 100 x -0.021)	

NOVA price: $14.96

Figure 12.3.

> You would be happy to buy one thousand shares at $12.50 and have $12,500 cash in your portfolio should the put be exercised and you are assigned stock, so you look to sell ten put options, since US options have multipliers of 100. You will maintain this cash position to back the short put options over the next twenty-two days. You submit an instruction on your broker platform to sell to open ten contracts of NOVA March 18, 2022, expiry 12.5 strike put options for $550 in premium (10 contracts × $0.55 put price × 100 multiplier), which is recorded as a liability on your portfolio.

The example above illustrates how put underwriting gives a return on the cash used to cover the put option. The $550 put premium equates to a 4.4 percent return over twenty-two days on the $12,500 set aside to cover it, which is 73 percent annualized. This is earned at an incremental rate every day in the form of theta, which whittles away the value of the short option premium.

The short put also gives positive exposure to the stock. Since a long put position has a negative delta and therefore negative exposure to moves in the stock price, a short put position has positive delta and therefore positive exposure to the stock price. In this example, a put option with a delta of -0.21 was sold short, creating a long stock equivalent position of 210 shares (-10 contracts × -0.21 delta × 100 multiplier) with a delta exposure of $3,142 (210 shares × $14.96 share price). If the stock were to fall closer to the strike shortly afterwards, the negative delta would increase toward -0.5, increasing the stock equivalent position to five hundred shares (-10 contracts × -0.5 delta × 100 multipier)—i.e., the delta exposure of a short put increases as the underlying stock falls in price. Correspondingly, the put rises in price as the stock price falls, creating a loss to the put seller who has sold it cheaper. This operates in reverse if the stock rises, causing the negative delta to get smaller. If, for example, the delta of the short put contracts to -0.1, the put seller would be long the equivalent of one hundred shares (-10 contracts × -0.10 delta × 100 multiplier) and the price of the put falls. This creates a profit, as it was originally sold at a higher price. At expiration, if the stock is above the 12.50 strike, it will be out-the-money and have a delta and a price of zero, thereby generating the maximum possible gain to the put seller, which is the entire premium amount. Alternatively, the delta will be -1.0 if the stock is below the 12.50 put strike and therefore in-the-money at expiration, obliging the put seller to buy one thousand shares at $12.50 each.

As with overwriting, underwriting produces the highest returns when selling consecutive short-dated options with high implied volatility, since this ensures a high theta and premium value. However, it is imperative to maintain cash to cover the short put and that the strike price corresponds to a price that the put seller is willing to buy the stock for. This is because short-dated, highly volatile options have an extremely high gamma, which means that the short put price can exponentially grow in very short order if the stock falls heavily beneath the put option strike, thereby increasing the probability of assignment of stock. Although unwelcome because a loss is likely generated as the sold put increases in value, the cash backing ensures that the liability of paying the strike price is met if stock is assigned. Therefore, a covered short put is not over leveraged—come what may, you have the means to cover the liability—which is not the case with naked put selling.

Selling naked puts

Naked short put options can leave a portfolio over leveraged and therefore exposed to potentially larger losses. The downside risk is similar to using a margin account to buy a quantity of stock in a portfolio that exceeds the cash available to invest. However, due to the negative asymmetry of a short put option payoff, there is not the benefit of a margin account in a rising market because the additional profit is limited to only the put premium received. Figure 12.4 differentiates portfolio returns arising from either using a margin account or naked put option selling.

Margined and unmargined portfolio versus unmargined portfolio with naked puts

(chart showing margined portfolio, unmargined portfolio, and unmargined portfolio with naked puts, with axes "portfolio P&L" vs "stock market")

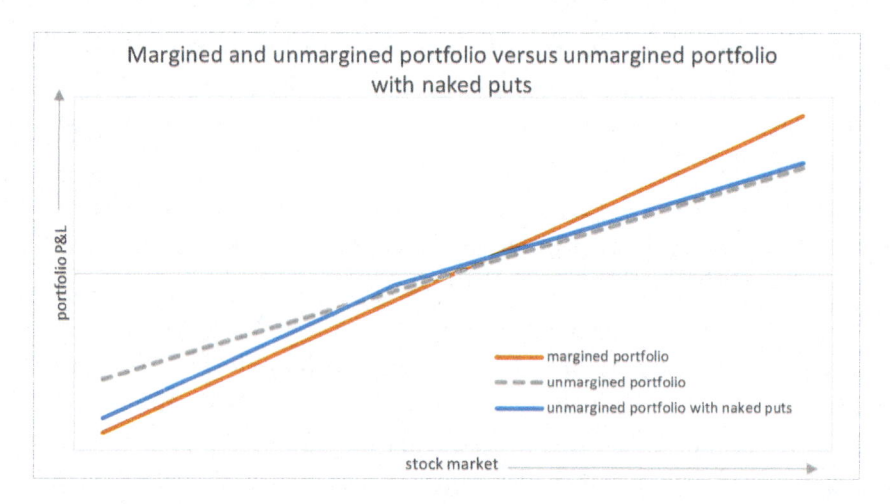

Figure 12.4.

Relative to a margined portfolio, although the profit potential is lower, a portfolio containing naked puts does at least receive premium from selling put options, which cushions losses to some extent if the market falls. If the short put strikes are below the current market price, the put seller also has less risk at expiry relative to an investor that has bought additional stock at the current market price, using a margin account.

Nevertheless, the focus of this book is on using options to generate superior returns and reduce risk on unmargined equity portfolios relative to using the stock market alone. The aim is not to emphasize strategies that compound risk, and from that perspective, investors with long-only equity portfolios should categorically not use naked option positions. However, investors already involved in shorting stocks, who are comfortable with the additional risk that this entails, are potentially able to use naked put options under two distinct circumstances in order to generate additional returns and reduce risk.

Firstly, a naked short put can be utilized as a means of closing out a short stock position whilst generating additional income, which is analogous to using a short call option to close a long stock position whilst generating income. This is because whereas an overwrite causes the stock to be "called away" under the assignment process if the short call is in-the-money at expiration, an underwrite causes the stock to be "put upon" the put seller under the assignment process if the short put is in-the-money at expiration. Furthermore, because a short stock and a short put option have opposing deltas, an underwritten short stock position has less risk than the short stock position alone, in the same way that an overwritten long stock has less risk than just the long stock position. This is because price movements in one offset price movements in the other, to an extent, thereby reducing overall price volatility of the position. Incidentally, a short put sold against a short stock position does not require cash to cover the short put strike, and assignment reduces the risk to the portfolio by closing the existing short stock position, so under these circumstances the short put is not overleveraging the portfolio.

Secondly, a portfolio that routinely constructs pairs trades can do so using put options to create a **put switch**, involving selling a naked put against a long put, in a similar way that a call switch is constructed. This is done in order to reduce the risk relative to the corresponding pairs trade in one of two ways: (1) Either by not participating intentionally if both underlying equities rise, because this is a scenario under which a loss is likely generated on the pairs trade but instead allowing for both put options to expire worthless. (2) Alternatively, because the implied volatility (and hence the cost) of the put options are different, this allows one-half of the trade to be in a larger size, whilst still keeping the trade costless.

Example

It is early March 2022, and you are investigating a potential pairs trade, selling the iShares MSCI India ETF (INDA) and buying the iShares China Large-Cap ETF (FXI) throughout the rest of the year. You believe the fundamental case to be quite compelling, as the Indian Index is much more overvalued, and you agree with the majority of equity strategists in believing that Chinese authorities will provide support to their equity markets. However, you are concerned that should emerging markets remain robust throughout the rest of 2022 INDA will inflect higher, since India still has stronger economic growth and the ETF has quite a high beta relative to other markets, which makes you wary of a pairs trade. Believing that markets might continue to be weak throughout the rest of the year, you decide to investigate a put switch—buying INDA puts and selling FXI puts.

Figure 12.5.

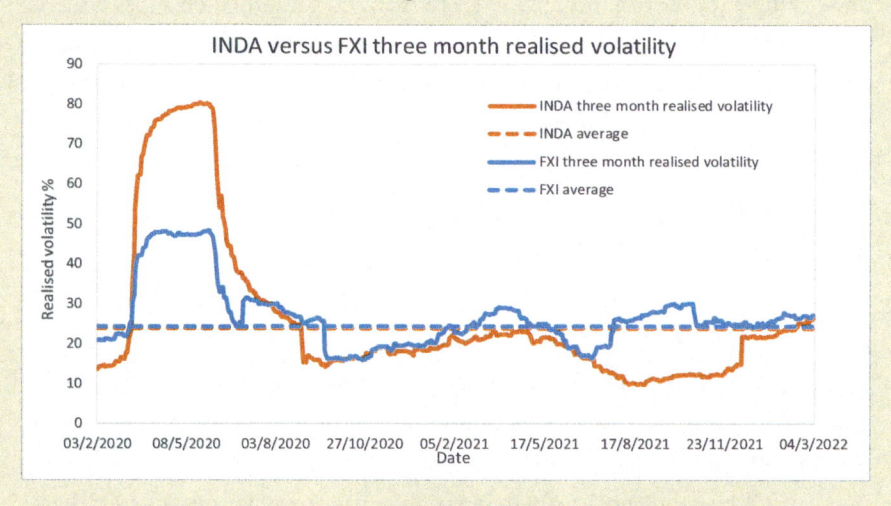

Figure 12.6.

You look at the listed options for each and judge that there is sufficient liquidity and open interest to trade January 20, 2023, expiry options on both but that INDA is probably the least liquid of the two. You want to consider options with strikes no more than 20 percent out-the-money (i.e., higher than 80 percent of the ETF price). You look at the out-the-money puts for INDA options for this expiry and match the deltas with corresponding FXI out-the-money put options as closely as possible, compiling the table in Figure 12.7.

INDA ETF		price: $41.50			FXI ETF		price: $32.97			Price ratio
put strike	delta	ask price	implied volatility	strike / ETF % strike	put strike	delta	bid price	implied volatility	strike / ETF % strike	INDA:FXI 0.79
41	-0.43	5.51	25.7%	98.8%	33	-0.44	3.80	29.0%	100.1%	0.69
40	-0.39	3.16	26.7%	96.4%	32	-0.40	3.26	29.1%	97.1%	1.03
39	-0.35	2.81	27.6%	94.0%	31	-0.35	2.75	29.3%	94.0%	0.98
38	-0.32	2.48	28.3%	91.6%	30	-0.32	2.37	29.8%	91.0%	0.96
37	-0.28	2.17	28.9%	89.2%	29	-0.28	2.02	30.5%	88.0%	0.93
36	-0.25	1.88	29.5%	86.7%	28	-0.25	1.72	31.3%	84.9%	0.91
35	-0.22	1.65	30.3%	84.3%	27	-0.21	1.46	32.0%	81.9%	0.88

Figure 12.7.

It is clear that despite INDA historically being prone to much greater realized volatility, FXI options for this expiry have higher implied volatility at present. This allows for implementing a put switch on beneficial terms. Were the pairs trade implemented for equal notional sizes—i.e., selling INDA ETF and buying FXI ETF for zero initial cost—the ratio would be 1:0.79, so less of the INDA ETF could be sold for each FXI ETF bought. Using the put switch allows for the ratio to be around 1:1. The best ratio appears to be buying the INDA 40 strike puts to achieve a short delta position and selling the FXI 32 strike puts to achieve a positive delta; however, the put deltas do not exactly match. In addition, the percentage strikes are 96.4 percent and 97.1 percent, respectively (i.e., 3.6 percent out-the-money and 2.9 percent out-the-money), to the slight disadvantage of the trade. Instead, you decide to buy the INDA 39 strike puts and sell the FXI 31 strike puts, which has the second-best ratio but has perfectly matched deltas and percentage strikes.

As the short option is always the riskiest part of the trade, you calculate the number of put options to sell, based upon the quantity of FXI ETFs you are willing to buy at the strike price. You would be comfortable owning $31,000 worth of the FXI ETF at the 31 put strike at expiry, which equates to ten contracts (10 contracts × $31 put strike × 100 multiplier = $31,000). You sell to open ten FXI January 20, 2023, expiry 31 strike put options at $2.75, generating a short put liability of $2,750 on your broker account (10 contracts × $2.75 put price × 100 multiplier). At the same time, you buy to open ten contracts of INDA January 20, 2023, expiry 39 strike put options at $2.81, costing $2,810 in premium (10 contracts × $2.81 put price × 100 multiplier). This gives you $39,000 worth of short exposure to the INDA ETF below the 39 strike at expiry.

In the example above, the resulting position carries considerably less risk than the corresponding pairs trade. At expiry, there will be no exposure if both ETFs are less than six percent below current levels, since both put options will expire worthless, and a small loss of $60 will be booked, which is the net premium spent on the trade (excluding trading costs). If both ETFs are over six percent lower at expiration, then the trade will be short $39,000 worth of the INDA ETF versus being long $31,000 worth of the FXI ETF at their respective strikes. This is a far better position to be in than being short $39,000 worth of the INDA ETF versus being long $49,000 of the FXI ETF as the market falls, which is the ratio implied by the pairs trade.

MULTIPLE OPTION STRATEGIES

CHAPTER 13: LONG CALL SPREAD

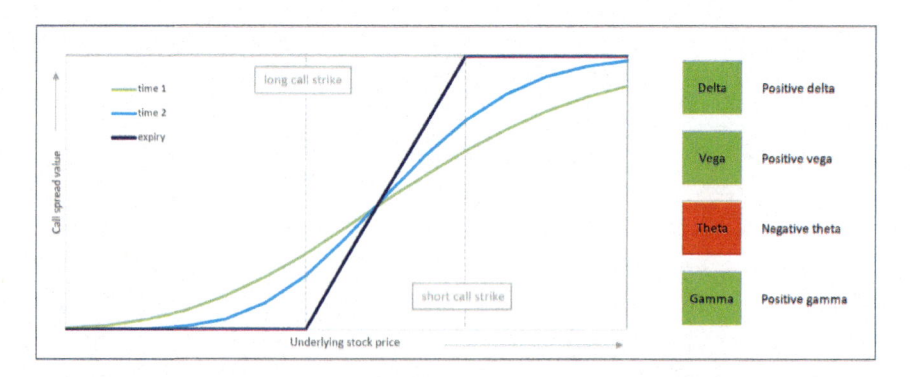

Figure 13.1.

A call spread is bought by simultaneously buying to open a call option and selling to open the same quantity of same expiry call options but with a higher strike price. These are often described as the **long leg** and the **short leg**, respectively, and the order to execute it is always submitted on a broker platform as a single instruction. A call spread is also referred to as a **bull spread**.

Unlike the single option strategies from previous chapters, the multiple option strategies covered in this book comprise both long and short options. Since each different option has its own Greek exposure, and short options have the opposite exposure to long options, the net Greek exposure for these strategies can change quite drastically over time, primarily due to which option strike is nearest to the underlying stock price at any point and the difference between their implied volatilities. A call spread, for example, can change from being net long vega if the stock is below the long call strike to being net short vega if the stock is above the short call strike. The Greek exposures shown in Figure 13.1 and with similar payoff diagrams at the beginning of all subsequent chapters are therefore just the most likely Greek exposures prevalent at the start of the trade.

The motivation to buy a call spread is similar to that of buying a call—risk is limited to the net premium paid, and it has a positive delta, so there is an expectation that the underlying stock will rise—but there are important distinctions due to the short call option leg.

1. It is cheaper—the call spread price is the lower strike call price minus the higher strike call price.
2. It has limited potential upside—the maximum value of a call spread at expiry is the higher strike minus the lower strike, unlike a call option, which has theoretically unlimited maximum value.
3. It will always have less delta, less vega, less theta, and less gamma than if just the long leg were bought because the short call (being the inverse of the long call) to some extent offsets all of these.
4. For a given expiry, "tighter" call spreads (i.e., where the long strike and the short strike are closer together) have smaller Greek exposures.
5. It will always have a positive delta and when bought at or out-the-money will have positive vega and gamma at the beginning, as shown in Figure 13.1. During the remaining life of the call spread though, whether the net vega, theta, and gamma are positive or negative is primarily determined by whether the underlying equity is closer to the long call strike or the short call strike at any point before expiry.

These distinctions help explain how a call spread will behave but also why it will sometimes make sense to speculate using (1) a call option or (2) a call spread.

Limited upside potential but less cost

When you buy a call option, you are paying for the opportunity to profit from the entire return distribution of the stock above the call strike. If, however, you believe that there is limited upside potential for the stock—say, you think the stock will not be able to appreciate more than 20 percent by expiry—then why pay for that part? The part of the distribution exclusively above 20 percent will also have a value, since there will likely also be a listed call option, which has a call strike 20 percent out-the-money. Assuming that the bid price for the 20 percent out-the-money call is meaningful enough in value to make it worthwhile selling, this can be used as the short leg of the call spread. This reduces the overall cost of the trade whilst tailoring it to fit your view more precisely, since you pay only for exposure to the extent of the stock move that you anticipate will happen.

Less exposure

As illustrated previously, an important factor to be mindful of when buying a call option is its implied volatility—especially with longer-dated and at-the-money call options, since they have a higher vega exposures. This makes it necessary to study implied volatility and realized volatility because if implied volatility is unusually high, the option will not only cost more but also have a higher daily theta. It may also generate a vega loss prior to expiration if implied volatility reverts back toward its average level.

These issues are somewhat allayed when buying a call spread, since all the Greek exposures in the long leg are offset to some extent by the inverse of those Greek exposures in the short leg. Consequently, the net exposures are comparatively smaller. The extent of the offset depends largely upon the distance between the strikes. A "tight" call spread where the short call strike is very close to the long call strike has much smaller overall net Greek exposures, since the size of the offsetting exposures from the short leg more closely resemble those of the long call leg. A call spread with strikes further apart has relatively greater net Greek exposures because the offsets from the short leg are smaller, since the short strike is much higher and hence further out-the-money. For this reason, call spreads (and often tight call spreads) are employed instead of long call option strategies when volatility is elevated.

Example

It is mid-March 2022, and there has been some extreme volatility in the oil market, having risen to multi-year highs and then collapsing over 20 percent during subsequent days. You want to speculate that the price will recover much of the subsequent collapse during the next thirty days or so and have identified the United States Oil Fund ETF (USO) as a vehicle for doing this, since it closely tracks oil price when it is in strong demand. It has liquid options and plenty of open interest, with acceptably tight bid/offer dealing spreads. Its recent peak was a daily closing price of $85.43, and it is currently trading at $70.10.

You see that the listed options have an unsurprisingly high implied volatility, exceeding 60 percent for the period in question, resulting in elevated prices for call options relative to the price of the USO ETF itself. Given the short time frame and the chunky call prices, this would result in large daily theta if you were to buy a call option outright. Although most likely warranted by the high volatility, the call option prices are unappealingly high, so you decide to investigate a call spread trade to see whether this is a better way to express your view.

You look at available listed option expiries and see that there is an April 14 expiry, which is thirty days away. This fits your time frame, which you do not want to exceed by too much because you are thinking about buying a call spread and not an outright call. You compile a list of available call options up to the 85 strike, which is just below the recent peak (Figure 13.3). Given the high degree of volatility in the ETF, you are happy to use mid-prices for the options and employ a limit order to attempt to trade at them.

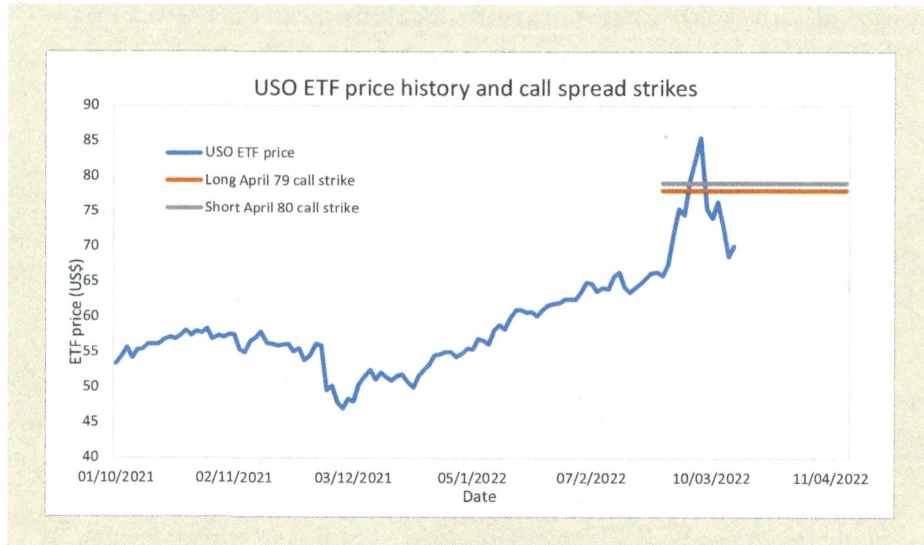

Figure 13.2.

USO April 14, 2022, expiry call option details				ETF price: $70.10		
strike	call mid price	implied vol	delta	vega	theta	gamma
85	1.26	66.7%	0.18	0.05	-0.06	0.02
84	1.36	66.0%	0.20	0.06	-0.06	0.02
83	1.48	65.4%	0.21	0.06	-0.06	0.02
82	1.61	64.8%	0.23	0.06	-0.06	0.02
81	1.75	64.1%	0.25	0.06	-0.07	0.03
80	1.90	63.3%	0.27	0.07	-0.07	0.03
79	2.08	62.7%	0.29	0.07	-0.07	0.03
78	2.29	62.4%	0.31	0.07	-0.07	0.03
77	2.51	61.8%	0.33	0.07	-0.07	0.03
76	2.75	61.2%	0.36	0.08	-0.08	0.03
75	3.01	60.6%	0.38	0.08	-0.08	0.03
74	3.29	59.9%	0.41	0.08	-0.08	0.03
73	3.59	59.2%	0.44	0.08	-0.08	0.03
72	3.95	58.8%	0.47	0.08	-0.08	0.03
71	4.35	58.6%	0.50	0.08	-0.08	0.03
70	4.78	58.4%	0.54	0.08	-0.08	0.03

Figure 13.3.

You then compile tables consisting of different call spread combinations. Figure 13.4 has 85 as the short call strike in each case, since you believe that the recent peak will likely be the upper bound of where you think the ETF might rise and that the $1.26 generated from selling the

85 strike call will meaningfully reduce the cost of the call spread. The call spreads in Figure 13.4 widen as the long call strike is lowered incrementally. Figure 13.5 shows "tight" call spread combinations, where the distance between the strikes is just one dollar.

Wide call spread details

(net = lower strike - higher strike)

call spread strikes	net cost	net delta	net vega	net theta	net gamma	maximum value	profit
83/85	0.22	0.03	0.01	0.00	0.00	2	809%
82/85	0.35	0.05	0.01	-0.01	0.00	3	757%
81/85	0.49	0.07	0.01	-0.01	0.01	4	716%
80/85	0.64	0.09	0.02	-0.01	0.01	5	681%
79/85	0.82	0.11	0.02	-0.01	0.01	6	632%
78/85	1.03	0.13	0.02	-0.01	0.01	7	580%
77/85	1.25	0.15	0.02	-0.02	0.01	8	540%
76/85	1.49	0.18	0.03	-0.02	0.01	9	504%
75/85	1.75	0.20	0.03	-0.02	0.01	10	471%
74/85	2.03	0.23	0.03	-0.02	0.01	11	442%
73/85	2.33	0.26	0.03	-0.02	0.01	12	415%
72/85	2.69	0.29	0.03	-0.02	0.01	13	383%
71/85	3.09	0.32	0.03	-0.02	0.01	14	353%
70/85	3.52	0.36	0.03	-0.02	0.01	15	326%

Figure 13.4.

Tight call spread details

(net = lower strike - higher strike)

call spread strikes	net cost	net delta	net vega	net theta	net gamma	maximum value	profit
84/85	0.10	0.02	0.01	0.00	0.00	1.00	900%
83/84	0.12	0.01	0.00	0.00	0.00	1.00	733%
82/83	0.13	0.02	0.00	0.00	0.00	1.00	669%
81/82	0.14	0.02	0.00	0.00	0.01	1.00	614%
80/81	0.15	0.02	0.01	0.00	0.00	1.00	567%
79/80	0.18	0.02	0.00	0.00	0.00	1.00	456%
78/79	0.21	0.02	0.00	0.00	0.00	1.00	376%
77/78	0.22	0.02	0.00	0.00	0.00	1.00	355%
76/77	0.24	0.03	0.01	-0.01	0.00	1.00	317%
75/76	0.26	0.02	0.00	0.00	0.00	1.00	285%
74/75	0.28	0.03	0.00	0.00	0.00	1.00	257%
73/74	0.30	0.03	0.00	0.00	0.00	1.00	233%
72/73	0.36	0.03	0.00	0.00	0.00	1.00	178%
71/72	0.40	0.03	0.00	0.00	0.00	1.00	150%

Figure 13.5.

HAPPY RETURNS

> You highlight in pink the call spreads that offer the required four-to-one profit potential (i.e., with a profit in the right-hand column exceeding 400 percent) and decide to buy the 79/80 call spread, which will offer the required return for the smallest rise in the USO ETF. You wish to allocate $1,000 to this trade, which will buy 55 call spreads, since each is $180 ($0.18 net cost × 100 multiplier). You submit a limit order to buy 55 USO April 14 expiry 79/80 call spreads at $0.18—simultaneously buying to open 55 USO April 14 expiry 79 calls and selling to open 55 USO April 14 expiry 80 calls as one order instruction on your broker platform.

The example above illustrates some important points about using call spreads. Firstly, the cost of the call spread is the lower strike call minus the higher strike call, and the maximum profit at expiry is the difference between the strike prices.

Call spread cost = lower strike call option price (long leg) – higher strike call option price (short leg)

Maximum call spread value = higher strike price (short strike) – lower strike price (long strike)

Maximum percentage profit = (maximum call spread value – call spread cost) / call spread cost

The maximum profit achievable for any call spread therefore is dictated by the price paid for it and the difference between the strike prices. As a rule of thumb, a four-to-one profit is the minimum desirable return when using a call spread—i.e., for every dollar risked in premium, a clear profit of four dollars is sought. Therefore, once an expiry is selected based upon the time frame believed for the underlying to move higher by the required amount (thirty days in this example), it is a matter of selecting a call spread that can generate a four-to-one profit. Notwithstanding this, the necessary move in the underlying equity clearly needs to be realistic and have a good reason to happen.

Moving down the table in Figure 13.4, the call spreads with the same short 85 call strike but with increasingly lower long call strikes become increasingly expensive, as the cost of the long call option increases along with its delta. Although the call spreads lower down the table have a higher potential maximum value at expiry because the difference between the strikes is greater, the net cost is increasing at a faster rate. Although the majority of the call spreads in Figure 13.4 will deliver the required profit, they all depend upon the ETF reaching $85 by expiry for that profit to be realized.

Fewer call spreads in Figure 13.5 meet the required profit hurdle, but they achieve it with a much smaller move in the underlying USO ETF price. The 70/85 call spread at the bottom of Figure 13.4 has a breakeven of just $73.52 (70 long call strike + $3.52 call spread cost) and is therefore more likely to make a profit than the chosen 79/80 call spread, which has a breakeven of $79.18 (79 long call strike + $0.18 call spread cost). However, if a required profit of 400 percent is set, the tight call spread will deliver that profit for the lowest possible move in the underlying equity. Of course, a greater potential profit is achieved from setting the strikes incrementally higher, but this requires a larger move in the underlying USO ETF.

Dealing costs require consideration as well, however. Tight call spreads necessitate trading a comparatively greater quantity of call option contracts than might ordinarily be the case, so broker's commissions per option contract also need factoring in. If these are too high (and you are unwilling to change your broker), then widening the call spread will greatly reduce the quantity of contracts required.

Incidentally, Figure 13.3 highlights an important aspect of option markets based on different asset classes. Almost without exception, option markets on equity underlying assets will exhibit a positive implied volatility skew—for any particular expiration date, implied volatility is higher for lower strikes than for higher strike options. This reflects the following fact: as equities fall in price, they become more volatile; as equities rise in price, they become less volatile. However, this is not necessarily the case for other

HAPPY RETURNS

asset classes. USO is an ETF and therefore trades as an equity on a stock exchange, but its price is derived from the price of oil futures. Oil is a commodity, not an equity, and commodities often become more volatile as their price rises, which is the opposite to equities. This can be seen in Figure 13.3, where the implied volatility of higher strike call options is greater than those of lower strike call options.

Figure 13.6 shows the profit and loss for the 79/80 call spread; and Figure 13.7 the 70 strike call, which is the call option from Figure 13.3 that offered the greatest possible profit at expiration if the USO ETF were to reach $85. Figure 13.7 shows the P&L for a similar investment of $1,000, which would allow of the purchase of two contracts (2 contracts × $4.78 call price × 100 multiplier = $956). This comparison illustrates several points.

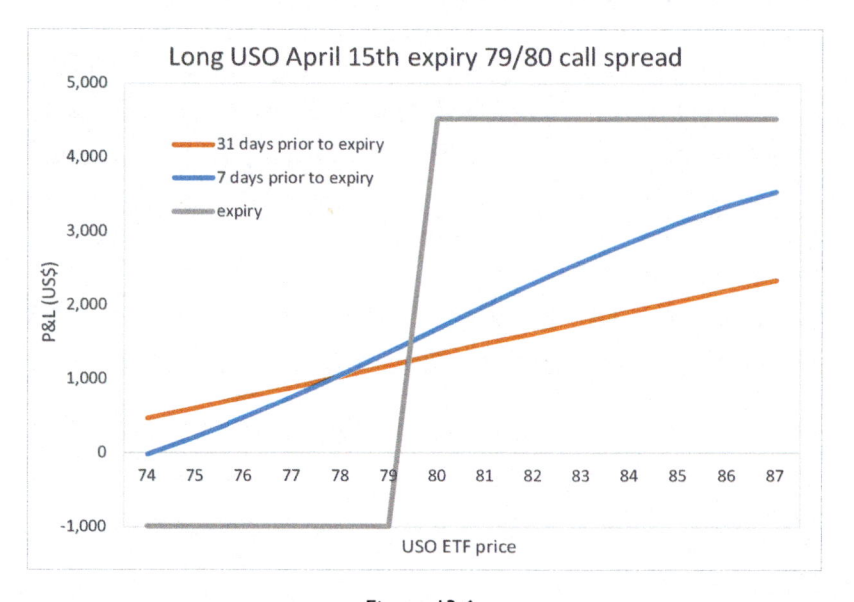

Figure 13.6.

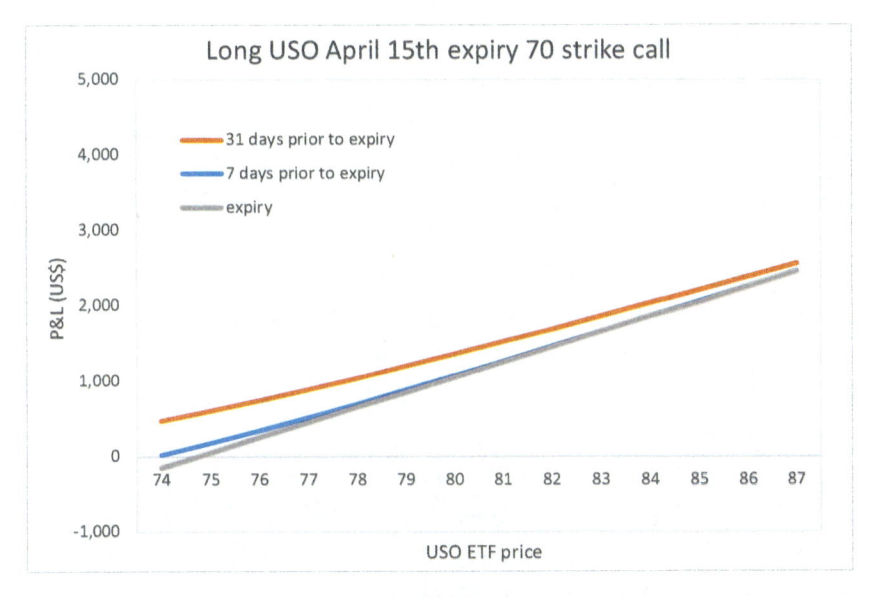

Figure 13.7.

The orange lines are remarkably similar and represent the P&L on the first day, assuming changes only in the USO ETF price up to and just above $85. The blue lines represent the P&Ls with one week remaining before expiry. In Figure 13.7, the move from the orange line to the blue line shows a fall in the premium value for the option as theta decay takes its toll on the 70 strike call option. On Figure 13.6, the move from orange to blue involves a steepening of the line as theta decays both options in the call spread. This steepening occurs because a call spread has two call options—one short and one long—and therefore has theta acting in opposite direction on each. The long call has negative theta decay and so is losing money incrementally every day, whilst the short call has positive theta so is making an incremental gain every day as the short liability gets smaller. The net effect of these two forces largely depends upon which of the two call options is closest to the underlying share price, because at-the-money calls have greater theta values. Consequently, when the underlying stock price is below the call spread strikes, the call spread has net negative theta because the long call option is decaying at a faster rate, and therefore the blue line falls below the orange line. However, when the underlying stock price is above the call spread strikes, the call spread has net positive theta because the sort call option is decaying at a faster rate, and therefore the blue line rises above the orange line.

In Figure 13.6 and Figure 13.7 the blue lines move towards the grey lines over the remaining seven days, as they decay to their intrinsic values. The breakeven for the long 70 call option is $74.78 (70 strike + $4.78 cost), and this is the point in Figure 13.7 where the grey line crosses zero, showing that a profit is made above that price at expiration. In Figure 13.6, the grey line shows that a loss is made below the breakeven for the call spread at $79.18 (long 70 strike + $0.18 net cost), but that profit rises steeply to a maximum at an ETF price of $80, where it plateaus. Above the short 80 call strike, the call spread P&L is vastly superior at every point on the graph relative to the long 70 strike call, whilst below a $79 ETF price, where the short call strike is located, the relative profit potential is inferior. It should be noted that call options have unlimited upside unlike call spreads, but in this example, the long 70 call option trade does not make more money than long 79/80 call spread trade until the ETF exceeds $97.33 in price.

An important aspect to appreciate when buying a call spread (especially a tight call spread) is that a large part of the potential profit occurs in the days and weeks before expiry. As shown in Figure 13.6, it takes twenty-eight days for the P&L to move from the orange line to the blue line, but just seven days for it to move from the blue line to the grey line. Consequently, determining which expiry date to use when buying a call spread takes greater precision than when buying a call option. Whereas it often makes sense to buy a call option with additional time in excess of what is strictly required, this is not quite the case when buying a call spread. With a call spread, any profit is only fully realised once both options expire. Therefore, being very clear about the timeframe within which the anticipated move in the equity will occur is even more important and the call spread expiry needs to fall immediately after this.

The net exposures for the call spread in this example are extremely small. Since the time to expiration is only thirty-one days, the vega exposures for the call options are already small, but the net delta, vega, theta, and gamma are greatly reduced even further within the call spread. These can be seen in Figure 13.5, where the negative theta value for all the tight call spreads are below half a cent a day (and therefore show a value 0.00), compared with eight cents of daily theta for the 70 strike call in Figure 13.3.

Indeed, the delta remains a very small positive number right up until expiry, given the close proximity of the strikes and the offsetting nature of the short call option. At expiry, the call spread will have a delta of only one between the strikes—i.e., if the USO ETF is above $79 or less than or equal to $80 at the point of expiry—otherwise the delta will be zero. With the ETF price between the strikes at expiration, then the long 79 call on its own will be automatically exercised and the owner liable to buy the ETF at $79. If this were undesirable, the call spread would need to be sold before or on the expiration date to avoid the risk of this happening. Expiration risk is explored further in the section on managing risks, in chapter 21.

Using longer-dated call spreads

Commonly, call spreads are used for speculation as outlined above. Expiration dates need not be quite so short but may cover several months if that more closely fits one's view, in which case the short call may play an even greater role in reducing unwanted Greek exposures. However, given the need to wait until theta decay has completely eroded the value of the short call leg at expiration before profits are fully realized, call spreads generally use relatively short-dated options. For this reason, call spreads are not generally used to invest in stocks in the same way that call options can be.

It may make sense to use a long-dated out-the-money call spread to speculate on a large move higher in a stock or index if there is a credible scenario for a stock to achieve a permanently higher trading range, but uncertainty about the time and likelihood of it occurring. For example, you suspect that a pharmaceutical company might deliver some news concerning a ground-breaking treatment under development over the next year that will transform their profitability. If there were a strong likelihood it will occur within a finite time frame, then it would be wiser to buy the stock or a long-dated call option if volatility was low. If there was less certainty, then a long-dated call spread might be a means of reducing the risk of speculating on its occurrence, assuming the potential payoff was appealing enough.

CHAPTER 14: LONG PUT SPREAD

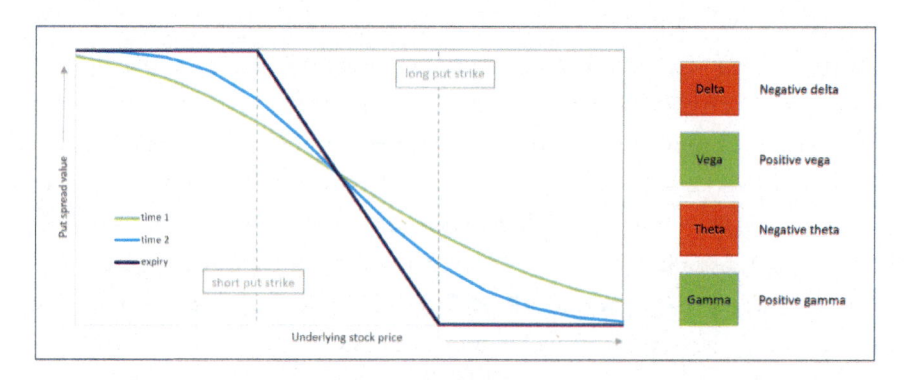

Figure 14.1.

A put spread is bought by simultaneously buying to open a put option and selling to open the same quantity of same expiry put options but with a lower strike price. As with a call spread, these are often referred to as the **long leg** and the **short leg**, respectively, and the order to execute it is always submitted on a broker platform as a single instruction. The motivation to buy a put spread is similar to that of buying a put—risk is limited to the net premium paid, and it has a negative delta so is used to hedge against or speculate on a stock or stock index falling in value. A put spread may also be referred to as a **bear spread**.

As is the case with a call spread, the short leg of a put spread conveys certain attributes to the trade, relative to simply buying a put option:

1. It is cheaper—the put spread price is the higher strike put price minus the lower strike put price.
2. It has limited potential profit—the maximum value of a put spread at expiry is the higher strike minus the lower strike, unlike a put option where maximum value is achieved if the underlying equity falls to zero.
3. It will always have a less negative delta, less vega, less theta, and less gamma than if just the long leg were bought because the short put (being the inverse of the long put) offsets all of these to an extent.
4. For a given expiry, "tighter" put spreads (i.e., where the long strike and the short strike are closer together) have smaller Greek exposures.
5. It will always have a negative delta and when bought at or out-the-money will have positive vega and gamma at the beginning, as shown in Figure 14.1. During the remaining life of the put spread though, whether the net vega, theta, and gamma are positive or negative is primarily determined by whether the underlying equity is closer to the long put strike or the short put strike at any point before expiry.

As was highlighted in the last chapter, an option spread that involves selling the same expiry option but at a different strike—as is the case with either a call spread or a put spread (sometimes also collectively referred to as a **vertical spread**)—is undertaken to reduce the overall exposures and cost associated with simply buying the long leg. This makes it a default choice when volatility is elevated, when all options are more expensive, and it is potentially undesirable to own too much vega exposure in case realized volatility falls again to more average levels.

Buying a put spread instead of a put under such circumstances also benefits from the fact that option skew, along with implied volatility itself, generally increases during bouts of higher realized volatility. Therefore, the lower strike put sold to create the short leg of the put spread will frequently have an even more elevated implied volatility than usual, as well as relative to that of the long leg. During more volatile market conditions, it is unavoidably more expensive to buy put options, but put spreads offer a much cheaper way of creating a desired short exposure.

Why not always buy put spreads instead of puts?

Indices or stocks that have listed liquid put options do not generally fall in value all the way to zero, so why not buy only put spreads instead of put options, and pay a smaller amount for a short exposure that relates to just the extent that the underlying stock might fall? For example, if you believe that a stock will realistically fall by a maximum of only 20 percent, why pay more for a put option instead of a smaller amount for a put spread with a short put strike sold 20 percent below the current price—a level where you do not believe the stock will actually fall beneath?

One reason already touched upon relates to levels of volatility. If realized volatility and the implied volatility priced into a put option is low, then it is desirable to have as much vega exposure as possible if it is more likely to increase. The optimal scenario is when an investor buys a slightly out-the-money put option with a low implied volatility, correctly assessing that imminently the underlying stock will fall. As the stock begins to fall and its volatility increases, the put holder benefits not just from the short delta but also from the long vega of the long put option. Put option skew is also potentially increasing as demand for lower strike put options increases. At this point, the put owner might be able to **leg into** a put spread by selling an equal amount of lower strike put contracts. In doing so, the put investor who originally bought some cheap slightly out-the-money put options, which have become in-the-money as the stock has fallen, can now sell some lower strike expensively priced put options as well. This greatly offsets or even negates the cost of the original put options, creating a valuable in-the-money put spread, which will make a maximum profit if the stock continues to fall to the short put leg by the expiration date. Hence, if implied volatility is already somewhat elevated, it makes sense to buy a put spread; however, if implied volatility is low, then buying a put option with the goal of legging into a put spread at a point in the future is a very effective strategy.

Another reason is the time taken for the entire potential profit of a long put spread to materialize. Similar to the discussion on theta decay of call spreads in the last chapter, if the underlying equity falls in price as far as the lower short put strike, the full profit from a put spread is only realized once the short put leg has decayed away to zero. Until then, the holder of the put spread is earning theta each day because the underlying equity price is closer to the short leg than the long leg, and hence the short put (positive) theta outweighs the long put (negative) theta. This is shown in the upper left of Figure 14.1, where the value of the put spread increases over time as it approaches expiration, represented by the dark blue line. This can present the put spread holder with a dilemma regarding taking an early profit if the underlying equity price is bouncing around quite erratically—whether to sell the put spread and lock in a potentially less significant profit, or hold the position and wait for the put spread to achieve its entire potential profit. Theta decay of the short put leg generates a daily incremental profit, but there is a risk that the underlying equity rallies back through both put strikes, and the put spread falls in value. Complicating the dilemma further is that as the put spread approaches expiry, the amount of profit lost resulting from a rise in the underlying equity increases, as shown in Figure 14.1 by the steepening payoff line between the option strikes as time progresses.

Put spread uses

Put spreads can be used effectively to speculate on an anticipated fall in an equity price, in which case "tight" spreads with out-the-money strikes will deliver the highest profit potential, as was shown in chapter 13. It usually makes little practical sense to buy longer-dated put spreads for this purpose due to the time taken for the short put to decay away to zero and for profits to be realized. One possible application of long-dated put spreads, however, concerns speculating on an event that would permanently depress the price of the underlying equity but where there is uncertainty regarding its actual occurrence or time frame. Frequently though, put spreads are also used to hedge an existing exposure, in preference to long puts, where volatility is elevated and the lower strike put can be sold for a meaningful amount, and if there is little perceived chance of the underlying equity falling far beneath it.

Example

It is mid-September 2022, and you own a portfolio of US stocks that have benefited from the strong gains in the US dollar relative to other currencies over the course of the last twelve months as it became apparent that the US Federal Reserve would aggressively hike interest rates to combat inflation. You are not a US-based investor but wish to maintain your US stock exposure whilst locking in some of the gains attributable to the rising US dollar.

Since the US dollar appreciation has been broadly against all major currencies, you identify the Invesco DB US Dollar Index Bullish Fund (UUP) as a suitable ETF for taking short exposure, which is currently trading at $29.38. Several scenarios could cause the US dollar to appreciate further to your mind, so you decide to look at buying put options instead of shorting the ETF itself, since this will allow you to benefit further if the currency continues to appreciate strongly.

You decide you wish to own some put protection between now and the start of next year and see that January 2023 expiry options are listed on the ETF. You calculate the realized volatility for the ETF, using a three-month realized volatility measure, since this is a decent enough approximation for the timespan between now and expiry, and see that it is over three percentage points above its two-year average (Figure 14.2).

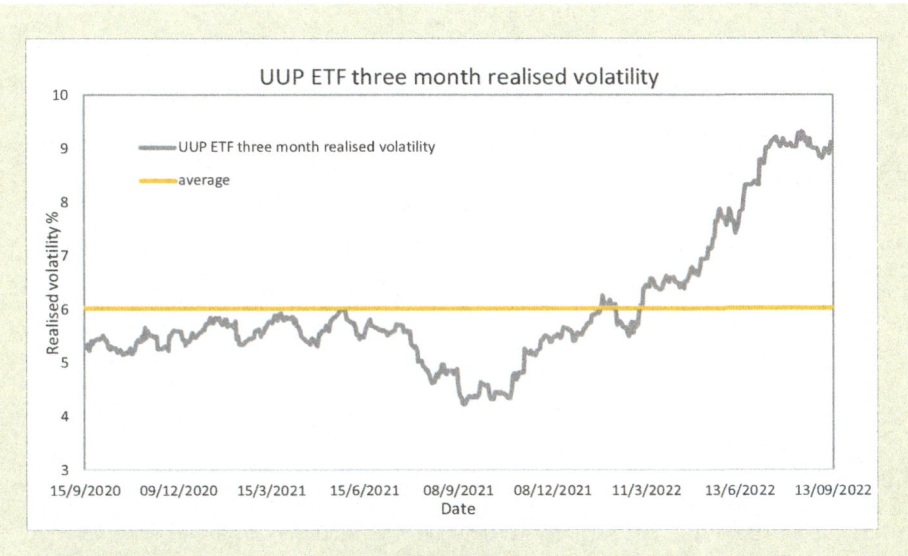

Figure 14.2.

UUP ETF Jaunaury 20 2023 expiry put option details

strike	put mid price	implied vol	delta	vega	theta	gamma
29	0.61	12.7%	-0.38	0.07	-0.003	0.17
28	0.27	12.9%	-0.21	0.05	-0.002	0.13
27	0.12	13.2%	-0.11	0.03	-0.001	0.08
26	0.07	14.9%	-0.06	0.02	-0.001	0.05

UUP ETF price = $29.38

Figure 14.3.

You collate a table of available listed January expiry put options, beginning with the strike immediately below where the ETF is currently trading (Figure 14.3). Unfortunately, your broker platform does not provide enough granularity to assess how historically extreme the put option implied volatility skew is, but at-the-money implied volatility is in excess of the elevated realized volatility.

This would suggest that if realized volatility were to return to its average, the at-the-money options might also fall in value by an even greater amount.

If the 29 strike put option's implied volatility were to fall from 12.7 percent to 7.7 percent, it would generate a vega loss of $0.35 (5 percentage points × 0.07 vega), which all else being equal would be over half of the option cost. This does suggest the options are expensive, and that negating some of the cost and vega exposure by also selling an option seems a sensible approach if using UUP put options as a hedging instrument. Buying a put spread might be better therefore, so you create a table of potential candidates, using the 29 strike for the long leg because you want to hedge as much of your current US dollar exposure as possible (Figure 14.4).

Put spread details

(net = higher strike - lower strike)

put spread strikes	net cost	net delta	net vega	net theta	net gamma	maximum value	profit
29/28	0.34	-0.17	0.02	-0.001	0.04	1	194%
29/27	0.49	-0.27	0.04	-0.001	0.09	2	308%
29/26	0.54	-0.32	0.05	-0.001	0.12	3	456%

Figure 14.4.

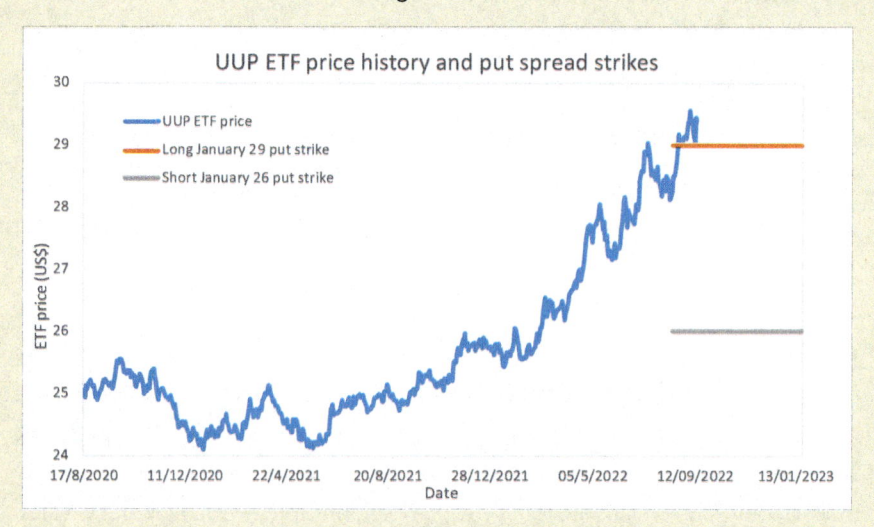

Figure 14.5.

Only the 29/26 strike put spread generates the required return in excess of four-to-one. Although a hedge and not a speculative trade, you still want to adhere to this principle and so dismiss the other potential put spreads. Relative to just buying the 29 strike put, the 29/26 strike put spread costs 10 percent less and has a vega exposure that is nearly 30 percent lower. Although happy selling the 26 strike put because you think it unlikely that UUP will fall lower than $26, ideally you would like to have received more than seven cents for doing so, thereby enabling an even lower cost and net vega. Nevertheless, you want to hedge your exposure, believe this is the best available method, and so decide to proceed.

You have $50,000 in US dollar–denominated equities, so need the same notional size of currency hedge, which requires 17 UUP ETF January 20, 2023, expiry 29/26 put spreads ($50,000 / ($29.38 ETF price × 100 multiplier)). You submit an order on your broker platform to buy 17 put spreads (buying to open seventeen contracts of the 29 strike puts and selling to open seventeen contracts of the 26 strike puts simultaneously as one order instruction) for a net cost of $0.54. Your total spend is $918 in premium (17 contracts × $0.54 cost × 100 multiplier) plus trading costs.

As mentioned earlier, the cost of a put spread is the higher strike put minus the lower strike put.

Put spread cost = higher strike put option price (long leg) – lower strike put option price (short leg)

Furthermore, the maximum value the put spread can have at any point in time is the difference between the strikes, and this is fully realized at expiry only.

Maximum put spread value = higher strike price (long strike) – lower strike price (short strike)

The maximum profit achievable for any put spread, therefore, is dictated by the price paid for it and the difference between the strike prices.

Maximum % profit = (maximum put spread value − put spread cost) / put spread cost

As is the case with a call spread, as a rule of thumb, a minimum four-to-one profit is desirable when using a put spread—i.e., for every $1 you risk in premium, you will look for a $4 clear profit. In this example, the maximum put spread value is achieved if UUP ETF falls to $26 or below by the expiry date, at which point the put spread would be worth $5,100 ((29 strike − 26 strike) × 17 contracts × 100 multiplier). The maximum profit that you can hope to achieve, therefore, is 456 percent (($5,100 − $918) / $918).

As the example illustrates, a put spread cannot provide a perfect hedge, partly because protection fully exists at expiry only and between the put option strikes. In the example, these are 1.3 percent and 11.5 percent below the current price of the UUP ETF for the long and short strikes, respectively (since UUP is $29.38, and the put strikes are 29 and 26). Furthermore, the breakeven for the trade is $28.46 (29 strike − $0.54 put spread cost), which is, in fact, 3.2 percent below the current UUP price. Therefore, the US dollar can fall by nearly 4.5 percent against a broad basket of other currencies by expiration of the put spread in January before the hedge gives any benefit. Sometimes, an attempt to compensate for such slippage is made by intentionally **over-hedging**—i.e., buying slightly more hedging contracts than strictly warranted by the size of the exposure. A judgement was also made that the UUP ETF would not fall below $26 by the expiration date (i.e., in excess of 11.5 percent). This could prove to be mistaken, however, in which case the hedge profits would be even smaller when compared with the loss on the US dollar–denominated portfolio to the overseas investor.

As touched upon also in chapter 10, an exposure mismatch will also likely exist between a hedging instrument and any investment portfolio. The UUP ETF chosen in the example tracks the performance of the US dollar versus a basket with specific percentages of euros, Japanese yen, British pounds, Canadian dollars, Swedish krona, and Swiss francs. These percentages will likely differ from those of an individual's international investment portfolio, allowing further potential slippage of hedge performance. Other ETFs exist that may provide closer fits for certain overseas investors (such as FXE for European investors or FXY for Japanese investors).

It is acknowledged, therefore, that a put or a put spread hedge, particularly when applied to a portfolio, will likely be imperfect for a variety of reasons. Although every reasonable attempt should be made to match the exposure being hedged with the most suitable and liquid put options, it is inevitable some slippage will occur.

CHAPTER 15: COLLAR

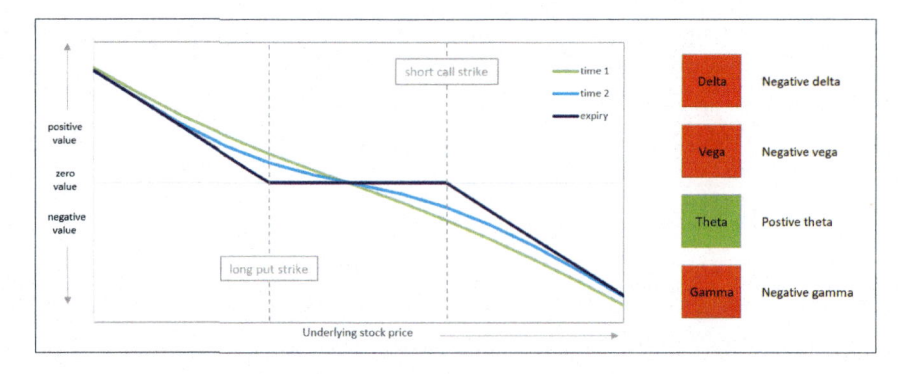

Figure 15.1.

A long collar is bought by simultaneously buying to open a put option and selling to open the same quantity of same expiry call options with a higher strike. A **zero cost collar** has its call option strike specifically selected to offset the put purchase cost, therefore making the overall cost zero. The order to execute a collar is always submitted as a single instruction on a broker platform.

The long put and short call options both contribute negative delta to a collar, making it commonly utilized as an inexpensive hedge when wishing to offset greatly the long exposure of an underlying stock. It is effective in doing so because, assuming the notional size of the trade correctly matches that of the underlying stock, the long put feature hedges drops in the stock price below the put strike, whilst the short call feature offsets any gains in the stock above the call strike. This is the obvious drawback also, since there is no benefit from a rise in price of the underlying equity above the short call option. The returns on your stock position are therefore "collared" to the upside and downside by the strategy due to the respective option strikes.

Zero cost collars have no potential wastage on paying for hedge protection that goes unused, as with buying puts or put spreads. Figure 15.2 and Figure 15.3 show the payoff profiles resulting from combining a long stock position with a zero cost collar.

Figure 15.2.

[Figure 15.3: payoff diagram showing P&L vs underlying stock price with long put strike and short call strike, plotted for time 1, time 2, and expiry]

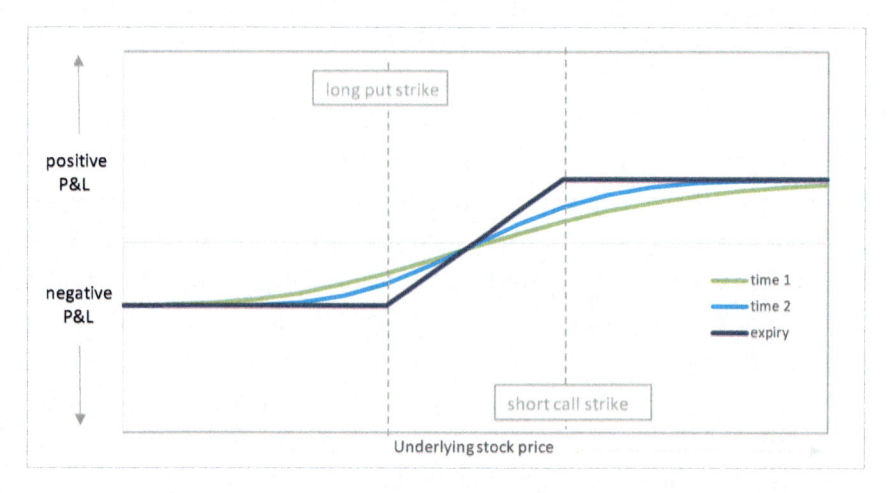

Figure 15.3.

The payoff diagram for a long stock position is simply a diagonal straight line from the bottom left to the top right: as the stock price increases, the P&L increases by the same percentage; as the stock price decreases, the P&L decreases by the same percentage. So when buying a zero cost collar to hedge a long stock position, it involves buying a put option with a strike some distance below the current market level and selling a **covered** call option (i.e., a short call option "covered" by a long stock position) some distance above the current market level. Assuming that the distances are the same and the purchase price of the put equals the sale price for the call, thereby making it costless (ignoring trading costs), Figure 15.2 and Figure 15.3 represent the combined position.

Note that in the left half of both diagrams, a loss is made due to the falling price of the long stock position. However, the loss is truncated by the long put strike, because if the stock is below the long put strike at expiry, the clearing house automatically exercises the option, thereby selling the stock for the value of the put strike. Prior to expiry, the put additionally has time value, which is eroded by theta from time 1 to time 2 to expiry. Conversely, the right-hand side of the diagrams shows a profit due to the long stock position rising in value. Gains are truncated by the covered call strike because if the stock price is above it at expiry, the clearing house will automatically "call away" the long stock position in exchange for the value of the short call strike price as part of the assignment process. Prior to expiry, the short call liability is eroded in value by theta, giving a profit uplift from time 1 to time 2 to expiry. Thus, a zero cost collared stock position can make a loss but only as far as the long put strike, or a profit but only as far as the short call strike.

The difference between the two zero cost collars in the diagrams are due to the distances between the strikes, with Figure 15.2 having put and call strikes that are wider apart than Figure 15.3. Consequently, the options in Figure 15.2 have smaller negative deltas and premium values individually, relative to those in Figure 15.3. As such, when combining the options with the stock position, which always has a positive delta of one, the collar in Figure 15.2 has a larger overall positive net delta and therefore more ability to go up and down in value because the offsetting negative deltas from the options are that much smaller than is the case in Figure 15.3. The table in Figure 15.4 shows this representatively.

	Figure 15.2	Figure 15.3	synthetic short
long put delta	-0.2	-0.35	-0.5
short call delta	-0.2	-0.35	-0.5
long stock delta	1	1	1
total delta	0.6	0.3	0

Figure 15.4.

Reducing the distance between the option strikes entirely so that the long put and short call option strikes are identical, creates a **synthetic short**. A synthetic short or synthetic long stock position (created by buying a call and selling a put with the same strike and expiry) are also known collectively as a **combo**. Since at-the-money options have deltas of roughly a half (i.e., either +0.5 for a long call or short put, or -0.5 for a short call or long put), as the table suggests, a synthetic short can be used to eliminate entirely the market exposure of owning the underlying stock until expiry of the options. A -0.5 delta put will also have the same implied volatility as a 0.5 delta call, meaning that the prices for each perfectly offset and the cost is zero. A synthetic short stock position also has no vega, theta, or gamma exposures, since the long leg of the option that provides the long vega, long gamma, and short theta exposures, is completely offset by the short vega, short gamma, and long theta exposures from the short leg, leaving just the delta exposure of minus one.

Although small-to-insignificant initially, the vega, gamma, and theta exposures of the long collars in Figure 15.2 and Figure 15.3 can grow prior to expiry. If the underlying equity rises more toward the short call strike, then the short call characteristics of short vega, short gamma, and long theta become dominant. If it falls more toward the long put strike, then the long put characteristics of long vega, long gamma, and short theta become dominant. Wider strikes, such as those in Figure 15.2, allow greater possible exposures to occur. Prior to expiry, therefore, a collar has increasingly positive net vega as the market falls and increasingly negative net vega as the market rises, which potentially also generates an additional vega profit if the market experiences extreme moves in either direction.

Lastly, a collar with a long stock position, as can be seen in Figure 15.2 and Figure 15.3, has the same payoff as owning a call spread, such as in Figure 13.1. This will come as no surprise thinking back to chapter 10, where Figure 10.7 showed that a long put combined with a long stock position creates a synthetic call option. A long collar used to protect a long stock position therefore is essentially a synthetic call option and a covered call option combined.

Option skew

There is one fly in the ointment, however, which is that equity options will almost certainly be priced with option skew—i.e., put options with lower strikes have higher implied volatilities than at-the-money options, which have higher volatilities than out-the-money call options. Whereas bonds, commodities, and FX markets (and therefore to an extent the ETFs available that invest in them) can often be priced with out-the-money call options that have equal or even higher implied volatilities than their respective out-the-money puts, this will almost certainly not be the case for equity options.

Option skew is of no concern for a synthetic short because the strikes, the implied volatilities and the option costs are the same, whereas it is increasingly a concern for the long collars in Figure 15.3 and Figure 15.2, respectively. This is because there is a larger distance between the option strikes and therefore potentially more option skew, making the difference in implied volatility between the long put and short call greater. Because a long collar involves buying the put, which has the higher implied volatility, and selling the call, which has the lower implied volatility, this means that inevitably there is a cost involved. In practical terms, this annoyance is resolved in one of two ways—either by paying a small amount for the collar or by adjusting the option strikes. This involves either selecting a slightly lower (and therefore cheaper) long put strike or selecting a lower (and therefore more expensive) short call strike to ensure that the collar remains zero cost.

Motivation for buying a collar

There are two main circumstances where a collar is used. Firstly, where you have an equity position that has performed strongly and you wish to "lock in" much of the performance but also want to benefit if it rises a little further. Relatively short-dated options are commonly used, setting the short call strike at the level at which you are willing to sell the stock if it were to be called away (i.e., if it were to finish above the call strike at expiry), then seeing what put strike can be bought with the proceeds to protect the long stock position. As outlined above, paying a small net premium can be easily justified on a stock that has made strong returns if you wish to have a higher put strike than the one afforded by selling the call option.

Long collars are also used when there is a strong belief in future market or specific stock weakness. This conviction is implicitly greater than the one that would motivate the purchase of puts or put spreads to protect a stock position, because selling the call implies that you are willing to forgo the chance of making reasonable positive returns on the stock, which would still be available had the equity position been hedged using put options alone. Whether the collar is traded for zero cost or for a small net cost is again determined by what current option pricing allows and how suitable the strikes are relative to your view on the severity of the future market weakness. Expiration dates selected are generally from short to medium term for this purpose (i.e., up to around six months). Collars generally have low vega exposures when initiated because the long vega exposure from the long put option is to a degree offset by the short vega exposure from the short call option, so can therefore be employed when market volatility is more elevated. However, periods of heightened volatility exhibit strong positive counter rallies, and collars implicitly limit potential positive stock returns, so it is important to be comfortable with this potential risk.

If the option pricing is such that it is not possible to buy the required collar for zero cost, a further variation to consider is a **zero cost put spread collar**. This essentially is a collar with an additional far out-the-money put sold, which turns the long put part of the collar into a put spread. The premium received from selling the far out-the-money put offsets the price of the collar, with the aim of making the entire put spread collar zero cost. These are generally employed during periods of heightened market volatility, so it is again important to be comfortable with the prospect of a very limited positive return if the market rebounds higher. The additional short put contributes further short vega exposure to the collar, so zero cost put spread collar prices benefit from both elevated implied volatility and put option skew. Although zero cost, however, the structure only provides a hedge to the long stock position between the put strike prices, as shown in Figure 15.5, leaving the position only partially hedged during extreme market sell-offs.

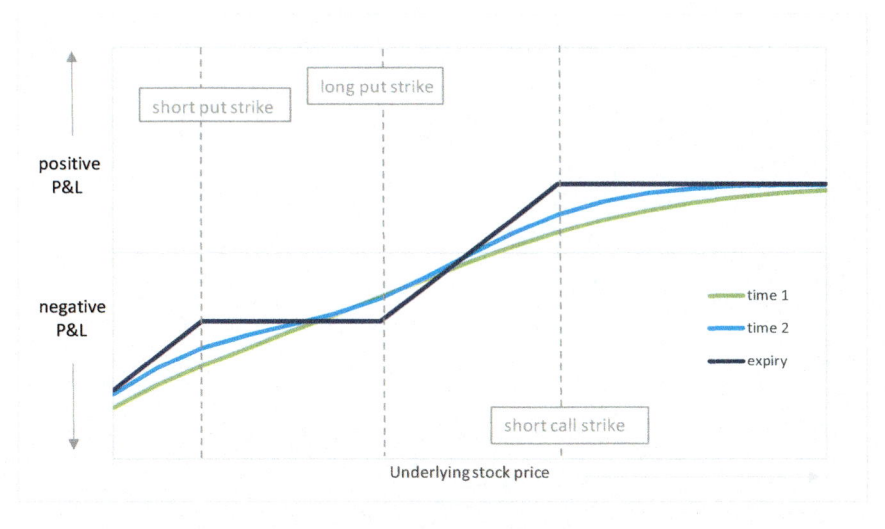

Figure 15.5

Example

It is late August 2022, and you recently bought two thousand British Petroleum (BP) ADRs at $27 when the price fell dramatically the previous month. You are keen on the stock due to the outlook for the oil price and profitability of the sector and the high stable dividend stream they provide. Indeed, your purchase was in part motivated in order to be eligible for the dividend on August 11. However, you have made over 20 percent, including the dividend, in under two months on the position, and as you foresee some market turbulence over the next few months, not least because September and October can be rather volatile, you decide to look for some protection.

You could sell the stock and book the profit, although you still think it could go higher and would like the next dividend, which you believe you would be eligible for on November 9 and to be around $0.36. However, you would also be happy selling it around this year's highs at $34, with the hope of buying it cheaper again in the future. You decide to look at the option market to see whether it can provide a solution.

November 18 2022 expiry option details

		CALL			strike			PUT		
gamma	theta	vega	delta	mid price ($)	strike	mid price ($)	delta	vega	theta	gamma
0.06	-0.011	0.05	0.27	0.80	36	4.71	-0.73	0.05	-0.011	0.06
0.07	-0.012	0.05	0.33	1.06	35	3.98	-0.67	0.06	-0.012	0.07
0.07	-0.013	0.06	0.40	1.39	34	3.30	-0.60	0.06	-0.013	0.07
0.07	-0.013	0.06	0.47	1.76	33	2.66	-0.53	0.06	-0.013	0.07
0.07	-0.013	0.06	0.54	2.23	32	2.15	-0.46	0.06	-0.013	0.07
0.07	-0.013	0.06	0.61	2.80	31	1.68	-0.39	0.06	-0.013	0.07
0.06	-0.013	0.05	0.68	3.47	30	1.31	-0.32	0.05	-0.012	0.06
0.05	-0.012	0.05	0.74	4.16	29	1.02	-0.26	0.05	-0.012	0.06
0.05	-0.011	0.04	0.79	4.95	28	0.79	-0.21	0.04	-0.011	0.05
0.04	-0.010	0.04	0.83	5.78	27	0.62	-0.17	0.04	-0.010	0.04
0.03	-0.010	0.03	0.86	6.66	26	0.48	-0.13	0.03	-0.009	0.03
0.03	-0.009	0.03	0.88	7.58	25	0.38	-0.10	0.03	-0.008	0.03

BP ADR price : $ 32.10

Figure 15.6.

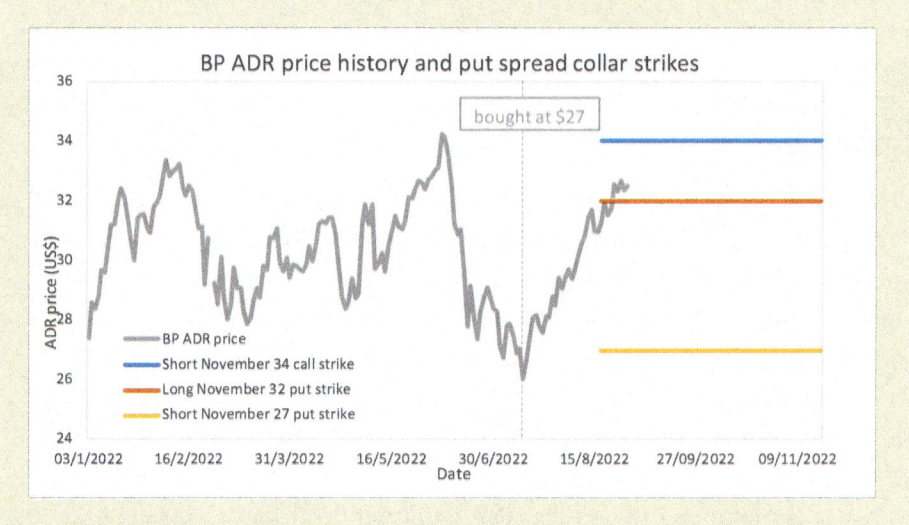

Figure 15.7.

Looking at your broker platform, you see that there is an option expiry on November 18, which would take you through the next couple of potentially turbulent months. You take a snapshot of the screen (Figure 15.6) to study the option pricing.

Ideally, you would like to buy a zero cost collar with the short call strike at 34, where you are happy to sell the stock. However, looking at the option pricing, you see that the 34 strike call has a mid-price of $1.39, which would allow you to buy the 30 strike put at $1.31 for a small net credit of $0.08 if you were able to trade at the mid-prices in each case. Although this looks reasonably priced for a zero cost collar—the strikes are roughly equidistant from the stock price—you ideally would like a little more protection, as the 30 strike (where your long put protection would begin at expiry) is 6.5 percent below where the stock is trading now. You decide to see whether a put spread collar looks any more appealing.

The lowest closing price for the year was $26.02, reached days after you bought the shares, but you would be happy effectively owning the share again if they reached around the $27 price that you originally paid. You see that the 27 strike put is priced at $0.62, which when added to the proceeds from selling the 34 strike call would generate $2.01 if each were sold at the mid-prices. This would almost cover the $2.15 cost of the 32 strike put if it were also traded at the mid-price, leaving a small $0.14 to pay. Since the 34 strike put would provide protection just 0.3 percent below where the stock is currently trading and the $0.14 cost is 0.4 percent of the stock price and hence small compared with the profits you have made, you decide to buy the BP ADR November 18, 2022, expiry 34/32/27 put spread collar for $0.14.

Since you own two thousand BP ADRs, and the option multiplier is 100 for US stocks, you place an order to sell to open twenty contracts of the November expiry 34 strike call, buy to open twenty contracts of the November expiry 32 strike puts, and sell to open twenty contracts of the November expiry 27 strike puts. This instruction is to be executed simultaneously as one order for a cost of $0.14. Once the instruction is executed, you pay $280 in premium (20 contracts × $0.14 net cost × 100 multiplier) plus trading costs.

The example above illustrates the flexibility that is possible when designing a hedge. The array of available strikes mean that a great variety of different potential permutations exists, which can be tailored to fit an individual's view. For example, some may prefer the long collar using the short 34 strike call and the long 30 strike put, which offers complete protection below the put strike, rather than the put spread collar selected in the example, which provides protection only between the long and short put strikes at $32 and $27, respectively. Another investor may favour a 34/31/25 put spread collar instead, for example, which offers protection between the long and short put strikes at $31 and $25, respectively. Hedges can therefore be fine-tuned to fit an individual's risk tolerance and expectations for a stock's return.

The long 34/30 collar and the 34/32/27 put spread collar in the example have somewhat different exposures up until expiry from the option Greeks. These, of course, change continually due to moves in the stock price, implied volatility, the passage of time, etc., but at trade initiation, the exposures for each are shown in Figure 15.8.

BP November expiry 34/30 collar

Option details

	price	delta	vega	theta	gamma
short 34 call	-1.39	-0.40	-0.06	0.013	-0.07
long 30 put	1.31	-0.32	0.05	-0.012	0.06
total	-0.08	-0.72	-0.01	0.000	-0.01

Trade details

	cost	delta shares	$ vega	$ theta
20 contracts	-160	-1440	-20	0.36
quantity of ADRs		2000		
net stock position		560		

BP November expiry 34/32/27 put spread collar

Option details

	price	delta	vega	theta	gamma
short 34 call	-1.39	-0.40	-0.06	0.013	-0.07
long 32 put	2.15	-0.46	0.06	-0.013	0.07
short 27 put	-0.62	0.17	-0.04	0.010	-0.04
total	0.14	-0.69	-0.04	0.009	-0.04

Trade details

	cost	delta shares	$ vega	$ theta
20 contracts	280	-1380	-80	17.92
quantity of ADRs		2000		
net stock position		620		

Figure 15.8.

The top sections show the prices and Greeks from each individual option, taken from Figure 15.6 in the example. The total values are then multiplied by two thousand (20 contracts × 100 multiplier) in the lower section to give the net exposure details of both potential trades of twenty contracts. Finally, the long two thousand ADRs are also added to the "delta shares" numbers in the lower sections to get an equivalent net stock position.

The collar has a small negative cost (i.e., you receive $160 in this example before trading costs) and small net negative vega and gamma and positive theta dollar exposures. This is due to the fact that the stock was at $32.10 in the example, which is fractionally closer to the short 34 call strike than the long 30 put strike, so the net vega, theta, and gamma have marginally more of the short option characteristics. The -0.72 short delta from

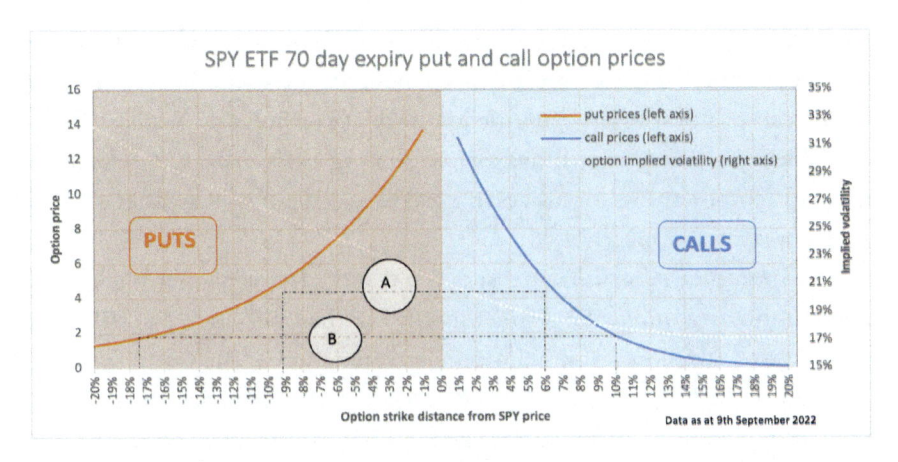

Figure 16.2.

Figure 16.2 shows the price of call and put options on the SPY ETF that have seventy days to expiration and strikes up to 20 percent above and 20 percent below, respectively. As the black dotted lines show, for this expiry at the time of writing, buying a call option with a strike 6 percent above the SPY ETF price can be fully paid for by selling a put option with a strike a little over 9 percent below (labelled A). Alternatively, a call option with a strike 10 percent above can be fully funded by selling a put option with a strike just over 17 percent below the SPY ETF price (labelled B). This is possible due to the option skew—as evidenced by the dotted white line—whereby lower strike options are priced with an increasingly higher implied volatility. By virtue of equity option skew therefore, a zero cost equity risk reversal constructed from out-the-money options offers positive asymmetry of returns. Figure 16.3 illustrates this using the SPY ETF risk reversal examples outlined above.

the two options gives an equivalent short stock position of -1,440 shares when twenty contracts of the collar are bought, reducing the overall stock equivalent position when combined with the two thousand ADRs to a net 560 shares. It therefore still has a residual long stock exposure, which can generate a profit or loss for moves in the $34 to $30 range (the short call and long put strikes, respectively).

The put spread collar has a cost of $280 and relatively larger vega, theta, and gamma exposures. This is because it also has the short 27 strike put, which gives additional short option characteristics to the trade. That includes a daily $17.92 earned by theta decay, although since the different options will decay at different rates and in a non-linear way, this will change over time. Also, the combined delta of -0.69 is smaller, which translates into a -1,380 share equivalent when trading twenty contracts, giving a net equivalent stock position of 620 shares when adding the ADRs. This is larger than the collar because the short 27 put also adds a positive delta to the overall position. Consequently, there is less of a hedge, which is only effective at expiry between a range of $32 and $27 in the ADR price only, as previously discussed.

Collar performance

Figure 15.9 and Figure 15.10 show the performance of the S&P 500 Total Return Index (SPXTR) and the CBOE S&P 500 Tail Risk Index (PPUT3M) as discussed in chapter 10, along with the CBOE S&P 500 3-Month Collar 95-110 Index (CLL3M). CLL3M is a hypothetical index maintained by CBOE, consisting of SPXTR and a three-month S&P 500 Index collar comprising a short call strike 10 percent out-the-money and a long put strike 5 percent out-the-money. The long collar is assumed to be held to expiration and a new one traded every quarter year (https://www.cboe.com/us/indices/dashboard/cll3m/). The long put feature of PPUT3M is not directly comparable with CLL3M, since PPUT3M's long put strike is 10 percent out-the-money, but the comparison is still informative.

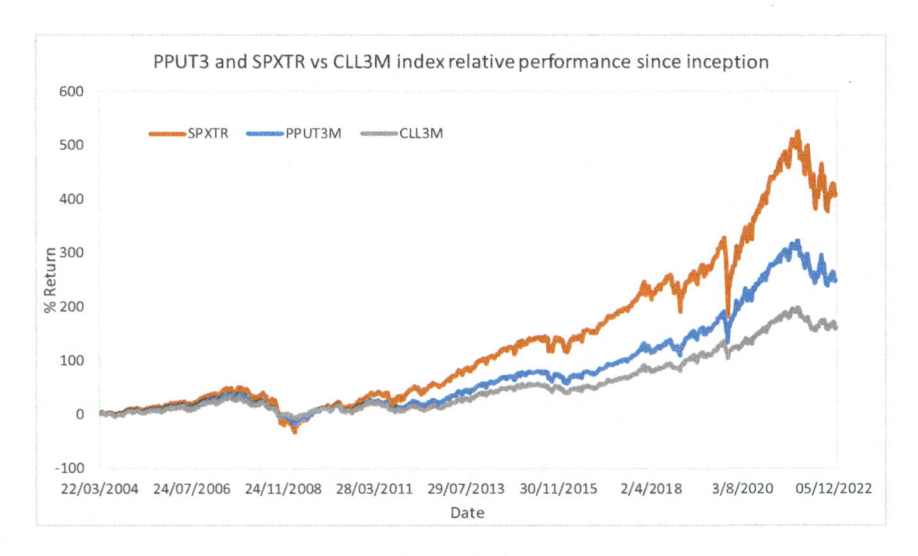

Figure 15.9.

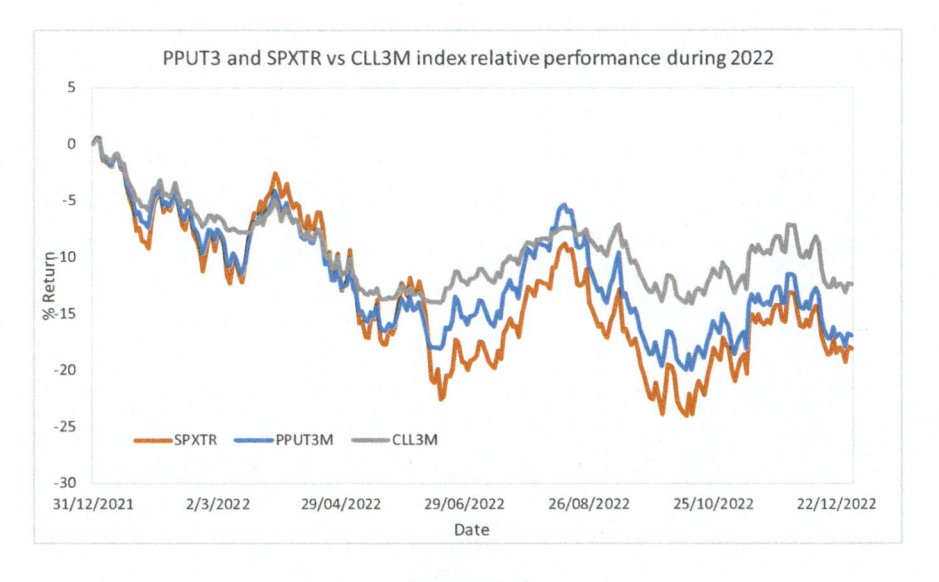

Figure 15.10.

As can be seen in Figure 15.9, the long collar strategy (CLL3M) has underperformed both the SPXTR and PPUT3M Indices since inception in 2004. As previously highlighted, this comes as little surprise because equity markets experience periodic long bull markets, and US equity markets in particular enjoyed the support of highly accommodative policies enacted by the US Federal Reserve during this period. Consequently, the quarter yearly purchase of unneeded put protection undermined the performance of PPUT3M, and the quarter yearly additional short call option feature further undermined the relative performance of CLL3M.

As accommodative policy ended in 2022 and equity markets fell, the simple systematic put protection offered by PPUT3M reduced the effect of some of the rout in the S&P 500 Index (Figure 15.10). However, CCL3M performed even better, because the short 10 percent out-the-money call option mitigated to some extent the cost of put protection, and a higher put strike was used. This illustrates the effectiveness of a long collar strategy in reducing the risk of investing in equity markets when they are especially weak.

CHAPTER 16: RISK REVERSAL

Figure 16.1.

A risk reversal involves buying to open a call option and selling to open the same quantity of same expiry put options with a lower strike. The order to execute a risk reversal is always submitted as a single instruction on a broker platform. It is therefore effectively a short collar and is usually traded at or near to zero cost, where the cost of the call option is fully offset by the premium received from selling the put option. They are therefore an effective and cheap way to gain long exposure to an underlying stock, since the long call and short put both contribute positive delta.

A risk reversal can be used as an alternative to investing directly in a stock and when used prudently can reduce the relative risk of doing so. As explained in chapter 12, when a short out-the-money put is "covered"—i.e., sufficient cash is maintained within an account to pay the strike price should the option be exercised—it is less risky than holding the same notional quantity of the stock. This is largely because at expiry, losses would begin to accrue below only the out-the-money short put strike rather than the current stock price. In this sense, a zero cost risk reversal that is "covered" is increasingly less risky relative to owning the underlying stock, the lower the short put strike used.

As was explored in chapter 15, a large put option skew works against the price of a long collar because it makes the long put option materially more expensive than the call option in implied volatility terms. This makes it necessary to either pay a cost for the collar or instead adjust the call or put strike lower to achieve zero cost. Since a risk reversal is the opposite of a collar, a large put option skew benefits the price of risk reversals because they involve **selling skew**—i.e., selling put options with higher implied volatility to fund the purchase of call options with lower implied volatility. Large option skews allow for zero cost risk reversals that have short put options with strikes that are further out-the-money than the long call option strikes.

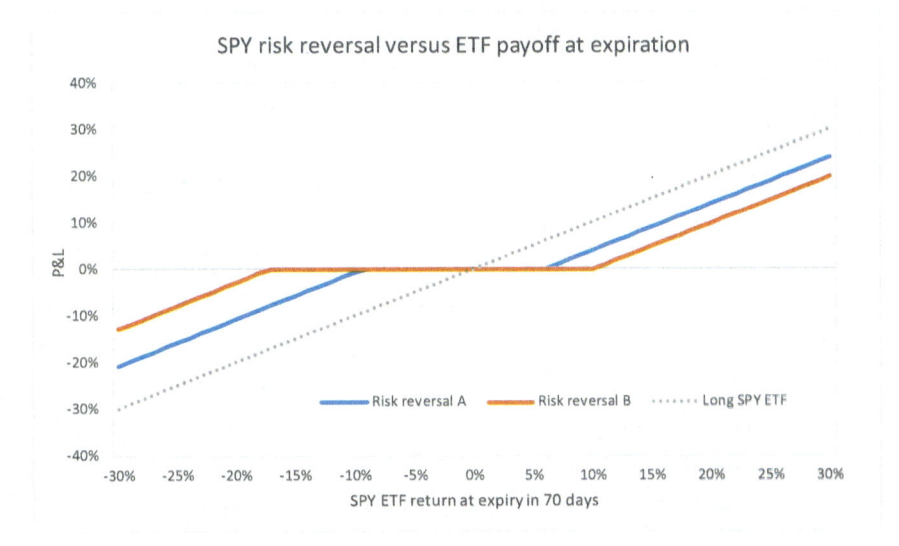

SPY risk reversal versus ETF payoff at expiration

Figure 16.3.

As can be seen (assuming all the notional sizes are the same), a risk reversal will not outperform the underlying stock in a rising market, since the options have out-the-money strikes. However, they will outperform the underlying stock in a falling market by a greater extent than their underperformance in a rising market, due to the short put strike being further out-the-money than the long call strike. Risk reversal A expires worthless if the SPY ETF is within the option strikes at expiry—either 6 percent higher or 9.25 percent lower. Above the long call and below the short put strikes, an option will expire in-the-money and be automatically exercised by the clearing house so, following the assignment process, a risk reversal owner will only have a long stock position above the call strike or below the put strike. Risk reversal B expires worthless if the SPY ETF is within the option strikes at expiry—either 10 percent higher or 17.2 percent lower, but outside of this range, the clearing house will assign a long stock position at either option strike. Assuming that the short put option is "covered" with sufficient cash, this is a less risky position than having instead bought the stock, albeit at the cost of a less positive return potential, because you are obligated to buy only at the much lower put strike. Note that sufficient cash would be required to buy the underlying shares at the call option strike if the stock is above the call strike at expiry, but there is also the choice of selling the risk reversal for a profit immediately prior to expiry if the risk reversal owner is unable or unwilling to be assigned.

Greater option skews therefore make buying a risk reversal more appealing (and a collar less so). Option skew is ultimately driven by a differing demand for put and call options, which can change radically over time. A greater relative demand for put options over call options will generally increase put skew. However, it does not necessarily follow that skew is at its highest during periods of market stress, as a variety of other factors are also at play, not least whether investors who would use the option market also have sufficient exposure in the underlying equity to necessitate buying put options for hedging.

Unfortunately, unlike professional investors who have access to highly detailed option market data, the ability of retail investors to assess whether option skew is attractive in an historical context is limited because the level of granularity is difficult to come across without paying large subscription fees. That said, the CBOE maintain an index on the S&P 500 called the **Skew Index**, which is calculated from one-month put and call option implied volatilities. The index history, which is available on their website ([https://www.cboe.com/us/indices/dashboard/skew/)](https://www.cboe.com/us/indices/dashboard/skew/), is shown in Figure 16.4. Unfortunately, similar skew indices based upon equity indices other than the S&P 500 Index are not widely available, and it is not possible to infer the degree of option skew on any index except the S&P 500 Index from the Skew Index.

CBOE Skew Index price history

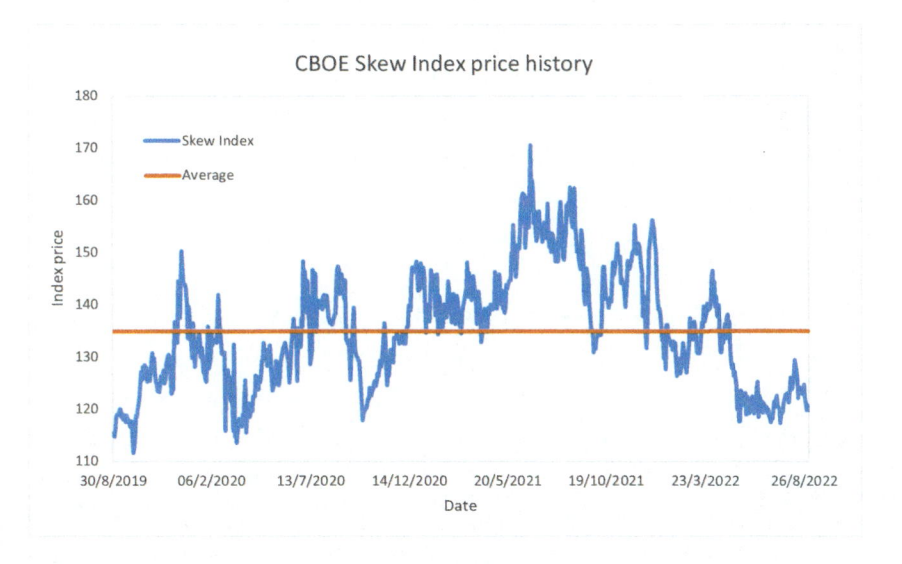

Figure 16.4.

Figure 16.4 shows that, at the time of writing, option skew for one-month put and call options on the S&P 500 Index is actually below its average and can be assumed to be the case for S&P 500 Index options with somewhat longer-dated expiries also. Therefore, although risk reversals on the SPY ETF that tracks the S&P 500 Index will currently offer a positive return asymmetry and therefore a less risky means of investing in the S&P 500 Index, it is actually one of the best times in the last three years to be doing the opposite—i.e., hedging long SPY EYF equity exposure with a long collar.

This illustrates how difficult it is for retail investors to judge whether option skew is historically cheap and therefore should favour protecting equity exposure with long collars, or expensive and therefore should favour taking equity exposure using risk reversals. Nevertheless, the asymmetry offered by SPY risk reversals is a consistent feature, even if greater asymmetry has been available at other times during the past three years.

Finally, especially when looking at zero cost risk reversals on single stocks, it is important to check that there is a genuine and meaningful difference in the option skew. If there is a sizable dividend with an ex-date prior to the option expiry, risk reversal pricing may give the appearance of offering attractive return asymmetry where none actually exists. This is because option prices incorporate the fact that a stock price automatically falls (away from the call strike and toward the put strike) on an ex-dividend date. For this reason, it is always worth studying the implied volatilities and deltas to ensure that there is a clear distinction between those of the puts and calls.

Example

It is September 2022, and you are a US investor eyeing European equity. Prices have fallen dramatically since the start of the year and are approaching levels you consider worth engaging in. Positioning and sentiment are universally bearish, which piques your interest, but which is understandable given the potentially bleak economic outlook heading into winter. However, you think that given the overwhelmingly negative sentiment, were economic activity prove to hold up better than feared, there could be a strong re-rating of the market into year-end and extending into the start of 2023. The euro has also fallen dramatically, which you view as excessive and a likely tailwind to a US dollar–denominated ETF of Eurozone equity, as well as providing some economic stimulation to the Continent.

You identify the Vanguard FTSE Europe (VGK) ETF as a suitable low-cost means of gaining the European equity exposure you want but loathe to buy it today, as the range of possible outcomes are too extreme over the next few months. You would be happy to buy the ETF a good deal lower but also want to have some immediate exposure to a rally in the ETF should sentiment brighten. You see that the ETF has liquid options and decide to investigate an option strategy.

Market volatility has been reasonably elevated recently, which argues against taking any sizable vega exposures and instead for selecting a strategy with both long and short VGK options. When studying the implied volatilities of options expiring in early 2023, you notice that there appears to be quite a pronounced option skew (Figure 16.5). Since you are a long-term investor and would be open to buying the ETF at the right price, this could make a risk reversal quite attractive. You generate a long-term price chart to see what price you would be happy owning the ETF for, and conclude that apart from the depths of the

Global Financial Crisis in 2008, $40 looks like an entry level that historically has offered positive subsequent returns (Figure 16.6). You decide to see what return asymmetry is available for risk reversals that have a short 40 strike put leg.

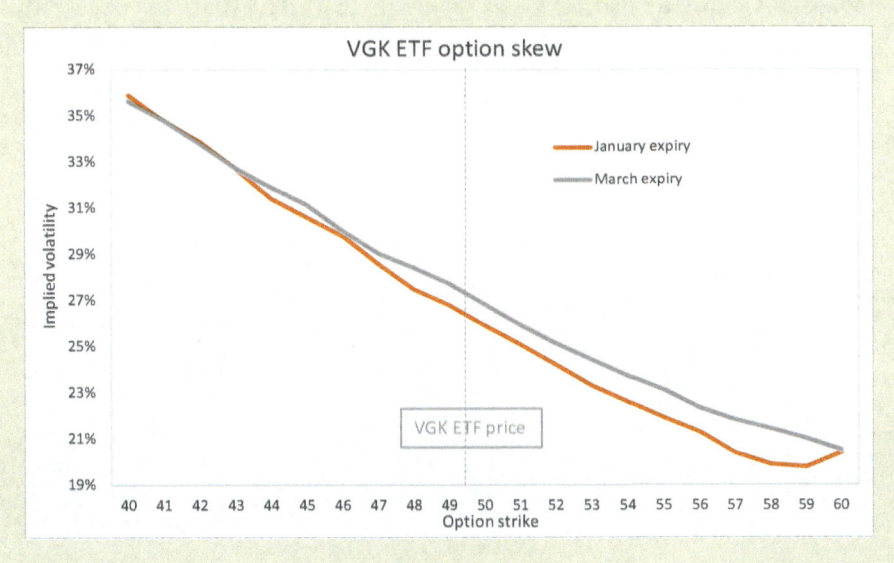

Figure 16.5.

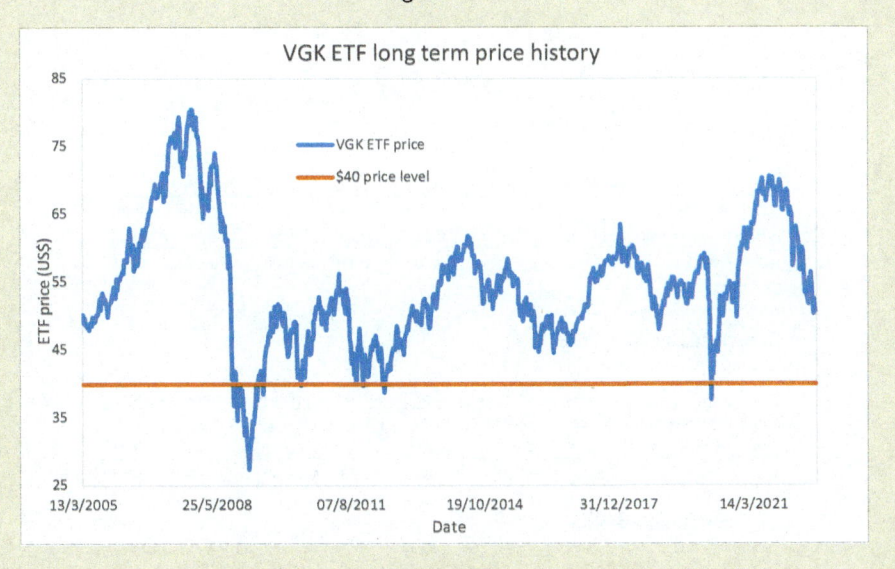

Figure 16.6.

In early 2023, there are listed expiries in both January and March and both have a 55 strike call option that is closest in cost to the 40 strike put option. In either case, a 40/55 risk reversal can be bought for a small residual cost with the VGK ETF currently trading at $49.35 (Figure 16.8). The 40 strike put is nearly 19 percent below the current stock price, while the call is 11.4 percent above the stock price, which offers sufficient return asymmetry for you (Figure 16.7).

Figure 16.7.

January 2023 expiry (122 days)

	% strike	implied vol	cost	delta	vega	theta	gamma
short 40 strike put	81.1%	35.9%	-0.75	0.13	-0.06	0.89	-0.02
long 55 strike call	111.4%	21.9%	0.81	0.23	0.09	-0.80	0.04
total			0.06	0.36	0.03	0.09	0.02

March 2023 expiry (178 days)

	% strike	implied vol	cost	delta	vega	theta	gamma
short 40 strike put	81.1%	35.6%	-1.12	0.16	-0.08	0.81	-0.02
long 55 strike call	111.4%	23.1%	1.21	0.27	0.12	-0.73	0.04
total			0.09	0.43	0.04	0.08	0.02

VGK ETF price 49.35

Figure 16.8.

Although the March risk reversal has a greater delta, you decide to err on the side of caution and select the January one, which is shorter-dated so will carry a lower vega risk. You decide to buy five contracts of the January 40/55 risk reversal, because you only want to risk the obligation to buy $20,000 worth of VGK ETFs should the price fall below the 40 strike at expiry on January 20, 2023 (i.e., 5 contracts × 40 short put strike × 100 multiplier). You will maintain this in cash in your broker account until expiry. You decide that the market looks weak enough to try to buy the risk reversal at zero cost rather than pay the $30 in premium (5 risk reversals × $0.06 cost × 100 multiplier). You expect this to be possible if the VGK ETF price falls to around $49.18 ($0.06 cost / 0.36 delta = 16.7c, which is approximately how much lower the VGK ETF needs to trade to make the risk reversal costless). You submit a limit order on your broker platform simultaneously to sell to open five contracts of VGK January 20, 2023, expiry 40 strike puts and to buy to open five contracts of VGK January 20 expiry 55 strike calls for a net cost of zero.

The example above illustrates how risk reversals can use large option skews to generate trades that have better return asymmetry than simply buying the underlying stock. It also demonstrates how to select the short put strike to ensure that if the trade goes wrong and the underlying stock falls heavily, you will only be obligated at expiry to buy the stock at a price that you believe offers genuine value and a good chance of positive future returns. As has been explained in previous chapters, the short put leg must be covered with sufficient cash to buy the stock should this eventuate and the sizing of the entire trade calculated with this in mind.

Whereas the long call option leg will generate the profits if there is a strong rally in the underlying stock, the focus must be on the short put leg when devising the strategy, since this is where the extreme market risk is. Even when the short put has sufficient cash covering it, there can be large "mark-to-market" losses generated from a short put position—i.e., when the short put position is revalued on a daily and intra-day basis due primarily to falls in the underlying stock (delta losses) and rises in the put option implied volatility (vega losses). These are concerns whenever a short put position is held, but especially so when trading a risk reversal, where a tendency may be to want to use somewhat longer-dated expiry options than would be the case when implementing a simple short put (underwriting) strategy.

As mentioned above, mark-to-market losses can accrue prior to expiry from both the vega and the delta of a short put position. Since volatility rises when markets fall heavily, this compounds the risk of a short put position. Note that this is the opposite of a long collar, where the long put leg can generate additional mark-to-market profits prior to expiry if the underlying stock falls heavily. While the cash covering the short put helps mitigate the riskiness of the delta by providing a means to pay for the potential obligation of buying a long stock position, the vega risk is controlled by ensuring that the short put's time to expiry is as low as practically possible.

In the example, the vegas for both risk reversals were small net positive values. This was because the 55 strike of the long calls was closer to the $49.35 VGK ETF price than the 40 strike of the short puts, therefore making the long vega exposure from the long call dominant. However, this would change if the ETF price were to fall.

Figure 16.9 shows the modelled P&L for the January and March risk reversal trades (in orange and blue, respectively) one week following the dates used in the example above. Both risk reversals have an extremely similar payoff profile. The option values are "modelled" because, unlike at expiry (shown by the solid grey line) where there is certainty of what the trade P&L will be for each possible price of the VGK ETF, at any time prior to expiry an option price can be affected by any of the Greeks. The modelled P&L therefore holds all other Greeks constant while (with the use of a BSM) changing the option value resulting only from movement of the ETF price along the horizontal axis. However, the Greeks are not constant and are liable to move also, so it is accepted that P&L graphs such as these are only a fair representation of how an option trade will behave prior to expiration under normal conditions.

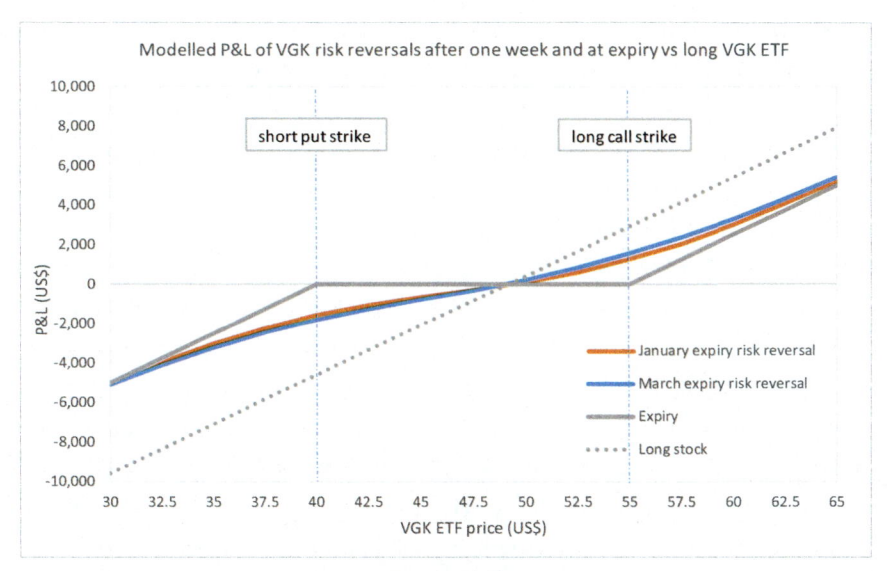

Figure 16.9.

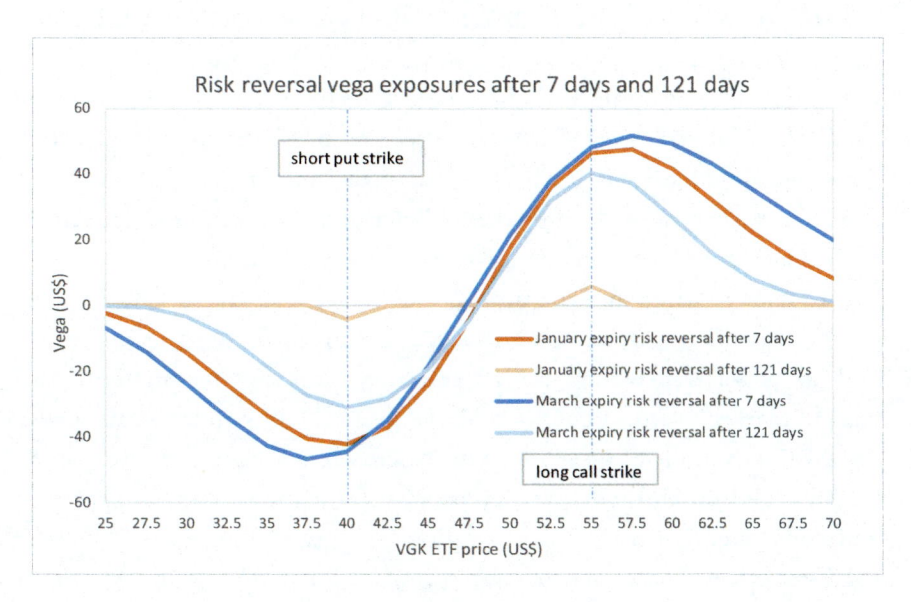

Figure 16.10.

In Figure 16.10, the modelled vega exposures of both risk reversals at two different points in time are shown. The dark blue and light blue lines are the vega exposures of the March risk reversal after 7 days and 121 days, respectively, and the dark orange and light orange are those of the January risk reversal after 7 days and 121 days, respectively. As discussed previously, an option's vega is greatest closer to its strike price and longer-dated options have comparatively greater vegas. Since short option positions have negative vegas, the greatest negative vega exposure is therefore that of the March expiry risk reversal when the ETF price is close to the 40 strike short put leg, and the greatest positive vega exposure is also the March expiry risk reversal when the ETF price is close to the 55 strike long call leg. This produces the sine wave shape of the darker blue line. Because the January risk reversal is shorter-dated than the March one (it had 122 days until expiry as opposed to 178 days in the example), it has a similar shape but with smaller magnitudes. After 121 days, the January risk reversal is just one day prior to expiration and so has almost no vega exposure (shown by the light orange line), whilst the March risk reversal still has 57 days until expiration, so still has a meaningful vega exposure (shown by the light blue line). The graph therefore illustrates that strategies that involve selling longer-dated options produce option structures that have larger negative potential vega exposures, even if these exposures appear small when the trade is initiated, and that their longer time to maturity means that these short vega exposures persist for a longer time into the future.

Any of this is only an issue if there is a fall in the underlying ETF and an associated rise in implied volatility, perhaps precipitated by a sizable market event. The onset of the COVID-19 pandemic in early 2020 is an example of such an event, where the enforced suppression of business and mobility wreaked enormous havoc on economies globally and consequently on the prices of global equities. Figure 16.11 shows three-month realized volatility for the VGK ETF, which jumped from around 10 percent to a high of almost 60 percent because of the market crash that the pandemic created.

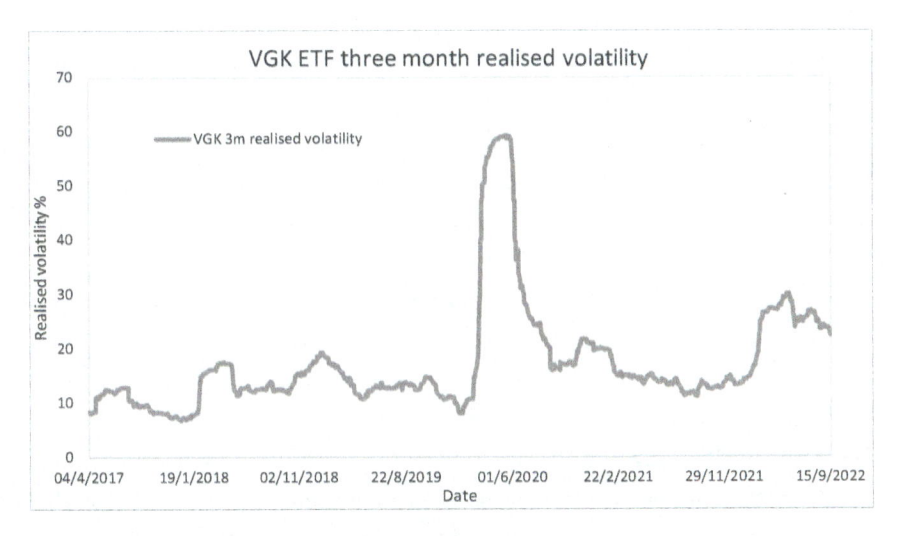

Figure 16.11.

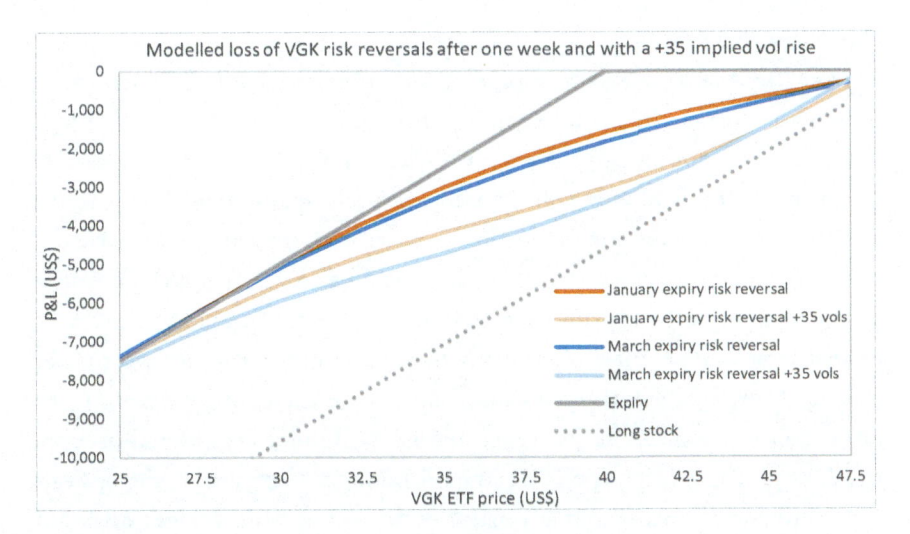

Figure 16.12.

Figure 16.12 is an enlargement of the left half of Figure 16.9—i.e., the loss-making side of the risk reversal P&L diagram, relating to a fall in the ETF price below $47.5. In addition to the original lines, it shows the approximate additional vega losses that would be generated for the January and March risk reversal trades (in light orange and light blue, respectively) if there was a rise in their implied volatilities by thirty-five implied volatility percentage points. A rise of this magnitude corresponds to the distance between the current VGK ETF three-month realized volatility and its pandemic-induced high in Figure 16.11. Focus is exclusively on the loss side of the original P&L graph because a rise in option implied volatility of such magnitudes is consistent only with large falls in equity prices.

Figure 16.12 illustrates the "double whammy" risk of the short put leg of the risk reversal prior to expiry—i.e., losses potentially occurring from a rise in implied volatility (vega loss) as well as a fall in the ETF price (delta loss). However, the potential loss in this example is smaller for the January than the March risk reversal, predominantly because it has a shorter time to expiry and therefore a lower vega exposure. Note also that although an increase in implied volatility amplifies the risk reversal loss, both still have a return superior to the long stock position in a falling market in this example.

Keeping risk reversals as short-dated as possible, while still achieving strikes that make the trade compelling, therefore helps control the vega risk. Not only does it cap the extent of the potential negative vega exposure at the outset (which may not be immediately apparent without careful analysis); the shorter time to expiry reduces the timespan over which a vega loss has the potential to occur. It should be remembered though that a vega loss only occurs prior to expiry, as options are "marked-to-market" in real time and over the days prior to their expiration date. No matter how high implied volatility rises and how large the consequent vega loss grows prior to expiry, the risk reversal P&L will move toward and become the dark grey line in Figure 16.12 at expiration, as theta decays the options on a daily basis. Ensuring that portfolios are not overly leveraged and that short put options, whether as part of risk reversal or not, are covered with sufficient cash ensures that positions that generate vega and delta losses to option portfolios can be maintained during adverse market moves. This reduces the risk that such positions need to be closed at inopportune times, potentially for a loss.

Risk reversal performance

The CBOE S&P 500 Risk Reversal Index (RXM) (www.cboe.com/us/indices/dashboard/RXM/) tracks the performance of a hypothetical index comprising a long one-month 25 delta call option and a short one-month 25 delta put option on the S&P 500 Index. It is assumed that these are traded every month and held to expiry, along with sufficient money (invested in one-month US government debt securities) to cover the liability of the short put leg. The S&P 500 Index option strikes and expiries are not the same as those used in the other CBOE Indices mentioned previously, so direct comparisons are imperfect but still illustrative.

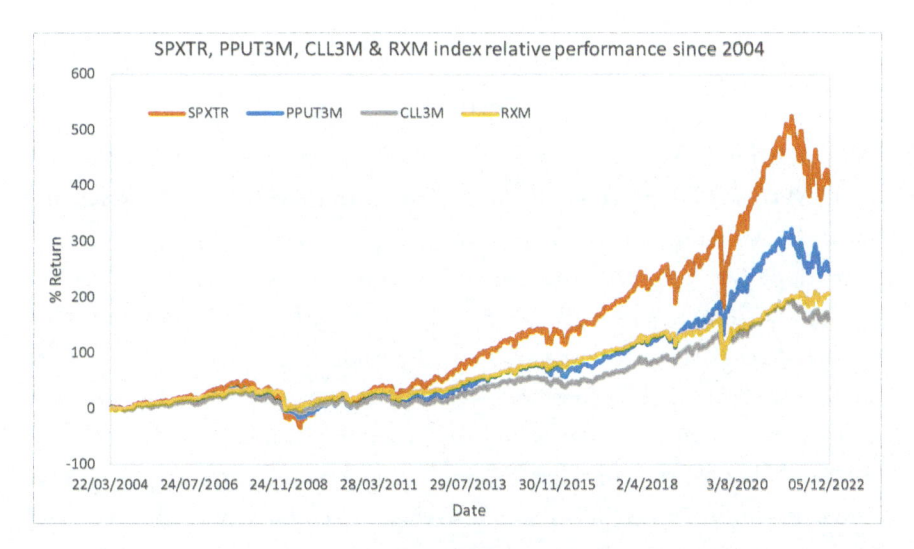

Figure 16.13.

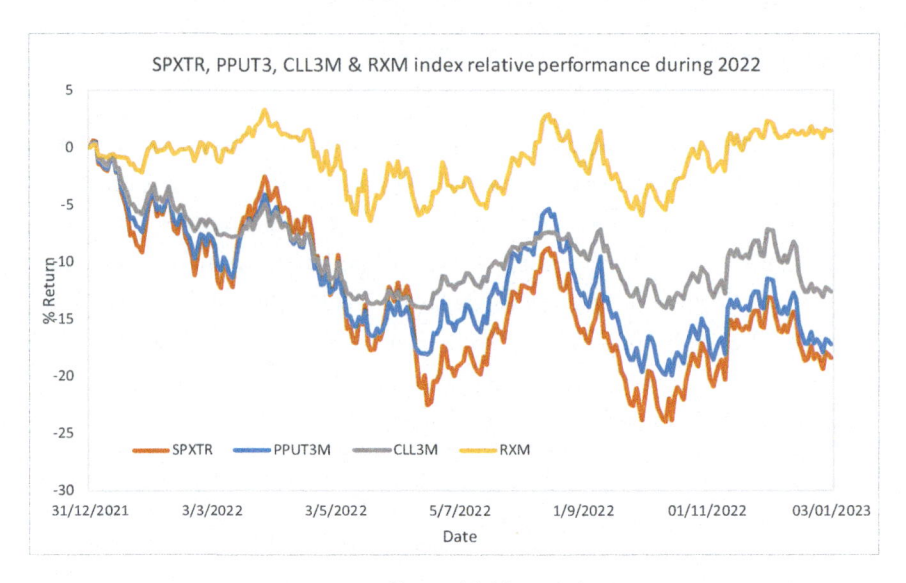

Figure 16.14.

Figure 16.13 shows a long-term graph for RXM as well as PPUT3M and CLL3M covered in previous chapters, along with the S&P 500 Total Return Index (SPXTR) in orange. As previously explained, this period covered an exceptionally strong performance by US equity markets, supported by accommodative policies by the US Federal Reserve. Figure 16.14 shows how these indices performed during 2022—a year during which the US Federal Reserve reversed their accommodative policies and actively worked to tighten financial conditions. Just as they underperformed in earlier years, during 2022 all the indices containing option positions outperformed the total return of the S&P 500 (SPXTR) due to their comparatively smaller net delta exposure. PPUT3M, which is SPXTR plus a long three-month 10 percent out-the-money (and therefore low negative delta) put option has the highest net delta exposure of the option-containing indices. This is followed by CCL3M, which contains SPXTR and a long three-month 5 percent out-the-money put and short three-month 10 percent out-the-money calls, which will give a marginally smaller (depending upon market conditions) net delta than RXM, which contains just a short 0.25 delta put and long 0.25 delta call, giving a net 0.5 delta for the index.

RXM performed extremely well on a relative basis during 2022, but this cannot be entirely attributable to the lower delta exposure of the index. Other factors will have played a part, such as higher implied volatility, which generates a larger net credit when selling 25 delta puts to buy 25 delta calls, as well as rapidly increasing interest rates, which provide greater additional return on the US government debt securities. Likely, the most important though was that despite the weakness throughout the year as a whole, the majority of one-month SPXTR returns were in excess of the short 25 delta put strike (which successively would have moved out-the-money each time a new short put position was established as implied volatility rose), causing the majority of short one-month put legs to expire worthless. This contrasts with CLL3M and PPUT3M, which both contain a long SPXTR position that would have generated a loss as the S&P 500 Index fell as far as their respective long put strikes.

CHAPTER 17: LONG CALL CONDOR AND BUTTERFLY

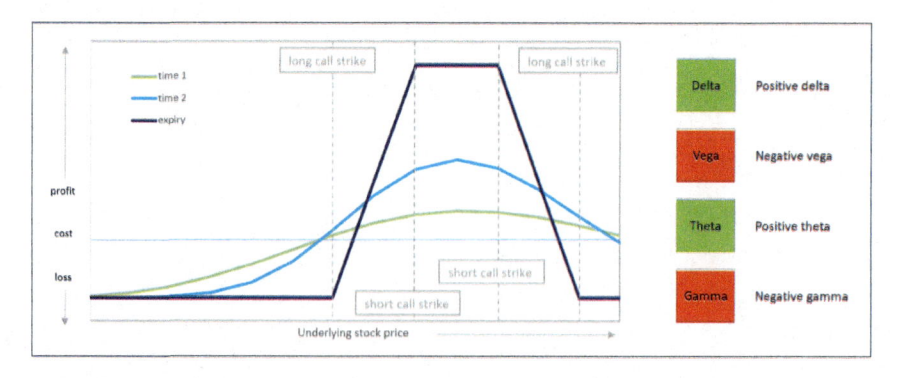

Figure 17.1.

A call condor is bought by simultaneously buying to open a call option, selling to open a call option with a higher strike, selling to open another call option with an even higher strikes, and buying to open another call option with an even higher strike. The same expiry and same quantity of contracts are traded for each of the four legs, and crucially, the distance between the strikes of the first two calls needs to be the same distance that is between the strikes for the final two calls. This makes the payoff and therefore the risk symmetrical as per Figure 17.1. The order to execute a condor is always submitted as a single instruction on a broker platform. Since a call condor has four different legs and therefore four separate bid/ask spreads, the order should be a limit order submitted at or near the overall mid-price for the trade.

The first two call options (long and short, respectively) form a long call spread, whilst the third and fourth call options (short and long, respectively) form a short call spread. Therefore, a call condor can be thought of as a call spread that is cheapened by selling a further out-the-money call spread against it.

A standard call spread makes its maximum profit at expiry once the upper short call option strike is reached, but makes this profit regardless of how much higher the underlying stock has moved from there. Not so with a call condor, since its short call spread begins eating into the profit generated by the long call spread once the stock has moved higher and through the second short call strike. A call condor therefore has two breakevens at expiration: (1) in between the long call spread strikes as the condor moves into profitability as the stock rises and (2) in between the short call spread strikes as the condor moves out of profitability as the stock continues to rise.

The profitable zone of a call condor is therefore much smaller than that of a call spread (which extends indefinitely above the short call strike), and so a very precise view is required to achieve a maximum payout—not just that the stock will move higher by a certain point in time but almost precisely by how much too. However, because the statistical probability of making a profit is that much smaller, the cost is lower and therefore the percentage profit achievable from a call condor can be extremely high. This makes them quite popular, and their low cost ensures that they are often traded in considerable size.

The maximum payout zone of a condor is therefore the flat area between the two short call strikes at expiry in Figure 17.1, which is the zone between the long call spread and the short call spread. Moving the short call spread (i.e., the top short and long respective call strikes) further out-the-money reduces the short call spread value and hence increases the net cost of the condor, because the short call spread has less of an offset to the overall cost. It also widens the maximum profitability zone, so logically makes the condor more expensive, since it increases the likelihood of making money.

Conversely, narrowing the maximum profitability zone by moving the short call spread nearer to at-the-money (lowering their strikes) increases the short call spread value, which provides a greater offset to the long call spread cost, thereby cheapening the overall net cost of the condor. Narrowing the maximum profitability zone between the long and short call spreads as much as possible would mean that there is no gap between them. This would result in twice the number of calls sold at the same short call strike. At this point, the call condor becomes a call butterfly, as shown in Figure 17.2.

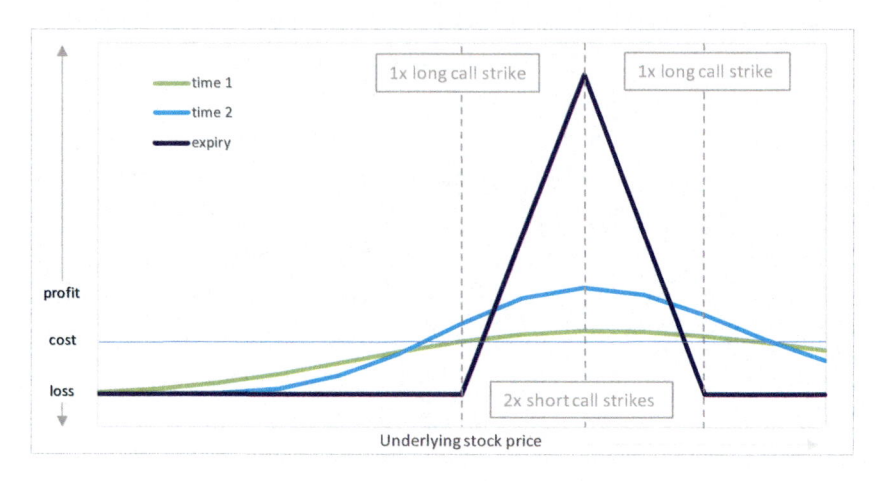

Figure 17.2.

The maximum profit for a long call butterfly is therefore exactly at the short call strike at exactly the moment of expiry. Its low cost and highly geared return reflect the small probability of a long call butterfly's maximum profit being realized. Indeed, any profit can be difficult to realize because the two breakevens are closely spaced, leaving very little room for error. Furthermore, a long call butterfly exposes the owner to a high degree of expiration risk. Assuming that the underlying stock is close to the short call strikes, it is necessary to hold the position right up until expiration to benefit from the high theta decay of the short call options and realize the full potential profit from the position. Leaving the option position to expire, however, could result in a long stock position, a short stock position, or no stock position, as well as the associated cash movements under the assignment process, depending upon exactly where the stock closes at on expiration day. Managing a profitable long call butterfly therefore requires a lot of vigilance around the expiration date. I discuss expiration risk in more detail in chapter 21.

In order to generate a return successfully, a long call condor and especially a long call butterfly therefore need a great deal of forecasting precision, since they require the underlying asset to be trading at a specific price at a specific point in time. They are often used with short-term **technical analysis**, where forecasts for future asset price movements are made from studying charts of their price history.

Example

It is the last few trading days of 2022, and you have noticed a wedge formation has been forming on a graph of the Nasdaq Index and the Invesco QQQ Trust Series 1 ETF (QQQ) that tracks it. Upside to the ETF has been capped by a descending trendline for the last twelve months, whilst a floor at $260 has been in place since late summer (denoted by the grey dotted lines in Figure 17.3). The ETF price has just reached the floor again, and you want to speculate that it will bounce and reach the descending trendline by the next monthly option expiration date on January 20, 2023, which will equate to a price level for the ETF of around $280 at that point in time.

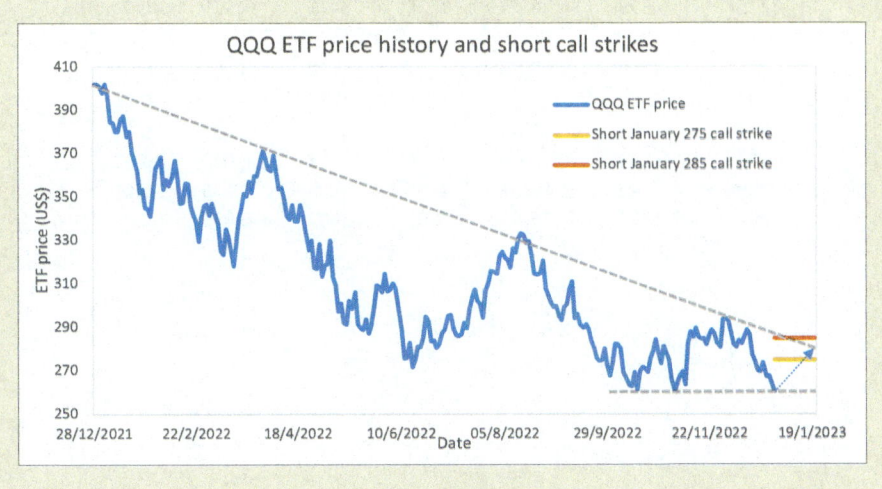

Figure 17.3.

You are not confident enough to attempt to pinpoint the exact price that you think the ETF will finish at on expiration, but anticipate that it will be in between $275 and $285. You are confident enough that the descending trendline will not be meaningfully broken though, so are willing to buy a call condor instead of a call spread but do not have sufficient confidence to buy a call butterfly. You decide therefore that the short call strikes of your call condor will be 275 and 285, which gives enough margin of error around your estimation of $280 for the closing price on January 20, and collate relevant call option prices from your broker platform (Figure 17.4) to determine pricing for call condors incorporating those short call strikes.

QQQ January 20th 2023 call option details

strike	call mid price	impl vol	delta	vega	theta	gamma
270	3.50	27.2%	0.32	0.23	-0.145	0.02
271	3.17	27.0%	0.29	0.23	-0.139	0.02
272	2.87	26.8%	0.27	0.22	-0.134	0.02
273	2.56	26.5%	0.25	0.21	-0.127	0.02
274	2.34	26.5%	0.24	0.20	-0.122	0.02
275	2.09	26.4%	0.22	0.19	-0.116	0.02
285	0.66	25.6%	0.09	0.10	-0.060	0.01
286	0.59	25.6%	0.08	0.10	-0.056	0.01
287	0.51	25.5%	0.07	0.09	-0.051	0.01
288	0.44	25.4%	0.06	0.08	-0.046	0.01
289	0.40	25.6%	0.06	0.08	-0.043	0.01
290	0.35	25.5%	0.05	0.07	-0.039	0.01

Figure 17.4.

Long call condor details

long condor strikes	mid price	net delta	net vega	net theta	net gamma	maximum value	profit
270/275/285/290	1.10	0.01	-0.01	0.00	0.06	5	355%
271/275/285/289	0.82	0.01	-0.01	0.00	0.05	4	388%
272/275/285/288	0.56	0.00	0.00	0.00	0.03	3	436%
273/275/285/287	0.32	0.00	0.00	0.00	0.02	2	525%
274/275/285/286	0.18	0.00	0.00	0.00	0.01	1	456%

(net = long call strike - 275 strike - 285 strike + long call strike)

Figure 17.5.

You find that the pricing for the long 273/275/285/287 call condor offers the best potential profit (Figure 17.5), which has a $2 spacing between the long and short call spread strikes. You wish to allocate $1,000 to this trade, which will buy thirty-one long call condor contracts, since each is $32 ($0.32 net cost x 100 multiplier). You submit a limit order on your broker platform to buy thirty-one QQQ January 20, 2023, expiry 273/275/285/287 call condors for $0.32—simultaneously buying to open thirty-one QQQ January 20, 2023, expiry 273 strike calls, selling to open thirty-one QQQ January 20, 2023, expiry 275 strike calls, selling to open thirty-one QQQ January 20, 2023, expiry 285 strike calls, buying to open thirty-one QQQ January 20, 2023, expiry 287 strike calls as one instruction on your broker platform.

The long call condor in the example is effectively made up of a long 273/275 call spread that costs $0.47 ($2.56 – $2.09), which is being bought, and a short 285/287 call spread, which is being sold for $0.15 ($0.66 – $0.51), giving a net cost of $0.32. The long 273/275 call spread would not have been bought on its own merit because its potential return is only 326 percent (($2.00 – $0.47) / $0.47), since the maximum profit for the call spread, as with the call condor, is $2, and this falls below the 400 percent return requirement for a call spread trade. It is only because there was conviction that the QQQ ETF would not move materially higher and through the descending trendline that the 285/287 call spread could safely be sold also for $0.15, which brought down the net cost for the condor to $0.32, thereby increasing the potential return for the trade to 525 percent (($2.00 − $0.32) / $0.32). However, it is especially important when buying call condors that trading costs are factored into the calculation of potential returns, since four different call option contracts are being traded and there will likely be a dealing cost for each. Trading costs vary from broker to broker and so should be studied to ensure they are competitive and subtracted from potential returns before a trading judgement is made.

The Greek exposures of the long call condor in the example are extremely small at the outset, since the options are short-dated and the strikes are relatively close together. Narrowing the long call strikes (the **condor wings**) and moving the condor further out-the-money generally reduce the cost, increasing potential profitability, and further reduce the net Greek exposures. Narrowing the short call strikes (the **condor body**) reduces the profitable zone and the cost, thereby also increasing potential profitability, as the condor begins to look more like a butterfly, as discussed previously.

RATIO OPTION STRATEGIES

CHAPTER 18: LONG RATIO CALL SPREAD

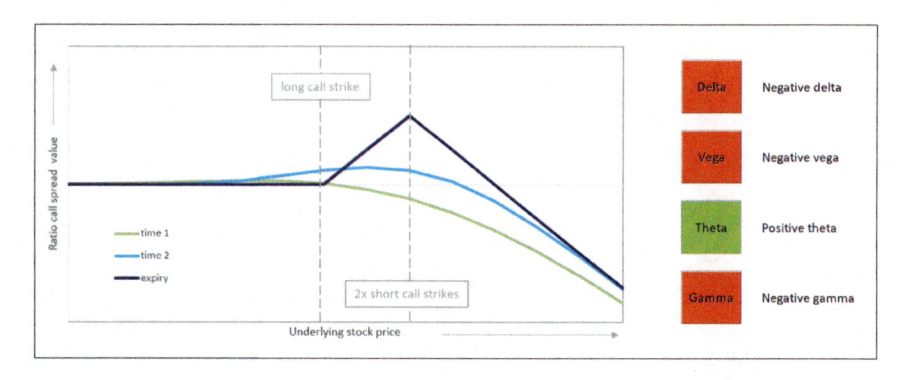

Figure 18.1.

A ratio call spread (Figure 18.1) is bought by simultaneously buying to open a call option and selling to open twice the number of further out-the-money call options with the same expiry. A covered ratio call spread describes a ratio call spread that additionally has sufficient stock to match the notional exposure of half of the short call options. Essentially therefore, a covered ratio call spread can be thought of as a call spread and one additional covered call option (i.e., a short call option and sufficient stock to cover it if the option is exercised). Therefore, at expiration there is no additional risk if the underlying stock is above the short call strikes of a long covered ratio call spread. The addition of a long stock position (which graphically is simply a diagonal upward sloping line) to a long ratio call spread gives a long covered ratio call spread payoff diagram a very different appearance (Figure 18.2).

Figure 18.2.

Ratio call spreads are commonly used as a **stock repair** to overlay an existing stock position that has fallen in value (thereby making it a covered ratio call spread), with the aim to sell the stock at the short call option strike if it bounces following its decline. The ratio call spread is traded at or close to costless, with the two short call options offsetting the cost of the long call option, so little or no further money is being committed to the stock trade. If the stock does subsequently rise above the short call spread strike by the expiration date, then the additional short call ensures that it is called away, while an extra return is generated by the call spread. This effectively repairs the loss made on the original long stock position by lowering the point at which it breaks even by the difference between the call spread strikes.

The option trade is aided by the fact that implied volatility usually rises after a stock falls in value and, since there are twice as many call options sold as bought, there is a net sale of elevated implied volatility. Positive theta from the additional short call option also provides an incremental benefit at the beginning of the trade. However, because there is no net income generated by a costless ratio call spread, theta is not positive throughout the trade's entire life, and if the stock does not bounce or indeed continues to fall, then all the options expire worthless and a ratio call spread will provide no benefit. It is therefore crucially important to have the belief that a stock's decline is more of a blip, albeit one that prompts exiting the stock, than a permanent de-rating of its prospects for future positive returns.

A variation on a covered ratio call spread is a **covered call ladder**. Here, a greater distinction is made between the call spread and the additional short call, which is given a higher strike by moving it a little further out-the-money. Consequently, there is sometimes a net premium paid for a covered call ladder if the two short call options do not fully offset the cost of the long call option. It is employed under similar circumstances, but in preference to the covered ratio call spread if the call strike implied volatilities look especially high and there is a realistic opportunity that the stock could bounce strongly prior to expiry. Under these conditions, the call spread would repair the loss the stock generated, and the short call is positioned higher in an attempt to capture the full extent of the stock bounce.

Example

It is early November 2022, and you are a US investor with a position in Nutrien Ltd (NTR) you bought for $85, attracted by its low P/E, high free cashflow yield, and belief that current extreme food inflation will underpin demand for its fertilizer products. However, the price has just plummeted over 14 percent on announcement of earnings for the second quarter of 2022 and now stands at $71.31 (Figure 18.3). The global macroeconomic picture is also looking challenging, with a potential recession on the cards next year that would induce indiscriminate further selling, so you decide you would like to lighten up on your shares.

Figure 18.3.

You believe you will see a bounce from their current drop in price, since $70 has acted as a floor over recent history, so do not wish to sell immediately. However, you would look to exit half your stock holding if you could get out at around flat. You decide to investigate the option market to see whether there is a suitable stock repair trade that could help you effectively lower the $85 entry price paid for originally buying the shares and thereby increase your chances of exiting the stock trade without loss.

You want to use short-dated options because, given the negative share price momentum and challenging macro backdrop, you are unsure how long the $70 floor will hold and so would like to reduce your holding over the next month or so. There are December-listed options with five-dollar strike increments expiring midway through the month, which appear suitable.

NTR share price history

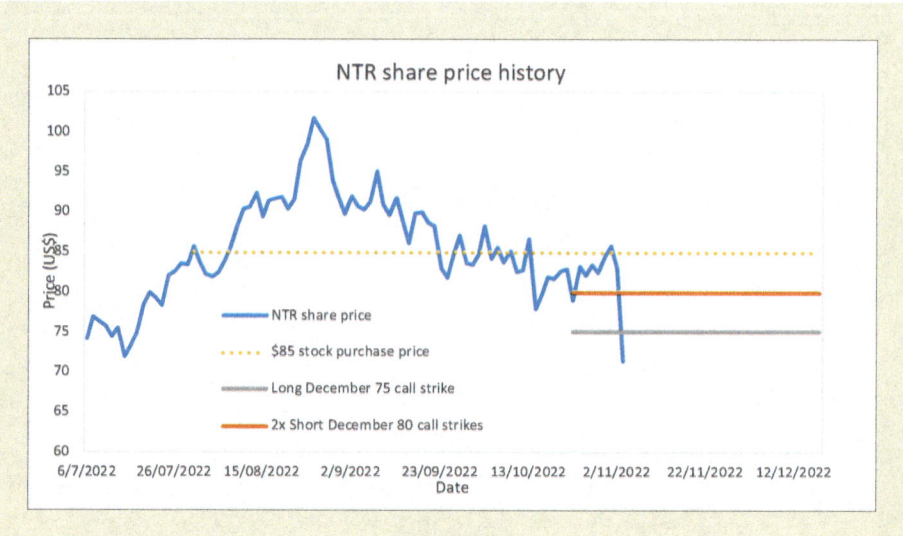

Figure 18.4.

NTR December 16th 2022 expiry call option details.

strike	call mid price	implied vol	delta	vega	theta	gamma
75	3.20	50.6%	0.42	0.09	-0.06	0.03
80	1.65	47.9%	0.27	0.08	-0.05	0.03
85	0.88	47.3%	0.16	0.06	-0.03	0.02

NTR share price: $71.31

Option trade details

strike	call mid price	contracts	$ cost	$ delta	$ vega	$ theta
75	3.20	2	640	5,987	19	-12
80	1.65	-4	-660	-7,641	-32	18
		Total	-20	-1,654	-13	7

Figure 18.5.

The 75 strike calls cost almost exactly twice as much as the 80 strike calls, so the covered ratio call spread pricing therefore lines up well (Figure 18.5). The covered 75/80/85 strike call ladder and the covered 75/85 ratio call spread also look attractive because call option implied volatility is elevated, but you are unwilling to pay more premium despite the greater potential return if NTR is much above $80 at expiry. You decide to attempt to repair your NTR trade, using the 75/80 ratio call spread.

You have two hundred shares that you would like to sell for no net loss, so place an order on your broker platform to buy to open two contracts of the NTR December 16, 2022, expiry 75 strike calls and simultaneously sell to open four contracts of the NTR December 16, 2022, expiry 80 strike calls. This will yield a credit of ten cents, which will help offset some of your dealing costs.

The example highlights how a covered ratio call spread can be used to attempt to repair a loss generated by a stock position. If at expiry the stock is at or above $80 in price, then all options are automatically exercised. This would involve a payment via the clearing house of $5 per share, being the difference between the 75 and 80 long and short call spread strikes, plus $80 per share due to the stock being called away at the additional short 80 call strike.

In other words, 2 contracts × (80 – 75) strikes × 100 multiplier = $1,000

Plus 2 contracts × 80 strike × 100 multiplier = $16,000

Total payment after expiry = $17,000

This is economically identical (ignoring any differences in transaction costs) to selling two hundred shares at $85 and illustrates how the breakeven for a stock trade can be lowered using a covered ratio call spread.

Figure 18.6 compares the P&L of the covered 75/80 ratio call spread, as well as the covered 75/80/85 call ladder and covered 75/85 ratio call spread considered in the example. As can be seen, the 75/85 ratio call spread has greatest upside potential, superior to just holding the NTR shares even up until nearly $95 in value, albeit at the cost of $1.44 a share additionally in premium ($3.20 – $0.88 – $0.88). This is because the stock is called away at $85 and not $80, as is the case with the 75/80 ratio call spread selected in the example. This allows for an additional $5-per-share profit, minus the $1.44 cost. The 75/80/85 call ladder performs in between the two ratio call spreads, having the shares also called away at $85 due to the short 85 call strike, but delivering just the $5 call spread return from between the 75 and 80 call option strikes. Consequently, it is also priced in the middle, costing $0.67 per share ($3.20 − $1.65 − $0.88). The 75/80 ratio call spread has the most modest upside return, since the stock is called away at the lowest price at the short 80 call option strike, but it is costless.

Covered ratio call spreads vs call ladder P&L

- Long stock
- Covered 75/80 ratio call spread
- Covered 75/80/85 call ladder
- Covered 75/85 ratio call spread

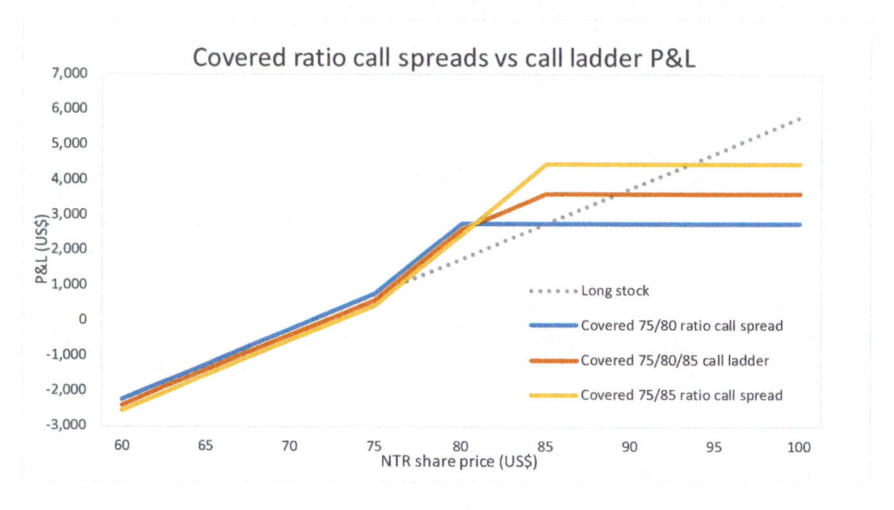

Figure 18.6.

The option deltas indicate the relative probabilities of where the stock will reach at option expiry. They suggest a roughly 27 percent probability and a 16 percent probability for stock to be called away at the 80 call strike and the 85 call strike, respectively. However, the premise for the trade is that the normal distribution of returns (on which these probability estimations rely) will not occur but instead will be skewed to the upside as the shares bounce from current oversold levels. The trade therefore is based upon the assumption that these probabilities should be higher.

The net Greek exposures for either a covered call ladder or a covered ratio call spread are governed by how much further out-the-money the short call strikes are positioned. The higher the short call strikes are, the less their short vega and positive theta exposures are, therefore providing less of an offset to the long vega and short theta of the long call option. Particularly if the expirations used are relatively short-dated, overwhelmingly the main risk is the inherent delta risk of owning the shares. Any covered call strategy has limited upside potential but much larger downside potential due to the long stock position.

Using somewhat longer-dated options than those employed in the example allows for the distance between the long and two short call option strikes to be widened and still derive a covered ratio call spread that is close to zero cost. Stocks that have fallen further in value and thus require more repair work, therefore will require using call options with more time to expiry.

Whatever the time to expiration of the options used, the call strike selection for a covered ratio call spread is reasonably standard. The long call option strike should be very close to at-the-money and the short call options about halfway between the long call option strike and the magnitude of the stock price fall that needs repairing, whilst keeping the expiry short enough to make the overall cost for the trade at or close to zero.

CHAPTER 19: LONG RATIO PUT SPREAD

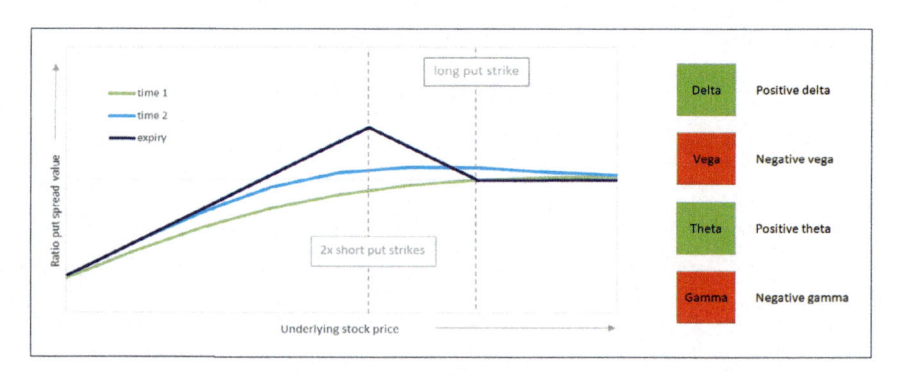

Figure 19.1.

A ratio put spread is bought by simultaneously buying to open a put option and selling to open twice the number of contracts of same expiry further out-the-money put options. The order to execute a ratio put spread is always submitted as a single trade instruction on a broker platform.

A ratio put spread is generally bought for around zero cost. The long put strike is situated very close to at-the-money and the two lower out-the-money short put option strikes determined by their cost, since they need to be around half the price of the long put option to make the entire trade as close to zero cost as possible. Using slightly longer-dated options generally allows the short puts to have a strike that is further out-the-money, though as explored in chapter 16, longer-dated short put options also carry much greater short vega risks. The expiry date and distance between the long and short put strikes greatly influence the net Greek exposures at the outset; however, often the delta is positive, but small and the short option characteristics of positive theta and negative vega and gamma dominate.

Just as a covered ratio call spread can be used to lower the effective breakeven when selling a stock, a ratio put spread can be used to lower the effective entry price for purchasing a stock. Since the intention is to attempt to buy the underlying stock at a lower price by being assigned shares at the short put strike, the expiry and short put strikes are selected to give this a reasonable probability.

The ratio put spread can therefore be thought of as a put spread, which generates a return if the stock falls, and an additional short put that facilitates buying the stock through the assignment process at the short put strike price if the stock has fallen sufficiently far. The put spread return offsets some of the stock cost, effectively discounting the purchase. As with a risk reversal or a put underwrite, a ratio put spread has a short put position that needs to be covered with cash (or a low-risk, liquid, interest-bearing investment) in order not to overleverage the portfolio. It is only the additional short put that needs to be covered, however, which is half of the total short put option quantity traded.

Unlike a short put underwrite, however, there is no net premium that is generated, since this has effectively been used to purchase the put spread. Therefore, unlike a put underwrite, if the shares rise in value, and the options expire worthless by the expiration date, then no benefit has been accrued from having traded a ratio put spread.

A variation on a covered ratio put spread is a **covered put ladder.** Here, instead of selling twice the out-the-money put options at the same strike, one of the short put strikes is moved lower (i.e., further out-the-money). Sometimes this is done if it is not possible to trade a ratio call spread for zero cost because the available listed put strikes do not have prices that allow it, while a zero cost trade is achievable if one of the put strikes is lowered. In any event, if the motivation for the trade is to buy stock at the lower short put strike, then it is important to ensure that the put strike has a realistic chance of being assigned at expiry.

As with any short put option strategy, the pricing of a ratio put spread or put ladder benefits from higher implied volatility and put option skew. This consequently makes them a useful strategy to employ when looking to buy stocks that have already experienced a meaningful sell-off. They are also used to great effect if market volatility is reasonably high, and, having just missed buying a stock at a level you think is a bargain, you are attempting to buy it at a discounted price closer to its previous valuation point.

Example

It is mid-November 2022, and most stock indices have been through a brutal bear market for the majority of the year, which you feel is creating some compellingly valued stocks. You have been watching Biogen Inc. (BIIB) for a few months with a view to buy the stock at a lower level, given its high free cashflow yield, low valuation, and position in a sector that you feel will have the ability to perform relatively well over the next few years. However, since news on its promising new Alzheimer's disease treatment was released and then solid third-quarter earnings results, the stock price has continued to climb. You do not want to chase it but would be keen to own the stock closer to the level it was trading at during the summer prior to its surge in late September (Figure 19.2). Volatility has been a feature of markets throughout the year, so you decide to study BIIB listed options to see whether a ratio put spread, which benefits from elevated levels of implied volatility, looks appealing.

The backdrop is uncertain enough not to want to take any particularly long-dated short put positions, and beyond a couple of months the bid/ask spreads begin to look particularly wide. However, since shorter-dated options will generally give narrower ratio put spread strikes, you focus on the January expiry put options, in preference to December (Figure 19.3).

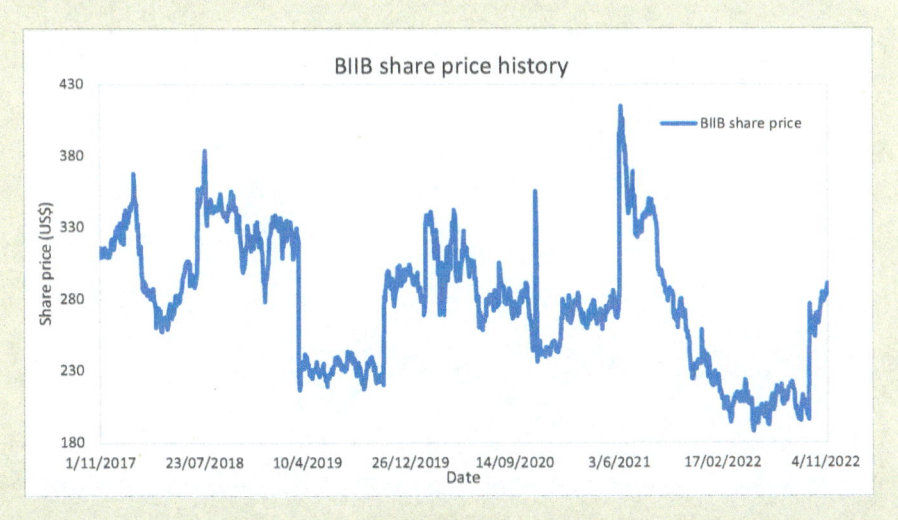

Figure 19.2.

BIIB January 20, 2023, expiry put option details.

strike	put mid price	implied vol	delta	vega	theta	gamma
290	24.05	49.3%	-0.45	0.50	-0.165	0.006
285	21.25	48.8%	-0.42	0.49	-0.162	0.006
280	19.15	49.5%	-0.39	0.48	-0.161	0.006
275	17.15	50.1%	-0.36	0.47	-0.159	0.006
270	15.63	51.3%	-0.33	0.45	-0.159	0.006
265	14.00	52.1%	-0.30	0.44	-0.156	0.005
260	12.01	51.1%	-0.27	0.41	-0.145	0.005
255	10.93	53.1%	-0.25	0.40	-0.145	0.005
250	8.70	51.2%	-0.21	0.37	-0.129	0.005

BIIB share price: $289.45

Figure 19.3.

The 290 strike put is slightly in-the-money but is almost exactly twice the cost of the 260 strike puts and therefore lines up well for a ratio put spread trade, giving an effective purchase price of $230 per share if assigned stock (Figure 19.4). You decide to proceed on this basis.

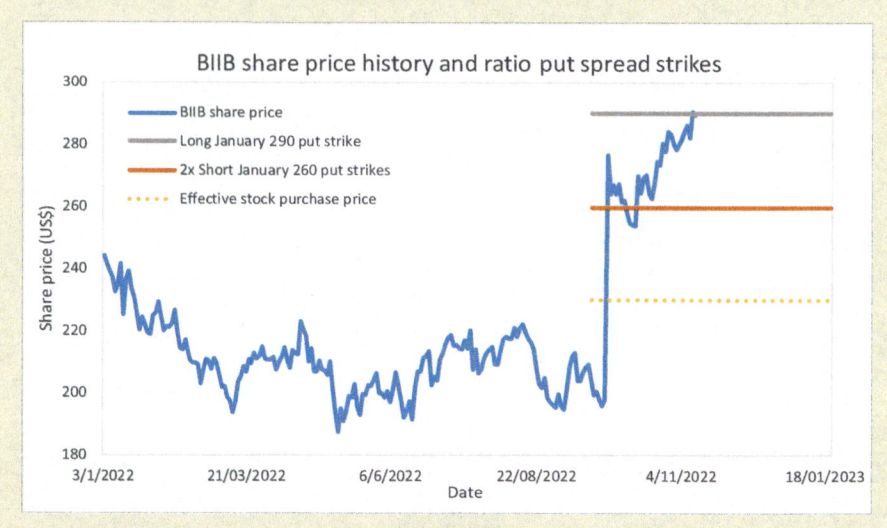

Figure 19.4.

Option trade details

strike	put mid price	contracts	$ cost	$ delta	$ vega	$ theta
290	24.05	1	2,405	-13,066	50	-16
260	12.01	-2	- 2,402	15,472	-83	29
		Total	3	2,406	-33	13

Figure 19.5.

Wishing to be at risk of being assigned just $26,000 in stock, you submit a trade order on your broker platform to buy to open one contract of the BIIB January 20, 2023, expiry 290 strike put options and sell to open two BIIB January 20, 2023, expiry 260 strike put options for a net premium cost of $3 (Figure 19.5). You ensure that you have at least $26,000 available in a money market fund that is liquid and earning an acceptable rate of return, to cover one short 260 strike put option.

The example illustrates how a covered ratio put spread trade is constructed and the circumstances under which it can be used. There is a three-dollar cost to the trade, which is lost if BIIB is above the 290 put strike at expiry. However, if the stock retreats and is below the short put strikes at expiry, shown by the red line in Figure 19.4, then stock assignment will automatically occur as intended. This would allow for the purchase of shares effectively at a net discounted price of $230 per share, shown by the dotted yellow line.

Specifically, net assignment flows to a brokerage account from the clearing house would entail a purchase of one hundred shares of BIIB for $26,000 from one short 260 strike put (1 contract × 260 strike × 100 multiplier), minus $3,000 profit received from one put spread (1 contract × (290 – 260) put strikes × 100 multiplier). The result is a $23,000 payment and receipt of one hundred shares, so effectively a net purchase of $230 per share.

Were the BIIB share price to remain reasonably static, positive theta would help the trade evolve beneficially over time. The light green line in Figure 19.1, which represents the value of the ratio put spread on the day it is purchased ("time 1"), moves up to the light blue line ("time 2") as time progresses to two-thirds of the way between purchase date and expiration date. In fact, the trade is in profit with the stock at both the long put and short put strikes at this point in time.

Furthermore, the remaining period between "time 2" and expiry (which is the final third of the total time) theta decay begins to accelerate, particularly if the stock is near the short put strikes. This forms a peak in the dark blue expiry line, where the maximum P&L from owning the covered ratio put spread is achieved. In the Biogen Inc. example, this would be if the BIIB share price were at the $260 short put strike at the close of the trading day on January 20, 2023. This is solely the profit from owning the 290/260 strike put spread, since at exactly $260 all the short put options expire worthless, leaving just the $30 profit per share from owning the 290 strike put. However, a covered ratio put spread is also in profit to the left of the peak of the dark blue expiry line if the stock falls below the short put strikes and as far as trade breakeven, which is the effective stock purchase price of $230 in the example above. The fall from the expiry peak profit occurs on a dollar-for-dollar basis, as the falling value of the long stock position (which is assigned at $260 per share in the example) denudes the return generated by the put spread. Thus, a long covered ratio put spread can be sold for a profit immediately prior to expiry of the options, if so desired, if the stock is anywhere between the long put strike and the breakeven, which would be if BIIB were between $290 and $230 in the example.

The profit generated between these two points as expiry approaches is the result of theta decay, which (assuming the stock has not moved considerably higher) is positive throughout much of the trade because there are two short puts decaying versus one long put. The flip side is that the net vega exposure is also negative, which as explored in chapter 16, can magnify the mark-to-market losses of a short put position. If there is a large sell-off in the stock, then implied volatility likely increases, but also an out-the-money put can become an at-the-money put as the share price falls to the short put strike. Since any individual option has its highest vega when the underlying stock is around the strike price, this compounds a vega loss.

Any vega loss that may occur is a mark-to-market loss, however, and, although uncomfortable in a portfolio context, increases the daily theta rate to reflect the fact that there is more option premium to decay, before the position ultimately returns to the dark blue line shown in Figure 19.1 at expiry. Since vega is also greater for long dated options, ratio put spreads are best employed when implied volatility is already high and expiration dates kept as short as practically possible, which reduces vega exposures whilst maximizing daily theta returns.

The main risk of a ratio put spread position comes from the net delta, however. Because cash is held to cover the short put, the risk is equivalent at expiry to having bought the underlying shares at the effective purchase price, which is the breakeven ($230 in the BIIB example). There is no additional risk at expiry other than the share price falling below this point, and therefore there is always less risk than having instead bought the shares at the prevailing market price (of $289.45 in the BIIB example). Prior to expiration, a ratio put spread generates a loss if the underlying stock price falls, but because the net delta exposure is initially small and at all times less than that of a corresponding stock purchase, the delta loss is always smaller. The light green line in Figure 19.1 shows the loss attributable to a moderate fall in the stock price immediately after purchase of a ratio put spread ("time 1"), which is when it is capable of generating its greatest mark-to-market loss for such a move, before time decay begins to erode the short put option.

CHAPTER 20: LONG RATIO CALL SPREAD RISK REVERSAL

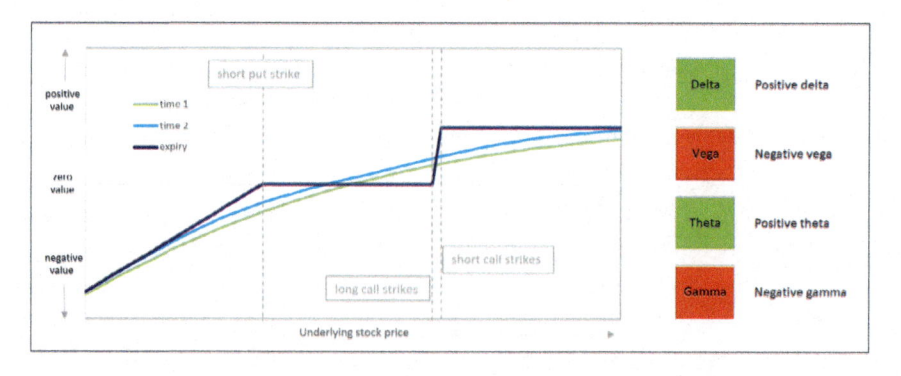

Figure 20.1.

Buying a ratio call spread risk reversal involves selling to open an out-the-money put option and buying to open a multiple number of out-the-money call spreads. It is unlikely that the order can be submitted on a broker platform as a single trade, so will likely require separate trade orders for the short put and the long call spreads. As with a risk reversal, it is generally bought for zero cost or thereabouts.

Essentially, it is a risk reversal but with the call option replaced with multiple call spreads, aimed at creating a highly geared return benefiting from a move higher in the underlying equity. As I discussed in chapter 13, greater percentage returns can be achieved from buying out-the-money call spreads with "tight" strikes—where the long and short call option strikes are close together. A ratio call spread risk reversal seeks to achieve these highly geared returns by funding the call spreads with a smaller notional of short put options for a net zero cost. As such, the motivation for undertaking the trade is an expectation that the underlying stock will move to or through the short call strike of the call spread by the expiration date.

The notional size of the call spreads are several times larger than that of the short put option, but because the call spread strikes are close together, their Greek exposures are relatively small, so it is therefore the short put that often dominates the overall Greeks. Thus, a long ratio call spread risk reversal generally has negative vega and positive theta when traded, while the majority of the positive delta exposure can sometimes come from the short put leg despite its smaller notional size. The positive theta is apparent in Figure 20.1, since the light green line moves higher to the light blue line, signifying an increase in value, solely due to the passage of time. A further feature of ratio call spread risk reversals is that due to the short net vega exposure, they can be bought more readily than risk reversals during periods of elevated market volatility.

As with a risk reversal, the short put option requires sufficient cash to cover the risk of being assigned stock. If done, it is inherently less risky than having instead bought the same notional quantity of the underlying stock, because at expiry, losses would begin to accrue only below the out-the-money short put strike rather than the current stock price. In this sense, a ratio call spread risk reversal that is bought for zero cost and is "covered" is increasingly less risky relative to owning the underlying stock, the lower the short put strike used.

Similar to a risk reversal, a pronounced put option skew benefits the price of ratio call spread risk reversals, since they also involve **selling skew**—i.e., selling put options with higher implied volatility to fund the purchase of call spreads with lower implied volatility. Large option skews allow for zero cost ratio call spread risk reversals that have short put options with strikes that are further out-the-money than the long call spread strikes.

One of the drawbacks inherent in a risk reversal, as explored in chapter 16, is that although there is a positive asymmetry of returns that allows it to perform significantly better (or less worse) than the underlying stock in a falling market, it will also always underperform the underlying stock in a rising market. A long ratio call spread risk reversal seeks to redress this to some extent, albeit at a very localized point immediately above the short call strike, by producing an outsized return from the multiple call spreads. This is shown in Figure 20.2, which is an augmentation of Figure 20.1.

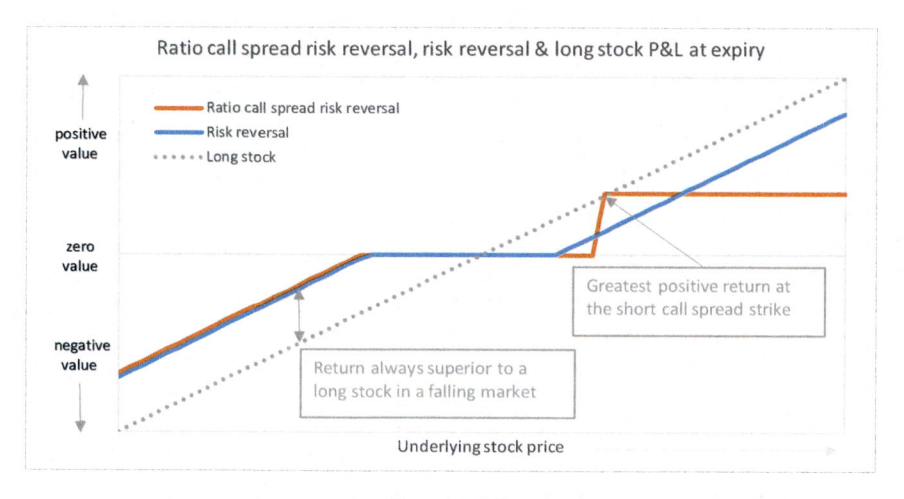

Figure 20.2.

Example

It is mid-October 2022, and you are a US-based investor. Markets are exceptionally volatile, and the US Federal Reserve continues to raise interest rates rapidly—both factors driving the US dollar (USD) to twenty-year highs. Stock markets have sold off dramatically, revealing areas of potential value. You wish to have exposure to cheap equity indices in countries that have had large negative moves in their currencies versus the USD, because you believe they will perform strongly when it stops rising and risk appetite returns to markets. The MSCI South Korea Index is in this category, having now a cyclically adjusted P/E (CAPE) of just 10.4, which is in its first percentile since

2005, whilst the Korean Won (KRW) has fallen 24 percent since the start of 2021. The iShares MSCI South Korea ETF (EWY) trades in USD and, since the equities in the index are traded in Korean won (KRW), has short exposure to the USDKRW exchange rate and long exposure to the equities in the index, making it a suitable vehicle to speculate on, in your view.

You think market weakness could persist and valuations fall further, however, so are hesitant buying even at current levels. It would offer exceptional value around 20 percent lower though (Figure 20.3), which was the 2020 pandemic-induced low and the cheapest point since 2009 before that, but you would also prefer some exposure today in case there is a turnaround in market sentiment through year-end and into early 2023. EWY has liquid options, so you decide to investigate them.

Figure 20.3.

You see that there are options listed with a January 20, 2020, expiry (Figure 20.4), which fits your time frame. There is also a $40 put strike, which is around 20 percent lower than the current ETF price where you would be happy to buy it. Market volatility is exceptionally high, and EWY looks to have a reasonable option skew and implied volatility that is correspondingly elevated. This makes you cautious about buying call options as part of a risk reversal and more inclined to own call spreads as part of a ratio call spread risk reversal.

		CALL							PUT				
gamma	theta	vega	delta	implied vol	mid price ($)	strike	% strike	mid price ($)	implied vol	delta	vega	theta	gamma
0.03	-0.007	0.06	0.13	27.2%	0.42	57	117.2%						
0.04	-0.008	0.06	0.16	27.2%	0.54	56	115.2%						
0.04	-0.009	0.07	0.20	27.5%	0.71	55	113.1%						
0.05	-0.011	0.08	0.25	28.4%	0.97	54	111.1%						
0.05	-0.012	0.09	0.30	29.1%	1.26	53	109.0%						
0.05	-0.013	0.10	0.35	29.6%	1.58	52	107.0%						
0.05	-0.014	0.10	0.40	30.1%	1.96	51	104.9%						
0.05	-0.014	0.10	0.46	30.5%	2.37	50	102.8%						
0.05	-0.015	0.10	0.51	31.5%	2.90	49	100.8%						
						48	98.7%	3.13	32.1%	-0.44	0.10	-0.017	0.05
						47	96.7%	2.68	32.4%	-0.39	0.10	-0.016	0.04
						46	94.6%	2.34	33.4%	-0.35	0.10	-0.016	0.04
						45	92.6%	2.03	34.4%	-0.31	0.09	-0.016	0.04
						40	82.3%	1.02	40.4%	-0.16	0.06	-0.013	0.02

EWY ETF price: 48.62

Figure 20.4.

Selling the 40 strike put yields $1.02 if you can trade at the mid-price. Using mid-prices also, the 55/56 call spread costs $0.17 ($0.71 – $0.54), or the 56/57 call spread costs $0.12 ($0.54 – $0.42). However, the 54/55 call spread costs $0.26 ($0.97 – $0.71) and therefore allows for only a 3.9:1 return ($1/$0.26), which is below the threshold for consideration. Despite the 57 call having a delta of only 0.13 and therefore technically only a 13 percent chance of profitability, you decide to opt for it because you feel that if EWY were to turn around, the price move higher would be dramatic enough to take it through the 57 call strike. You consult a graph to sense-check this choice and are encouraged to see EWY was trading at $57 just at the beginning of last month.

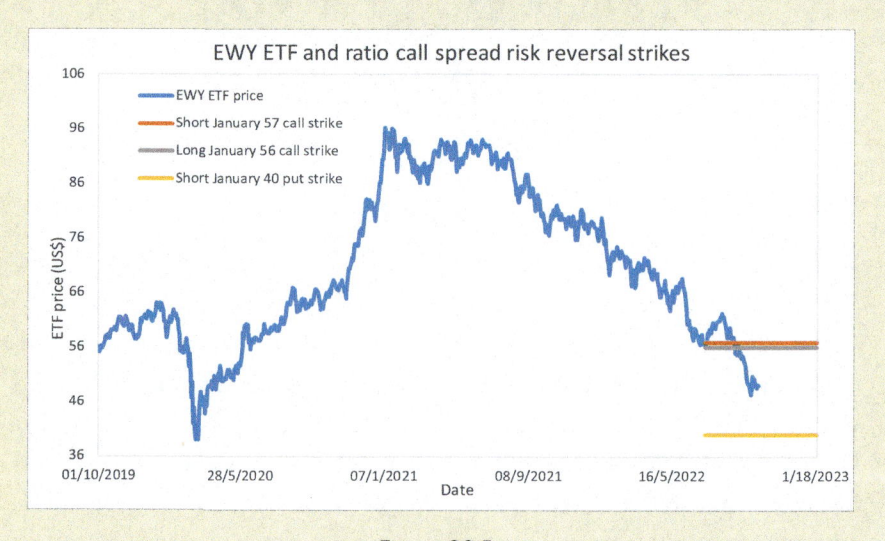

Figure 20.5.

OPTION DETAILS

option	strike	% strike	mid price ($)	implied vol	delta	vega	theta
short call	57	117.2%	-0.42	27.2%	-0.13	-0.06	0.007
long call	56	115.2%	0.54	27.2%	0.16	0.06	-0.008
			0.12				
short put	40	82.3%	1.02	40.4%	0.16	-0.06	0.013

TRADE DETAILS

option	strike	% strike	contracts	cost	$ delta	$ vega	$ theta
short call	57	117.2%	-34	-1,428	-21,490	-204	23.73
long call	56	115.2%	34	1,836	26,449	204	-27.06
				408	4,959	0	-3.33
short put	40	82.3%	-4	-408	3,112	-24	5.16
			TOTAL	$0	$8,071	-$24	$1.83

Figure 20.6.

Assuming you can successfully trade at mid-prices, the ratio between call spreads and short put options will therefore be 8.5:1 ($1.02 put price / $0.12 call spread price). You would happily invest $16,000 in EWY should the ETF fall to $40, so place a limit order to sell to open four contracts (4 contracts × 40 put strike × 100 multiplier) of EWY January 20, 2023, expiry 40 strike put options at $1.02, which will raise $408 (4 contract × $1.02 put price × 100 multiplier). You maintain this $16,000 in a liquid, low-risk money market fund. You also place a limit order to buy to open 34 EWY January 20, 2023, expiry 56/57 call spreads at $0.12, which costs $408 (34 contracts × $1.02 net cost × 100 multiplier). In time, you are filled on both orders.

The above example illustrates how a long ratio call spread risk reversal can be designed and implemented. As covered in chapter 16 when discussing risk reversals, the short put leg is the greatest source of potential risk. The entire trade must be prudently sized according to the quantity of stock you are happy to buy at the short put strike should the market fall heavily under a worst-case scenario. Sufficient cash must be set aside or kept in a very low-risk, short-dated, liquid investment to cover the short put in the event of being assigned the underlying stock and expirations kept as near-dated as possible to control vega exposures.

The orange line in Figure 20.7 shows the P&L at expiry for the long ratio call spread risk reversal detailed in the example above. Also shown in blue is the P&L that would have derived from buying the (almost) zero cost 40/54 risk reversal as well as from simply buying 400 shares of the ETF at the prevailing price of $48.62. Note that the blue risk reversal P&L line is identical to and therefore obscured by the orange ratio call spread risk reversal P&L below a price of $54. This gives some numbers and context to the similar schematic in Figure 20.2.

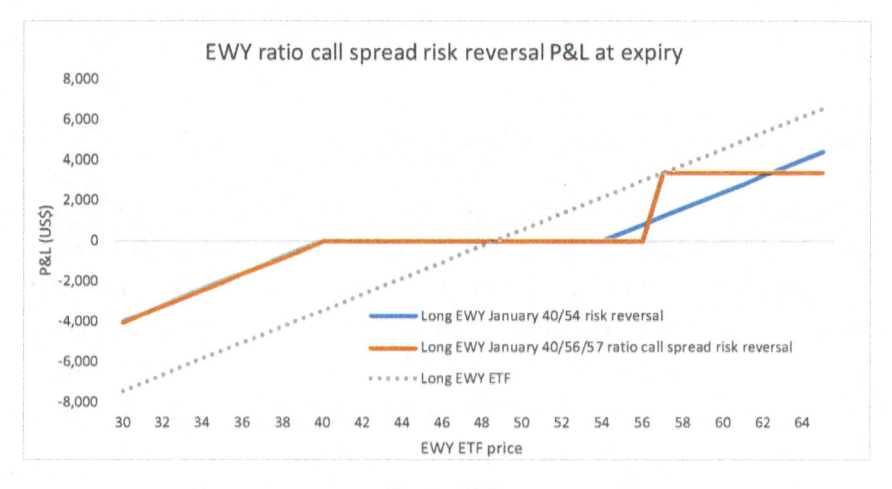

Figure 20.7.

The maximum return for the trade is $3,400, which is achieved at or above the short 57 call strike at expiry (34 contracts × (57 − 56) call strikes × 100 multiplier). This would have slightly bettered the EWY ETF return if it had been at $57 or thereabouts at the close of the day that the options expire. Aside that one price point, if the ETF had risen in value by expiry, then its return would have been superior. However, owning the ETF means accruing losses immediately, if instead it had fallen in value. The ratio call spread risk reversal, alternatively, would have made no loss above the $40 short put strike, whilst any point below that have produced a return $3,448 better than the loss from owning the ETF.

The risk reversal P&L is almost identical to that of the ratio call spread risk reversal in a falling market, since both are (almost) zero cost and both have four short 40 strike put option contracts. It is only what the proceeds from selling these 40 strike put options are invested in that differentiates the two strategies and hence their respective returns in a rising market. The risk reversal begins to make a profit above the 54 long call strike, and, because the notional size of the four call options is the same as the 400 long EWY ETFs, the profit line in blue runs parallel with the dotted line in Figure 20.7, but at a lower level. The ratio call spread risk reversal does not make a profit until the long 56 call strike is reached and then makes its entire profit at the 57 call strike. Since the notional size of call spreads is 8.5 times greater than that of the risk reversal or long EWY ETF, the orange profit line rises extremely steeply relative to them, and this occurs entirely between the call spreads. Consequently, the ratio call spread risk reversal has a superior return between an EWY ETF price of $56.30 and $62.50 at expiry, relative to the risk reversal in this example. An ETF price of $62.50 would require a 28.5 percent return during the period in question, or put differently, a call option with that strike would have a calculated delta of 4 percent, implying a very low chance of the EWY ETF reaching there by the expiry date.

Using the same logic, the 54 strike call had a delta of 0.25, and therefore the risk reversal would have roughly a 25 percent chance of its call option ending up in-the-money at expiry. As Figure 20.7 shows, the risk reversal makes a small profit with an ETF price between $54 and $56.30 at expiry, whereas the ratio call spread risk reversal does not. Aside from this area, for the remaining returns below $62.50 in the ETF (which has only an estimated 4 percent chance of being reached), the ratio call spread risk reversal has either a superior or (almost) equal return to the risk reversal.

Evidently, many different permutations are possible by varying option strikes, and this is purely an illustrative example. It shows, however, that a risk reversal, which can offer greater asymmetry albeit with a lower return than simply buying the underlying stock, can be improved upon further by a ratio call spread risk reversal if a specific view is held regarding the stock's return potential. A ratio call spread risk reversal also maintains the huge capacity to reduce risk relative to owning the underlying stock in a falling market, whilst also potentially generating a comparable return at a specific point if the market rises.

PORTFOLIO CONSIDERATIONS

CHAPTER 21: MANAGING RISK

A portfolio of options contains many more risks than a standard stock portfolio. As covered in chapters 3–6, the Greeks quantify the risks (both positive and negative) to an option, and the main ones of concern to a retail investor are delta, vega, and theta. These quantify the risk to the price of an option due to the change in another variable—namely, the price of the underlying stock, implied volatility, and time, respectively. There is also **rho**, which in 2022 especially had an effect on longer-dated option prices as a result of rapidly rising interest rates, as well as second-order Greeks, which quantify the change in the value of one of the Greeks due to a change in another variable. There are also varieties of other risks that require consideration when any portfolio of equity exposures is managed. Collectively, all risk that affects the value of equity and equity options in a portfolio through movements in market variables is termed **market risk**. However, there are other risks such as those around option trading, expiration, and assignment, for example, which are termed **operational risk**. This chapter aims to address both in sufficient detail for a retail investor.

Of utmost importance, however, is having a broker platform that is up to the job. Managing market risks across a portfolio of options is not possible unless they are quantified precisely and accessible in sufficient detail, and operational risk cannot be mitigated unless operating the platform is intuitive and easily manageable. As covered in chapter 8, it is therefore imperative to spend a great deal of time selecting the most appropriate platform for you and utilizing the tuition it offers to understand how to use it properly.

I. Market risks
Equity risk

As alluded to above, market risk is a broad term covering how movements in market variables and prices affect a financial asset. **Equity risk** is the subset of market risk that pertains specifically to equity investments. Equity risk is divided into **systematic risk** and **unsystematic risk**.

Systematic risk is the risk inherent in an investment that is impossible to avoid completely and that comes from the impact of external shocks, such as wars, or macroeconomic events, such as recessions, inflation, and policy rate changes by central banks. Beta measures the systematic risk of an equity by quantifying how volatile it is relative to a broad equity market index, such as the S&P 500 Index. Systematic risk cannot be diversified away (although it can be hedged away using long put strategies) but can be reduced within a portfolio by spreading risk across different asset classes that historically tend to respond in somewhat different ways to shocks. The growth of equity ETFs over the last few decades provide a means of reducing (though not completely mitigating) systematic risk in equity portfolios. This is because the ubiquity of ETFs gives equity investors easy access to a range of non-equity market risks. For example, there are equity ETFs that just have exposure to government bonds (short, medium, or long maturity), to corporate bonds (investment grade or high yield), to an array of different commodities, or purely to baskets of currencies. ETFs traded in one currency that contain equity investments that are denominated in another currency also implicitly package up currency risk with equity risk (such the EWY ETF used in the chapter 20 example). Blending exposures within an equity portfolio to these different asset classes aids diversification because they historically have had low, or at times negative, correlations to each other, meaning that their prices move in different ways to the same stimulus. Harry Markowitz, the Nobel prize–winning economist, is attributed as saying that "diversification is the only free lunch" in investing. Incorporating exposures from other asset classes is capable of reducing the systematic risk of equity portfolios to an extent.

Unsystematic risk is the risk attributable to a specific stock or industry. Investing an entire portfolio in the stock of a single company exposes the investor to large unsystematic risk, since a negative event pertaining to that one company, such as a profit warning, would have a significant impact on the entire stock portfolio. Similarly, investing entirely in the technology sector had a significant negative impact on risky portfolios due to the "dot-com bubble" bursting in early 2000. Unsystematic risk is mitigated by ensuring that an equity portfolio is well diversified across a range of industry sectors and geographical regions.

Although most of the time unsystematic risk from an equity portfolio can be eliminated by diversification and systematic risk reduced by incorporating exposures from other asset classes, severe macroeconomic conditions such as recessions cause correlations within equity markets to rise as investors collectively rush for the exit. This reduces the benefit of diversification within equity portfolios. Stagflationary fears during 2022 also increased the correlation of stocks and bonds, which historically had been inversely correlated for decades and therefore had offered hugely beneficial portfolio diversification, thereby negating the effectiveness of cross-asset diversification too. Clearly, although the less pernicious consequences of equity risk are managed by diversification, systematic risks are never eliminated and have the ability to intensify during extreme unfavourable market conditions as correlations between and within asset classes increase. During such episodes, the choice comes down to either accepting the equity risk and the price volatility that it comes with, reducing equity risk by selling positions, or hedging equity risk using some variation of a put option strategy.

Greek risks

The character and nature of individual Greek risks were covered in chapters 3–6. The following seeks to focus on the aggregated risk that is created for each when owning a portfolio of options, as well as on useful ways to think about managing each risk.

Delta risk

Delta risk at any point is a snapshot of stock equivalent exposure in your portfolio. An equity option notional (or gross) exposure is shown by the equation below:

Notional exposure = number of option contracts × stock price × option multiplier

The delta risk or "delta-adjusted exposure" is shown below:

Delta-adjusted exposure = notional exposure × option delta

Thus, during the life of a call option, the delta-adjusted exposure will always be a fraction of the notional exposure, which increases (decreases) in size as the option delta increases (decreases). At expiration, the delta-adjusted exposure becomes equal to the notional exposure if the call ends up in-the-money (and therefore has a delta of one), or zero if the call ends up out-the-money (and therefore has a delta of zero). Similarly, a put option will have a negative delta-adjusted exposure that is always a fraction of the notional exposure, which increases (decreases) in size as the put delta increases (decreases). At expiration, it equals the negative notional exposure if the put ends up in-the-money (and its delta is minus one), or zero if the put ends up out-the-money (and its delta is zero). Because option deltas are constantly moving throughout each trading day, the delta risk is just a snapshot of how much "equity-like" exposure there is at any point. For example, if you owned ten SPY at-the-money call options, you would have the equivalent of 500 SPY shares, since at-the-money calls roughly have a delta of 0.5, and US options have a multiplier of 100. If SPY was trading at 370, you would have $185,000 of delta-adjusted exposure or delta risk. Note that this is also called $ delta for shorthand, in the same way that € delta is shorthand for the delta-adjusted exposure of an option on a euro-denominated stock.

A portfolio's total delta risk is therefore the aggregate of all the long delta-adjusted exposures, plus the notional exposure of any long stock positions, minus the aggregate of all the short delta-adjusted exposures, minus the notional exposure of any short stock positions. However, different stocks also have different betas, so a portfolio that has a $250,000 delta risk made up of low beta stocks will experience a lot less volatility than a portfolio with a $250,000 delta risk made up of high beta stocks. It is therefore useful that the broker platform is able to **beta-adjust** each of the deltas in a portfolio, relative to a broad equity index such as the S&P 500 Index. This beta-adjusted delta risk will more clearly indicate the exposure of a portfolio's equity risk, since you are able to think of the aggregate delta in terms of a well-defined market index.

Managing delta risk also requires ensuring that the size of this is commensurate with your view on how equity markets will perform. There is little sense in having a portfolio just of various long delta strategies on stocks that you are very bullish on, whilst harbouring a negative view on the overall market. Reducing portfolio delta by using call spread type exposures instead of long call exposures at the individual stock level, or if you have enough conviction in your negative market view, using a put strategy on the relevant equity index ETF, both will help reduce a portfolio's beta-adjusted delta risk to more comfortable levels.

Of course, delta risk of option positions can change quickly if a portfolio contains a number of different options on a variety of different underlying equities. In addition to ensuring you are comfortable with the beta-adjusted delta risk size, it is important to monitor the size of delta risk of individual positions to ensure that there is not excessive concentrations building within one area. As discussed in the section on equity risk, diversification of delta risk exposures across different sectors, geographies, and even asset classes will help reduce unsystematic and even systematic risk to an extent.

It is important also that the delta of option positions is used to realistically assess the chance of profitability for a trade. As mentioned before, an option's delta gives an approximate probability of an option ending up in-the-money at expiry. A portfolio of call options that consists entirely of very low delta options with larger numbers of contracts may have the same delta risk as a portfolio of call options that consists entirely of larger delta options with a smaller contract quantity. This is akin to either putting large bets on a number of outsiders in a horse race or putting smaller bets on a number of horses with shorter odds. Unless you are very fortunate or very good at playing the stock market, although you have the possibility of winning big using the first approach, you are far more likely to lose your entire option premium, whereas the second approach makes you more likely to make smaller amounts of money. Deltas of long option positions require continual review and any low delta option positions assessed to ensure that the investment thesis is still valid. This is because a portfolio containing a large number of long low delta option positions, that hence have a low probability of making a profit, tends to bleed P&L over time, a topic explored in more detail below in the section on theta.

Vega risk

This is the aggregated vega exposures of each option position in a portfolio and is denoted at $ vega in shorthand if all the options are traded in dollars. Vega risk for a single option position is calculated as follows:

Option vega × number of contracts × option multiplier

Retail investors should predominantly trade options with shorter-dated maturities, which have greater liquidity and also lower vegas, unless specifically buying call options as investments and then only with the caveats discussed previously. As illustrated in chapter 16, longer-dated options that have lower vegas because their strikes are out-the-money are at risk of their vega exposures climbing dramatically if the underlying stock moves toward the strike.

Essentially, managing a large vega exposure is not within the remit of the large majority of retail option traders. However, long options have positive vega exposures, and short options have negative vega exposures, so a portfolio of options will inherently have an aggregate vega risk. Maintaining it within a range that is small enough not to have an oversized impact on performance is sensible by keeping it within a set percentage range of the total value of a portfolio. As individual traders become more comfortable with managing vega exposures and develop a more intuitive understanding of how market implied volatility moves over time, this percentage range can be increased if desired. Studying the VIX Index will help, which shows the behaviour of 30-day implied volatility (and put option skew) on the S&P 500 Index.

Nevertheless, keeping in mind some of the broad concepts of volatility that were explored in chapter 4 will also offer some guidance when thinking about the appropriate level of portfolio vega risk. Volatility is mean reverting over longer-time horizons, clusters over short-time horizons and shows distinct regimes that may persist for several years, which can be categorized as high, medium, and low. Also, volatility generally increases as equities fall in value and decreases as they rise in value and thus have an inverse relationship with equity prices. Tying this into an economic cycle, volatility generally increases with the onset of and during a recession and collapses as stocks rebound out of recession. These precepts can help form a judgement on whether at a portfolio level, a slight positive, flat, or negative vega exposure might be most appropriate.

However, since different equities have different betas, they also exhibit different volatilities. Furthermore, it might not be immediately apparent when comparing current levels of realized volatility that one stock might have the propensity to exhibit higher volatility than another. For example, Figure 21.1 and Figure 21.2 show one-month realized volatility for Facebook (META) and International Business Machines Crop (IBM), respectively.

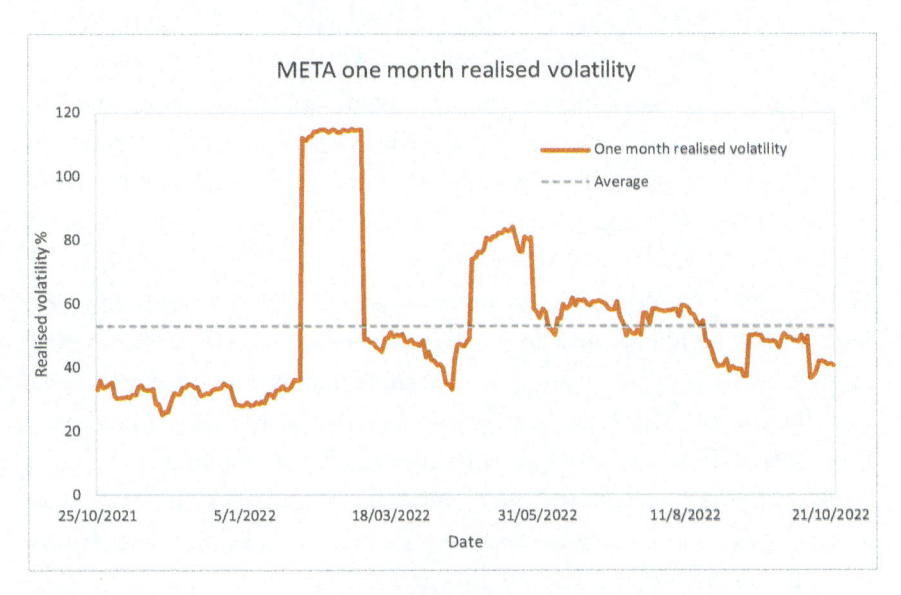

Figure 21.1.

Figure 21.2.

META at the time of writing has a one-month realized volatility that is around nine percentage points higher than IBM. However, that is low relative to its recent history, since the stock experienced dramatic sell-offs around earnings announcements during 2022 (i.e., displayed a high degree of unsystematic equity risk). Conversely, IBM has a lower realized volatility, but this is currently near the top of its twelve-month range and is ordinarily much less volatile.

The option market is where participants determine where to price the implied volatility of META, IBM, and all other equity. This example highlights an issue with aggregating different individual vegas from a range of different underlying stocks, in the same way as it's difficult to aggregate delta risks from a range of different underlying stocks, without beta-adjusting them. It also highlights that (due to unsystematic equity risk) it is far riskier to manage the vega risk of an individual stock than it is to manage an equal quantity of vega risk for a diversified stock index. Managing large vega exposures of individual stocks requires detailed understanding of the way a stock trades, its corporate structure, and its upcoming schedule of corporate announcement, to name but a few factors, and is outside of the expertise of the large majority of retail option investors.

In all, this argues for retail investors to keep vega risks relatively small, gain exposures only from short- to medium-dated options and primarily from diversified underlyings such as ETFs on equity indices. Call or put spreads can also be used instead of single option strategies to limit excessive accumulation of vega risk in a portfolio when necessary, and large vega exposures should especially be eschewed when volatility is elevated relative to history. Even when market volatility is stuck in a low-volatility regime, caution should still prevail when considering a large vega exposure, because volatility can remain at extreme low levels for several years at a time.

In any case, an analysis of implied volatility is necessary prior to undertaking any option trade on any underlying stock or ETF. This should involve any functionality provided by your elected broker platform, as well as an analysis of recent realized volatility, in order to form a judgement on whether a long-volatility or short-volatility strategy is most appropriate for the underlying stock or ETF.

Theta risk

This is the aggregated theta exposures of each option position in a portfolio and is denoted at $ theta in shorthand if all the options are traded in dollars. Theta risk for a single option position is calculated as follows:

Option theta × number of contracts × option multiplier

Ideally, it is, of course, beneficial to an option portfolio to have a high positive theta, as this implies that the portfolio is generating a positive return on a daily basis whilst the market is doing nothing (or even closed for the weekend). Whilst this is true, positive theta occurs from the decay of short option positions, and short option positions expose the seller to the greatest risks (technically, infinite risk in the case of selling naked call options).

As has been explored in earlier chapters, however, short put and short call strategies that are covered with cash or stock, respectively, potentially generate greater return with less volatility under certain conditions compared with simply buying shares. A ratio call spread risk reversal and a put spread collar also generate positive theta, whilst risk reversals, collars, and put or call spreads generally will if the short put option leg is closer to the stock price. All these are examples of where short options are used either covered or as part of a multi-option strategy where the seller is not exposed to undue risk.

In the earlier section on delta risk, it was mentioned that a portfolio consisting predominantly of low delta options would generally bleed money over time and have just a small chance of profitability. Since an option's delta is an approximate probability of whether it will expire in-the-money, this stands to reason. However, options generally have a **volatility risk premium**, which is to say that because stocks have the capacity to experience spikes in realized volatility, the implied volatility that is priced into an option by the market is generally in excess of the usual realized volatility that it experiences month by month. Therefore, call options that have a ten delta will have a roughly 10 percent probability of expiring in-the-money. However, in reality, because the implied volatility is generally higher than the realized volatility that occurs, the actual percentage of call options that expire in-the-money is lower than that over the long run.

The existence of the volatility risk premium in option markets argues for the sale of options to generate theta, since it tilts the profitability probabilities marginally in favour of option selling and away from option buying. Indeed, there are short volatility funds that sell implied volatility systematically in order to profit from these and other mispricings, and individual investors who just sell options to generate an investment yield. However, such investment strategies, although generally profitable over very long time horizons, can leave investors exposed to large losses over shorter periods and as such are outside of the parameters of this book.

Nevertheless, selling options where possible to increase theta is beneficial to the long run performance of an option portfolio. Holding long option positions with large negative theta exposures for any length of time should be discouraged, as they easily become a drag on a portfolio's ability to make a profit. For this reason, closing out or rolling long option positions that are within the last month or so prior to expiry into something longer-dated is a sensible way of managing the theta bill of a portfolio. Negative theta exposures can also be managed by either taking profits on long option positions that have performed strongly or selling another option slightly further out-the-money to create a put or call spread from a single option strategy. This is not to say that low delta option positions are never permitted, but a realistic and rational assessment of their likelihood of bearing fruit is mandatory, because over the long run it is often more beneficial to be short the option than to own it.

Gamma risk

Calculating gamma risk, or $ gamma in shorthand if all the options in a portfolio are traded in dollars, is mathematically rather more complicated than computing the first order Greek risks covered so far in this chapter, but your selected broker platform will compute portfolio gamma risk for you.

The interpretation of gamma risk is also somewhat more complicated. Gamma risk is the change in delta risk, resulting from a 1 percent move in its underlying stock (assuming the portfolio contains just options on dollar-denominated stocks). This becomes less intuitive at a portfolio level when all gamma risks are aggregated, primarily because a 1 percent move in stock X is not the same as a 1 percent move in stock Y.

It is still an important measure to monitor nevertheless, even if its magnitude can be difficult to interpret. This is because a positive gamma risk suggests that as the market rises, the portfolio is gaining delta, and as the market falls, the portfolio is losing delta, which implies that the portfolio will profit from an increase in market volatility and lose from a decrease in volatility. Conversely, a negative gamma risk implies the opposite—that a portfolio is getting longer delta as the market falls and getting shorter delta as the market rises and will therefore lose from an increase in market volatility and gain from a decrease in market volatility. There is a subtle distinction here that we are talking about increases and decreases in realized market volatility, instead of implied volatility, which instead respectively requires either a long or a short vega exposure to turn a profit.

Remember though that gamma is a second order derivative. It quantifies the change in the delta for a 1 percent change in the price of the underlying stock and does not quantify any changes to the option price itself and therefore the value of options in a portfolio. So how does an option price that has negative gamma make money due to a decrease in market volatility, and how does an option price that has positive gamma lose money due to a decrease in market volatility? The answer is that gamma and theta are almost always of opposite sign—that is to say that an option that has a positive gamma will have a negative theta, and vice versa. Their respective magnitudes are also quite similar—a high gamma option will have a large theta, and a low gamma option will have a low theta. An option trader who wishes to be long gamma in order to make money from trading the movement in an option delta that it provides will think of theta as **gamma rent**—i.e., the cost required to own gamma for a period of time. As was explained in chapter 6, it is at its greatest for at-the-money options that are about to expire, since the delta (and hence the probability that the option will end in-the-money) will swing dramatically as the stock moves into and out of being in-the-money.

When combining options within a strategy, creating positions that are long gamma and theta is relatively easy though. The risk reversal example in chapter 16 that used options on the VGK ETF, for instance, has these characteristics, where steep option skew allowed for selling far out-the-money puts with a high implied volatility, to buy less far out-the-money calls with lower implied volatility. It is therefore entirely feasible to have long gamma and long theta within a portfolio.

Since the intention for strategies contained in this book, particularly with short options, is that they can be held to expiry, both theta and gamma of option positions will likely show reasonably large moves within a portfolio context. Short gamma risk is extremely hazardous around expiries when an option is naked and at-the-money, but not so when a short option is covered, because implicitly as part of the short option strategy, there is a predetermined level at which you are willing and able to buy or sell the stock. Around option expiries, therefore, a large negative gamma risk (and therefore most likely a large positive theta) indicates a covered short option position that is close to expiry.

Long option positions approaching expiry—associated with a large positive gamma risk and corresponding negative theta—require a little more attention. This is because instead of having the option exercised, you may instead wish to sell it, which can be done up to the very day of expiration. Expiration risk is an operational risk, which is covered in the next section.

2. Operational risks

This broad term will be used to cover risks that do not directly act upon the price of financial assets such as equities and equity options, but are "the risk of loss resulting from inadequate or failed internal processes, people and systems or from external events." (*Principles for the Sound Management of Operational Risk*, Basel Committee on Banking Supervision, 2012)

Early exercise and expiration risk

The fluctuation of underlying stocks on the day of option expiration can expose investors with expiring option positions to unexpected outcomes. Outsized moves can happen any day in any financial market, but the mechanics of option expiration means that any investor with an expiring long or short option position needs to be especially vigilant on expiry days.

The requirement at all times throughout the life of the trade is to cover short call options with sufficient stock and short put options with sufficient cash to meet the obligations of option assignment. This eliminates expiration risk for short options on the day of expiry as well as largely negating the risk of needing to post additional margin at any point during the life of the trade.

However, **early exercise risk** describes the risk that short option positions at times can be exercised early. The majority of listed equity options are **American style options**, which means that the buyer can exercise them at any time prior to expiry by submitting an instruction to the clearing house (via the broker platform for retail investors). The clearing house will then pro rata these at random across the holders of the corresponding short option positions. In the case of short put options, this results in receiving stock in exchange for the strike price, as well as expiration of the option on a day prior to its expiration date. Although this makes little economic sense for a long put holder to exercise early (unless the stock has fallen considerably through the strike price with little chance of recovery and additional incremental daily interest can be earned on receiving funds early), it does occur at times. It is more common for short in-the-money call options to be assigned early, however, so that the long call holder is able to take ownership of the stock at an earlier point in time. This may be either because there is a dividend due on the stock, or ownership allows the stockholder certain voting rights, etc. Unless these incentives to own the stock are especially large, early exercise is mainly a risk in the days prior to expiration because once an option is exercised it no longer exists, so any residual time value is lost. To mitigate this risk, it is advisable to check prior to selling a call option that the expiration date does not fall immediately prior to the ex-dividend date of a stock.

As an option buyer, you can choose to exercise prior to expiry if you wish (ordinarily for one of the reasons outlined above) by a request sent via your broker platform. If held to expiration, long option positions will automatically be exercised if they are in-the-money by the clearing house. In the case of long put options, this involves receiving the strike price in exchange for selling stock; in the case of long call options, this involves buying stock at the strike price.

Long call options, therefore, also require sufficient funds in a brokerage account if the intention is that they are to be exercised. Commonly though, the goal of a long call option position is not to take ownership of the underlying stock but instead to simply profit from an anticipated short-term stock movement. The majority of long call option trades are therefore sold in the market prior to expiration to monetize their value if they are in-the-money, or left to expire worthless if they are far out-the-money.

Buying a call option does not necessitate holding sufficient cash to pay for stock at expiration in the same way that a short put option does, because there is no loss that can be created other than losing the call premium paid, and the call option value can always be monetized prior to expiration by selling it in the market. **Expiration risk** for long call options can occur when you overlook to sell a call option before the close of trading on the day of expiration, which subsequently expires in-the-money, thereby triggering automatic exercise and an unwanted long stock position and associated debit on your brokerage account. This can cause monetary loss because your broker may be forced to liquidate positions in your account to cover the funds due for the assignment of stock, or since assignment occurs after close of the trading day, the stock might fall in value before the following trading day begins and you are able to liquidate it. Expiration risk is therefore mitigated by staying on top of open positions and selling to close long call options when exercise is not desired, which is something that can be done right up until the last hours of trading on the day of expiry. Since a long option position will always have value in excess of its intrinsic value, there should not be an issue with doing so, provided there is sufficient liquidity in the underlying stock.

This gets slightly more complicated when dealing with a call or put spread. If the spread is in-the-money and remains in-the-money at expiration, then there is not an issue, and you effectively receive the intrinsic value of the spread (number of contracts × difference between option strikes × multiplier). For a call spread, the mechanics involve buying stock at the long (lower) call strike and selling stock at the short (higher) call strike, which nets off as no movement in stock and a receipt of money from the clearing house equal to the intrinsic value of the call spread. For a put spread, the mechanics involve a sale of stock at the long (higher) put strike and a purchase of stock at the short (lower) put strike, which nets off as no movement of stock and a receipt of the intrinsic value of the put spread from the clearing house also.

The only issue occurs when there is an early exercise of one of the short option strikes, or at expiration the stock ends up in between the option strikes. Again, vigilance is required every day, leading up to and on expiry day so that necessary corrective steps can be taken. If you are assigned a position resulting from early exercise of a short option as part of a spread, this might look alarming when you view your broker account the next morning, but it is easily corrected. It is likely that the options are very in-the-money because otherwise there is a large time value remaining on your short option, which the option exerciser could have monetized by selling the option in the market rather than exercising it early. If the short leg of a call spread is exercised early, this would leave you with a long call option and a short stock position, and if the short leg of a put spread is exercised early, this would leave you with a long put and a long stock position. In either case, your long option is hedging the stock position and should not be sold. Either your long option can also be exercised early by submitting a request via your broker account, which will close out both the stock or option position at intrinsic the next morning. Alternatively, submit a covered stock transaction for the option and stock position simultaneously as one order, using your broker platform, which will let you monetize any remaining time value in your long option in excess of its intrinsic value whilst closing out the stock and option position at the same time immediately during the trading day. Check the costs involved and which method is cheapest for you on the broker platform you are using, which should also give guidance on how these transactions are submitted.

If you are approaching expiry, and the stock price is trading close to or in between the strikes of an option spread, the safest way to manage it if you do not want to be assigned on just the long leg is to sell the whole position. This can be done at or better than intrinsic value of the spread right up until expiration of the options, which occurs at the close of trading for US stock options (although this does differ at exchanges in other countries).

Option trading

Human error is the greatest source of operational risk whilst trading option positions. Orders can be miskeyed on broker platforms or mistakenly submitted in the wrong expiry, or strike or buy orders can be submitted as sell orders, etc. Dealing errors like these are made just as easily on trading desks in large financial hubs throughout the world, and much focus is made on reducing these as much as practically possible (since they can never be entirely eliminated), because they can lead to severe financial loss under nightmare scenarios.

Once you select a broker platform, the first investment should be the necessary time to thoroughly understand how to use it correctly. Demos are usually available to allow you to submit orders on dummy accounts and to practice selecting options by expiry and strike. Do not use a platform you do not feel entirely comfortable using when submitting orders to the market. Many will have online video tutorials to help guide you through how trades are submitted using their correct safeguards. Following these closely will reduce the risk of incurring financial losses arising from dealing errors.

Once an order has been created for submission to the market, there should always be a final checking stage built into the platform. This allows you to make one final verification that you have correctly selected the underlying equity, the strike, the expiry, and whether you are intending to buy or sell the contract and at what price. Taking time to do this before finally submitting an order for trading, especially during fast-moving markets or when stress levels may be elevated, will greatly reduce potentially costly human errors. Never submit trade orders if your reasoning is in any way impaired.

Checking your portfolio positions to ensure that they are behaving as you would expect once they have been traded also helps identify any mistakes you have made during trading. Closing out any mistakes quickly is an important rule to abide by. Do not run with any unintended positions created in error, as they are capable of snowballing into greater problems. Being able to take such missteps on the chin and dealing with them quickly is an important part of becoming a resilient option trader.

Position sizing

A crucial aspect of controlling the risk of any portfolio is correctly sizing each position. Whatever investment approach you have to generate the ideas to allocate your money to, it is important to have a consistent and considered framework for sizing trades. A portfolio that has returns dominated by a small number of positions is excessively risky, just as unsystematic risk is at its greatest due to a lack of diversification. However, equity option prices are far more volatile than prices of the underlying stocks because options have leverage. Furthermore, premiums amounts vary considerably due to differences in implied volatility, delta, time to expiry and strategy, etc. So while some strategies have high premiums, others are generators of income (such as short calls or short puts). How is trade sizing best implemented, given these variations?

A useful approach considers the notional exposures of underlying stock for each trade. This is especially useful for sizing trades that include short put option exposures and the only way for sizing overwriting trades using short call options. Examples covered in previous chapters that involve a short put option have all been sized in this way—using the quantity of notional stock that the investor would be willing to buy if assigned on the short put (which is, of course, equal to the sum of money set aside to cover the short put liability).

However, should each underlying stock deserve the same notional exposure? Large investment portfolios size stock exposures according to their volatility and correlations with each other, so that more volatile stocks are given smaller notional exposures and allocations among more correlated stocks, which may, for example, be in the same sector, are shared. This can get overly technical, but a means of diversifying the size of underlying stock exposures as discussed in the market risk section is generally a good idea.

Whilst this may be a good way to think about exposures arising from short option positions, which carry obligations to buy or sell specific quantities of stock, it doesn't necessarily work so well for long option trades, especially speculative short-term ones where there is no desire to result in a position in the underlying stock. Here, the focus is more likely to be on the quantity of money necessary to generate a specific anticipated leveraged return from a long option strategy. As such, it is often easier to size a trade entirely upon the amount of money you are prepared to risk in order to make an anticipated return and use the same premium value for each long option trade you undertake. It is also useful to have two "usual bet" sizes: (1) a slightly higher one for higher conviction trades or ones that you deem to be less risky and (2) a lower-standard size for trades that are more speculative.

A combination of the two approaches for long and short option trades is a good basis to use as long as there is consistency. The resulting option portfolio, however, will be subject to all the risks outlined in the market risk section, so sizing of new trades and managing existing ones both require thinking about the portfolio as a whole, with primary focus upon diversifying delta risk.

GLOSSARY

Account fees	Fees charged by a broker to use certain parts of their broker platform.
ADR	"American Depositary Receipts" are certificates issued by a US depositary bank traded on US stock exchanges like a regular share, which have the exposure of shares in a foreign company's stock.
American style options	An option that can be exercised on any day up to and including its expiration date.
Asymmetric payoff	Where the return potential of an asset is different depending on whether the market rises or falls. Long options have a positive asymmetric payoff at expiration so potential gains are greater than potential loses, whilst short options have a negative asymmetric payoff at expiration so potential gains are smaller than potential losses.

Assignment	The process that follows the exercise of an option by its owner or automatically by the clearing house, under which the seller of a call option is required to take a short position in the underlying stock, or the seller of a put option is required to take a long position in the underlying stock.
At-the-money	Describes any listed option whose strike price is closest to the price of the underlying asset.
Automatic exercise	Whereby the clearing house exercises any option at expiration that is even marginally in-the-money, unless the option holder has given instruction to the contrary.
Bear spread	A put spread.
Beta	A measure of the volatility of an asset relative to a reference asset, such as the S&P 500 Index.
Beta adjusted exposure	The notional exposure of an asset multiplied by its beta.
Black-Scholes Model (BSM)	An option-pricing model based upon the input of implied volatility developed by Fischer Black and Myron Scholes in 1973.
Bonds	Debt securities traded on capital markets —essentially IOUs — issued by governments, companies and other entities to raise capital from financial markets, that provide a return through fixed periodic interest payments.
Breakeven	The price in the underlying asset at expiry at which an option trade has neither made nor lost money.
Broker platform	Downloadable software from an option broker made available when an account has been set up that facilitates trading of option orders and provides market data, news and analytical tools to help manage a portfolio.
Bull spread	A call spread.

Buy to close	An order submitted via a broker platform to buy an option to offset (close out) some or all of an identical existing short option position i.e., with the same underlying, strike and expiration date.
Buy to open	An order submitted via a broker platform to buy an option where no identical existing short position already exists.
Buying on margin	Buying assets with funds borrowed through a broker margin account.
Buy-write	A covered call strategy.
Call butterfly	A multiple call option strategy with a single expiration date involving a long call option, two short call options with a higher strike and a long call option with an even higher strike. The long call option strikes must be equidistantly spaced around the short call option strikes.
Call condor	A multiple call option strategy with a single expiration date involving a long call option, a short call options with a higher strike, a short call option with an even higher strike and a final long call option with an even higher strike. The long call option strikes must be equidistantly spaced around their closest short call option strikes.
Call ladder	A multiple call option strategy with a single expiration date involving a call spread and a further out-the-money short call option.
Call option	A financial derivative contract that bestows the buyer with right but not the obligation to buy an underlying asset at a strike price prior to an expiration date.
Call spread	A multiple call option strategy with a single expiration date involving a long call option and a short further out-the-money call option.
Call switch	A relative value call option strategy whereby a call option is bought on an underlying asset and a call option sold on a different underlying asset.

Called away	The sale of stock at a short call option strike price following the assignment process conducted by the clearing house, resulting from the exercise of the corresponding long call option.
Cash-settled options	Options that only involve the transfer of cash under the assignment process e.g., listed equity index options.
CBOE	The Chicago Board Options Exchange.
Charm	A second-order option Greek quantifying the change in an option's delta resulting from the passage of time.
Clearing house	The corporation or agency of an options exchange that acts as intermediary between buyers and sellers of all option trades to reduce counterparty risk, responsible also for reporting and clearing trades and margining accounts.
Collar	A multiple option strategy with a single expiration date comprising a long out-the-money put and short out-the-money call.
Combo	A synthetic long or synthetic short stock position.
Condor body	The middle two short call options of a call condor option strategy.
Conor wings	The long call options of a condor call option strategy, which are the lowest strike and the highest strike call options.
Contract	A single tradable unit of an option.
Convexity	Positive convexity describes an asset's return that increases in value at a faster rate as its price increases and decreases in value at a slower rate as its price decreases. Negative convexity describes an asset's return that increases in value at a slower rate as its price increases and decreases in value at a faster rate as its price decreases.

Correlation	A statistical measure of the degree to which the price of two assets move in relation to each other.
Covered call	A call option strategy comprising a short call and sufficient stock to meet the obligation if the option is exercised.
Covered put	A put option strategy comprising a short put and sufficient cash to meet the obligation if the option is exercised.
Delta	The sensitivity of an option price to a change in the price of the underlying asset.
Delta-adjusted exposure	The notional exposure of an option position multiplied by its net option delta.
Derivative	A financial instrument with a value that is derived from the price of another underlying asset.
Dividend	Monies that a company regularly distributes to its shareholders from its profits or reserves.
Early exercise risk	The risk to an option seller that the option is exercised prior to its expiration date by its owner.
Equity	The net worth of a company once all debts have been paid. Ownership of a company's equity equates to ownership of the company. Equity ownership is divided into and traded as shares.
Equity index	A grouping of stocks selected by country, sector or other criteria and weighted by an accepted methodology to calculate a single price.
Equity risk	The risk inherent in owning any stock or share exposure. Equity risk can be further subdivided into systematic risk and unsystematic risk.
ETF	An "Exchange Traded Fund" is an investment fund that can contain any variety of different assets and asset classes, which is subdivided into units that trade on a stock exchange like a regular equity.
European style options	An option that can only be exercised on its expiration date.

Ex-date	The date on which a stock is no longer trading with the right to receive its next dividend payment.
Expiration date / expiry date	The date on which an option expires.
Expiration risk	The risk an option position poses on its expiration date, that due to an undesired movement in the underlying stock the option may move in or out-the-money.
Gamma	A second-order option Greek quantifying the change in an option's delta resulting from change in the underlying asset price.
Gamma rent	Theta decay of an option position from the perspective of an option trader attempting to profit from hedging an option's delta exposure.
Gross exposure	See notional exposure.
Hedge / hedging	Use of a financial asset to offset the market risk inherent in another financial asset.
Implied volatility	The expected average annualized volatility of an asset's price, as determined by market participants in the option market.
Implied volatility surface	A three-dimensional plot of implied volatility versus time to expiration and option skew for an underlying asset.
In-the-money	Describes any listed option that has intrinsic value i.e., a call option with a strike below the underlying asset price, or a put option with a strike above the underlying asset price.
Intrinsic value	The amount by which an option is in-the-money.
Kappa	See vega.
Leg into	The process of trading an option to open, in order to create a multiple option strategy out of an existing position.

Leverage	Having exposure to a larger notional value of an asset than the value of the funds invested. Leverage is most commonly achieved with using either: 1) options; 2) or a margin account.
Limit order	A trade instruction submitted through a broker platform to buy or sell an asset but only at a specific pre-determined price or better.
Liner payoff	The return of an asset that exhibits no asymmetry, such as an equity.
Listed	An asset that meets the sufficient requirements to be officially traded on a recognized investment exchange.
Long exposure	A position with a positive delta, such as a long stock, long call option or short put option.
Long leg	The long option in a multiple option strategy.
Lot	See contract.
Margin	Collateral demanded by a clearing house in the form of cash to back open option positions.
Margin call	Demand for additional collateral on a margin account due to adverse market moves affecting open positions.
Market order	A trade instruction submitted through a broker platform to buy or sell an asset immediately at the prevailing market price.
Market risk	A broad term to cover the risk inherent in any financial asset resulting from moves in market variables.
Mean reversion	The movement in any variable toward its long-term average level.
Moneyness	Whether an option is in, at or out-the-money and often expressed as the option strike price in percentage terms relative to the market price of the underlying asset.

Multiplier	The standardized quantity of stock that underlies an option contract, as determined by the options exchange.
Naked call	A short call option position that is not covered with the underlying stock.
Naked put	A short put option that is not covered by cash or very low-risk, liquid, interest-bearing assets in a portfolio.
Notional exposure	The current market value of the underlying equity.
Open interest	The quantity of open option positions that exist of a specific strike and expiry on an underlying asset, as calculated by the options exchange.
Operational risk	A broad term to cover "the risk of loss resulting from inadequate or failed internal processes, people and systems or from external events." (Principles for the Sound Management of Operational Risk, Basel Committee on Banking Supervision, 2012)
Option exercise	The process by which the option holder or the clearing house executes the terms of the option contract and begins the assignment process.
Option skew	Describes the tendency for lower strike equity options to trade with a higher implied volatility than higher strike equity options.
Options exchange	A regulated market that lists and facilitates the trading of option contracts.
OTC option	"Over The Counter" options are not listed, but are traded predominantly between investment banks and their clients away from an options exchange.
Out-the-money	Describes any listed option that has no intrinsic value i.e., a call option with a strike above the underlying asset price, or a put option with a strike below the underlying asset price.
Over-hedging	Establishing a greater quantity of a hedging position than is strictly warranted within a portfolio.

Overwrite	A short call stock option that is covered with an equivalent long stock position.
Pairs trade	A long stock position that is matched with an equivalent short position in a different stock.
Payoff	The return potential for an asset under different scenarios.
Plain vanilla	A term used to describe listed put and call options.
Premium	The total money spent or received on an option.
Profit or loss (P&L)	The projected or actual return on a financial asset.
Put ladder	A multiple put option strategy with a single expiration date involving a put spread and a further out-the-money short put option.
Put option	A financial derivative contract that bestows the buyer with the right but not the obligation to sell an underlying asset at a strike price prior to an expiration date.
Put spread	A multiple put option strategy with a single expiration date involving a long put option and a short further out-the-money put option.
Put spread collar	A multiple option strategy with a single expiration date comprising a put spread and a short call.
Put switch	A relative value put option strategy whereby a put option is bought on an underlying asset and a put option sold on a different underlying asset.
Put upon	The purchase of stock at a short put option strike price resulting from the assignment process conducted by the clearing house, following the exercise of the corresponding long put option.
Put-write	See underwrite.

Ratio call spread	A call spread with twice the quantity of short call option contracts relative to long call option contracts.
Ratio call spread risk reversal	A multiple option strategy with a single expiration date comprising a short put and larger notional quantity of long call spreads.
Ratio put spread	A put spread with twice the quantity of short put option contracts relative to long put option contracts.
Realized volatility	The annualized standard deviation of daily returns of an asset.
Retail investor	Any investor not classified as a professional investor by the relevant regulatory body.
Rho	The sensitivity of an option price to a change in the risk-free rate.
Risk reversal	A multiple option strategy with a single expiration date comprising a short put and long call.
Risk-free rate	An interest rate based upon the highest-rated government bond with lowest probability of default risk.
Rolling an option position	An option trade involving the simultaneous closure of an existing position and the opening of a new position.
Rule of 16	A useful observation that an annualized volatility of 16% equates to roughly a 1% daily move in the underlying asset during a given time period, and that this relationship holds in multiples or fractions thereof.
Sell to close	An order submitted via a broker platform to sell an option to offset (and therefore close out) some or all of an identical existing long position in an account with the same underlying, strike and expiration date.
Sell to open	An order submitted via a broker platform to sell an option short where no identical long position already exists in an account.
Selling skew	Any option strategy that involves selling low-strike options.

Sell-write	A covered put strategy.
Settlement price	The price of the underlying asset calculated by the exchange that is used for option expirations.
Share	The smallest denomination of a company's tradable equity, which entitles the owner to dividend payments if distributed and only to a share of any residual value of a company once all other parties have been paid, in the event of the company's liquidation.
Short leg	The short option in a multiple option strategy.
Short squeeze	A sharp move higher in the price of a stock resulting from a number of investors closing out their short stock positions.
Skew index	An index maintained by the CBOE that is calculated from the price of one-month options on the S&P 500 Index to show the degree of option skew it exhibits.
Statistical arbitrage	A pair trade constructed from a long and short position in two correlated assets to profit from their re-converging in price.
Stock	A publically traded company that has shares issued.
Stock exchange	A regulated investment exchange that lists and facilitates the trading of equity shares.
Stock repair	A ratio call spread.
Stop loss	A trade instruction to close out a position in an asset that is submitted to a broker, which will only be executed at a pre-determined price in order to eliminate the market risk of the position making further losses.
Strike price	The price at which the owner of a call option is able to buy the underlying asset or the owner of a put option is able to sell the underlying asset by exercising the option.

Synthetic long call	A long call option exposure synthetically created by combining a long stock and long put option position.
Synthetic long	A long stock position that is synthetically created by combining a long call option and short put option with the same strike and expiration date. This is a type of combo.
Synthetic long put	A long put option exposure synthetically created by combining a short stock and long call option position.
Synthetic short	A short stock position that is synthetically created by combining a short call option and long put option with the same strike and expiration date. This is a type of combo.
Systematic risk	Equity risk that cannot be reduced or eliminated by diversification.
Technical analysis	The study of historical chart patterns of an asset in order to make forecasts about its future price returns.
The Greeks	A collective name for the variety of different risk factors affecting an option.
Theta	The sensitivity of an option price resulting from a change in the remaining time an option has to expiry.
Time decay	See theta.
Time value	The remaining value of an option once intrinsic value is subtracted.
Trading commissions	Commissions levied by a broker for execution of trade orders.
Underlying asset	The financial asset that is delivered when an option is exercised.
Underwrite	A short put stock option that is covered with a sufficient cash or very low-risk, liquid, interest-bearing asset in a portfolio.

Unsystematic risk	Equity risk pertaining to an individual stock or sector that can be reduced or eliminated by diversification.
Vega	The sensitivity of an option price to a change in the option's implied volatility.
Vertical spread	A broad term for either a put spread or a call spread.
Vix Index	An index calculated by the CBOE from S&P 500 Index short-dated put and call options to produce a measure of constant thirty-day implied volatility for the index.
Volatility	The extent to which the price on an asset fluctuates over a period of time.
Volatility clustering	The observed phenomena in equity markets that over short time horizons, daily bouts of high realized equity volatility tend to group together.
Volatility regime	Usually retrospectively classified as low, medium or high and occurring in long (often multi-year) phases, the average realized volatility level that prevails between periods.
Volatility risk premium	The premium that is usually priced into implied volatility over and above realized volatility, to compensate option sellers for the risk that realized volatility has the capacity to spike higher unexpectedly.
Vstoxx Index	An index calculated by the Eurex from Eurotsoxx Index short-dated put and call options to produce a measure of constant thirty-day implied volatility for the index, using the same methodology as the Vix Index.

Printed in Great Britain
by Amazon